IMAGES
of America

HAWKINS COUNTY

Rodney L. Ferrell

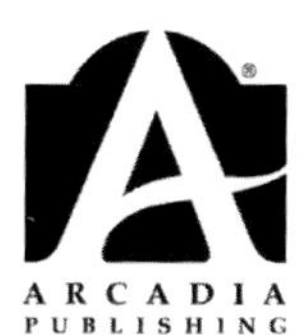

ISBN 978-0-7385-6780-8

Published by Arcadia Publishing
Charleston, South Carolina

Printed in the United States of America

Library of Congress Control Number: 2009921625

For all general information contact Arcadia Publishing at:
Telephone 843-853-2070
Fax 843-853-0044
E-mail sales@arcadiapublishing.com
For customer service and orders:
Toll-Free 1-888-313-2665

Visit us on the Internet at www.arcadiapublishing.com

For my mother, Georgia Ferrell, and in memory of my father, Paul, and my grandparents Harvey and Maude Ferrell. They have instilled in me a deep and loving appreciation of the people and history of Hawkins County.

Contents

ACKNOWLEDGMENTS

First and foremost, I would like to thank George Webb, who for many years has generously shared his vast collection of photographs, postcards, and knowledge of the history of Hawkins County with me. Unless otherwise noted, all images appearing in this book are courtesy of Webb. Thanks to fellow historian and author Justin Guess for his invaluable assistance and vast knowledge of Hawkins County; Mike Ringley, for his constant encouragement; and former county historian Henry R. Price, who initially gave me the idea for this book.

I would also like to thank author and photographer Randy Ball for the images and information he provided. Special thanks go to Maggie Bullwinkel and Arcadia Publishing for their constant support and for allowing me to do this project. Others who contributed photographs are the following: Stella Gudger, Norma Bowers, Diane Venable, Cary Lewis Barton, Levi Ringley, Stella Pyles, Buddy Russell, Barbara Combs, Jim Caswell, Susan Farrow, Zachary Ferrell, Eileen Absher, Bill Davidson, Richard and Marty Beets, Shane Bailey, Universal Studios, and the Swift Museum.

INTRODUCTION

Tucked away in the Appalachian Mountain region of East Tennessee is historic Hawkins County, an area so rich and diverse in history that it is actually 10 years older than the state itself. The county was named for Benjamin Hawkins, a member of the Continental Congress. It was organized in 1786 and was originally a part of the State of Franklin and later North Carolina, but there were settlers in the area as early as 1752. The original Hawkins County extended from the North Fork of the Holston River southwestward to present-day Chattanooga in Hamilton County. Other counties or parts of counties that came from the original Hawkins boundaries included Hamilton, Bledsoe, Rhea, Anderson, Hancock, Grainger, Jefferson, Knox, and Claiborne. This earned Hawkins the nickname of "Mother of Counties."

Rogersville, the county seat, was established in 1787 and is considered Tennessee's second oldest town. American Indians massacred the grandparents of Alamo hero Davy Crockett near the original town site in 1777. They lie buried next to town founders Joseph and Mary Rogers. On a nearby hill, the Rogers family ran a tavern for many years. A young Andrew Jackson was a frequent guest. Built in 1836, the state's oldest courthouse still stands on the town square. Next door is the historic Hale Springs Inn, known first as the Hale Springs Hotel, built in 1824 by Irishman John A McKinney; for many years, it was the oldest operated inn in Tennessee. Presidents Andrew Jackson, James Polk, and Andrew Johnson were frequent visitors there. The town square is on the National Register of Historic Places. Rogersville once boasted three major educational institutions: the Rogersville Synodical College, a private Presbyterian finishing school for women; McMinn Military Academy for boys; and Swift Memorial College, one of the most prestigious African American educational institutions in the South. Today the town retains much of the rich history and heritage that has drawn visitors and residents for over 200 years. The town's annual Heritage Days Festival draws in over 40,000 visitors.

The Holston River was named for Stephen Holston, an early long hunter who settled its headwaters in 1748. Other names for the river were Hogohegee, Cherokee, and Indian, and the Creek Indians called it Callamacco. The Holston River played a large part in the history of Hawkins County. American Indian villages and ancient forts have been excavated along its banks. The river provided both food and a means of early transportation for earlier civilization. Another major waterway was Big Creek. Dr. Thomas Walker discovered the small-scale river in 1750, and he called it Holly Creek. A fort was built in the 1700s at the mouth of where the creek runs into the river to protect the early settlers against sporadic American Indian raids. During the Civil War, the Battle of Big Creek was fought on the banks of the Holston River a few miles south of Surgoinsville. Also near Big Creek is Ebbing and Flowing Spring, another natural occurring phenomenon in Hawkins County. The waters of the spring rise, flood, and then return to normal again. It is one of two such springs in the world—the other being in France.

There are several other interesting communities and towns in Hawkins County. In the west, there is the town of Bulls Gap. Besides being a major railroad junction after the Civil War, the town is also the birthplace of Grand Ole Opry legend Archie Campbell. A festival named in memory of the entertainer is held every Labor Day. The community of Stony Point in Surgoinsville is one of the oldest in Tennessee. Nearby, New Providence Presbyterian Church was founded in 1780, and the neighboring Armstrong Mansion once entertained Prince Louis Philippe Duc De Orleans, a future king of France. Mooresburg in the south section is renowned for its marble quarries and the special type of pink marble found there. A large block of the beautiful marble is in the Washington National Cathedral, located in Washington, D.C.

The county once boasted over 11 resort mineral springs including Galbraith Springs and nearby Tate Springs, which hosted such notables as the Rockefellers, the Melons, and the Fords. Mineral waters from these springs were shipped all over the world.

The Allandale community in the northern section boasts Rotherwood Mansion, the ancestral home of Motown legend Diana Ross. Nearby, Churchill boasts the county's first settlers and several historic sites.

At the eastern end of the county between Stone and Pine Mountains lies Pressmen's Home. This town was once the headquarters for the International Printing Pressmen and Assistants' Union of North America (IPPAU). Under the direction of IPPAU president George L. Berry, a former Tennessee senator, Pressmen's Home boasted a large six-story resort hotel, a sanitarium, a retirement home for former pressmen, a four-story trade school, an administration building, and various recreational facilities, including swimming pools, tennis courts, and horseback-riding stables. The town was also self-sufficient with its own powerhouse and telephone company. The headquarters moved to Washington, D.C., in 1967 and later became a resort named Camelot. Today Pressmen's Home is a virtual ghost town.

Major celebrities and politicians also have roots in Hawkins County. Pres. Harry S. Truman has ancestral ties to the Young family in Carters Valley. Built in 1762, Long Meadow, the Young homestead, is considered the oldest wooden structure in Tennessee. The first white child in Hawkins County was born there in 1763. Charlie Chase of Crook and Chase fame also grew up in Rogersville.

The natural beauty of the area attracted Hollywood in 1983. *The River*, starring Mel Gibson and Sissy Spacek, was filmed at Laurel Run in Churchill. Many local county people were used as extras in the film including a young boy named Shane Bailey who had a major role.

Today Hawkins County retains much of the character and charm that has drawn visitors and residents for over 200 years. Readers of this book may not unlock all of Hawkins County's secrets, but they are sure to be swept up in its spell.

One

Rogersville Through the Years

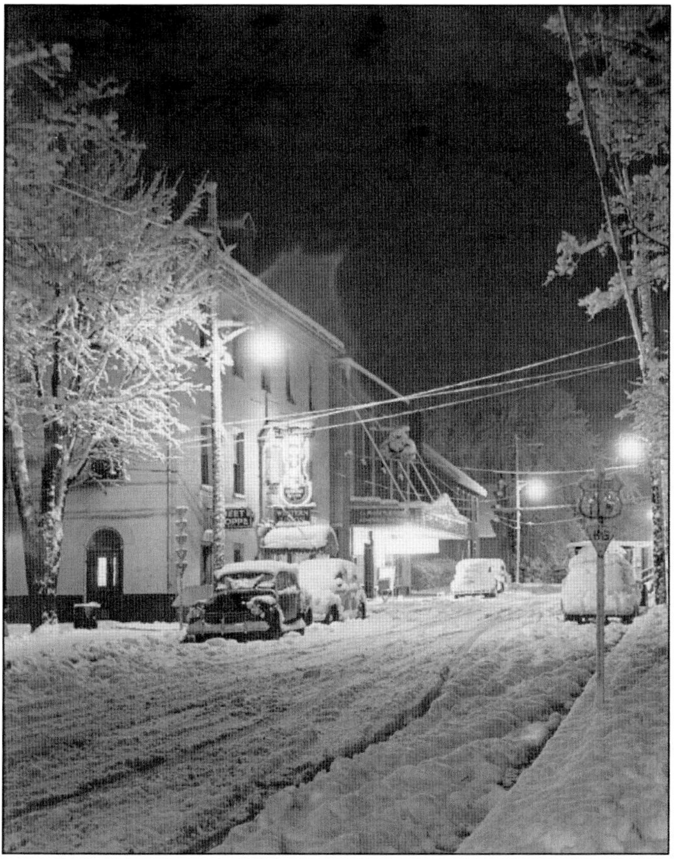

Snowy Night. Here is a snowy February night in downtown Rogersville in 1936. In days of yore, heavy snows were very prominent in Hawkins County, but since then, milder winters have prevailed. The old Rogersville Theater can be seen in the background, and in the foreground is the Hale Springs Hotel, which is now known as the Hale Springs Inn. The Sweet Shoppe was a very popular restaurant run by the Phipps family.

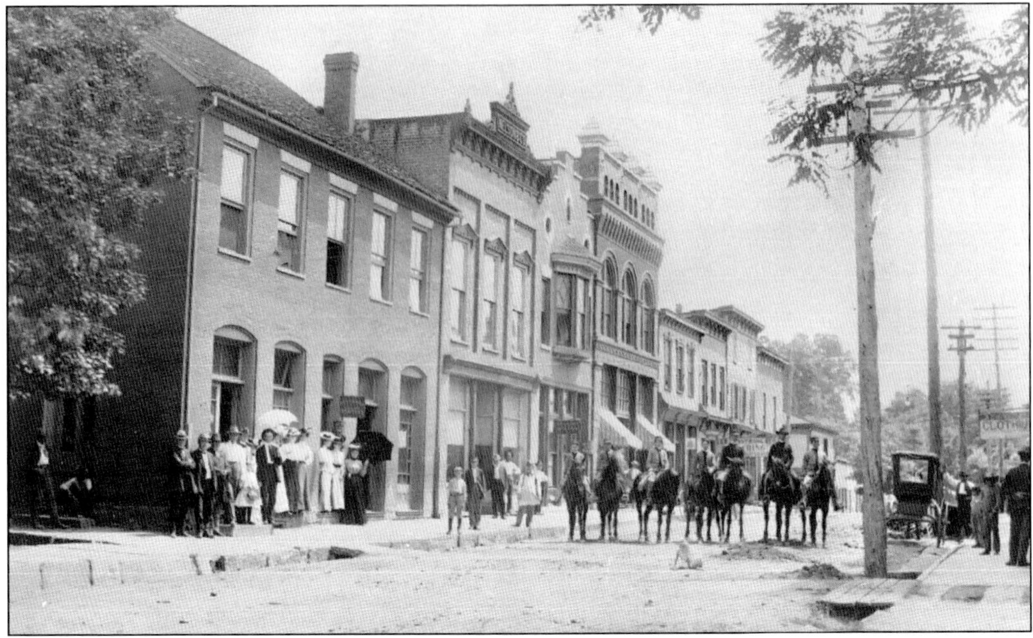

1902 STREET SCENE. This photograph of Main Street in Rogersville shows, from left to right, the old Simpson store, formerly the James K. Neil building, later the Citizens Bank; Nelson's Drug Store; the Hawkins County Bank; Rogans Hardware; Rod Armstrong Store; Hassan's Millinery Store; Rod Armstrong Company; and the George Hale Hardware Store. Young men from McMinn Military Academy are seen doing maneuvers down Main Street.

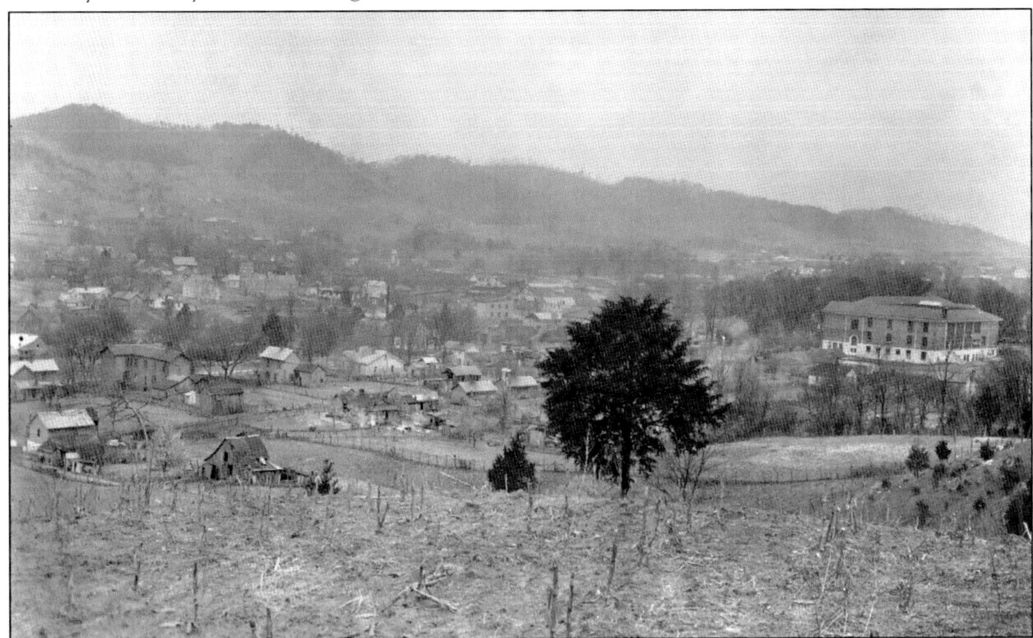

BIRDS'-EYE VIEW. This is a panoramic view of Rogersville taken around 1910 from a ridge above the town. Pictured at the right is the old Rogersville Synodical College, and presently the Rogersville City School at the left is the Wade Hampton house on Broadway. The beauty and charm of the tranquil little valley have drawn visitors for over 200 years.

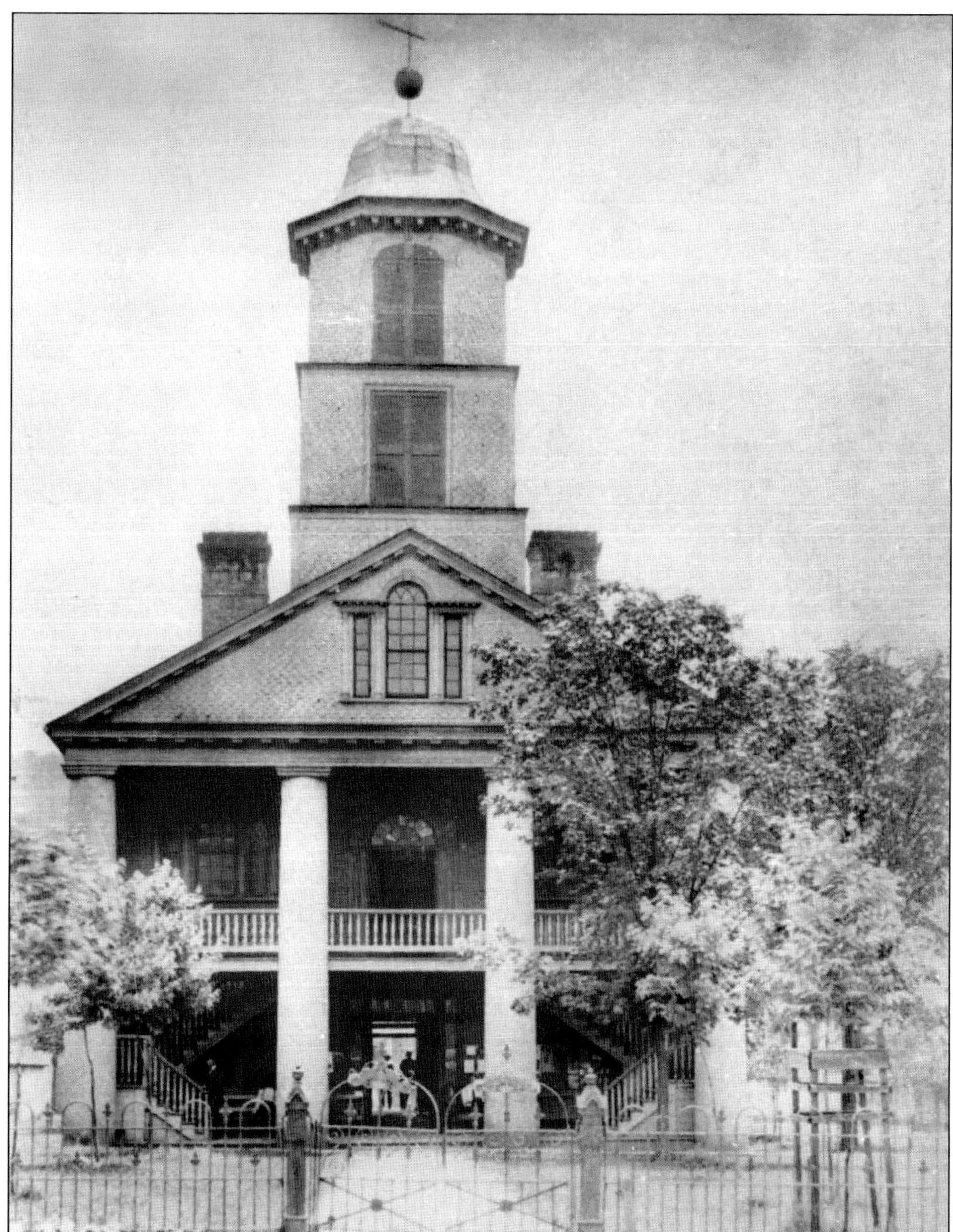

State's Oldest Courthouse. On the town square in Rogersville stands the oldest occupied courthouse in Tennessee. Designed by renowned architect James Dameron in 1836, it replaced a wooden structure in the same vicinity. In 1824, there was a controversy over whether to build the new courthouse in Surgoinsville or Rogersville. An election was held, and it was decided to build the structure on the town square.

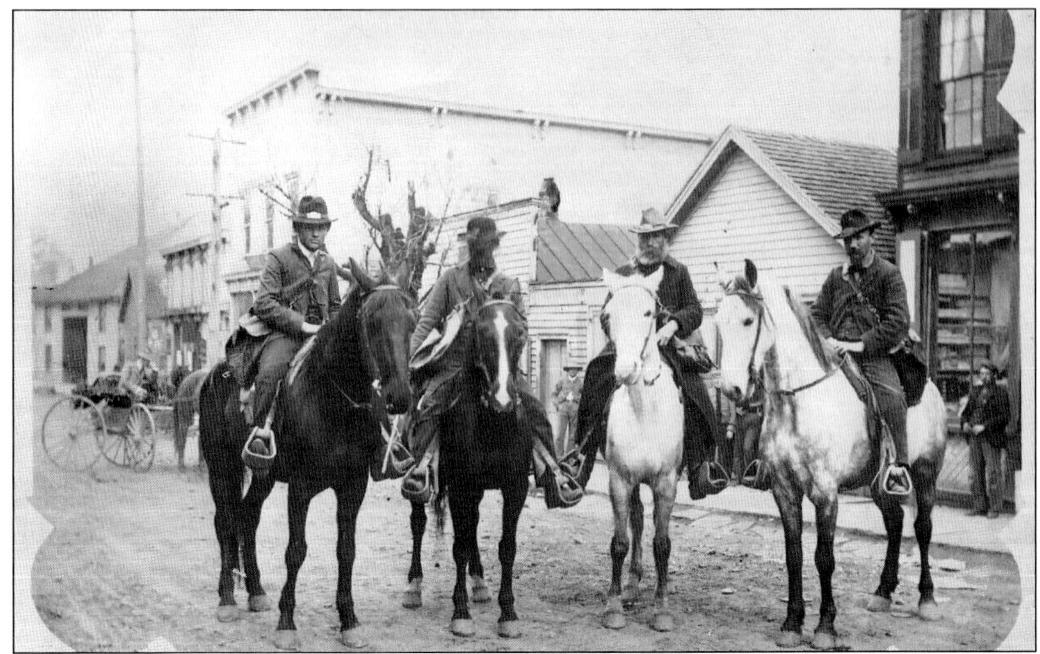

Early Postmen. In the early days, mail was carried via horseback to residents all over Hawkins County. This photograph taken in 1902 shows rural mail carriers leaving the Rogersville Post Office for their individual destinations. From left to right are Win S. Armstrong, Frank Lee Shanks, Ed Lee, and Stockley Donelson Mitchell.

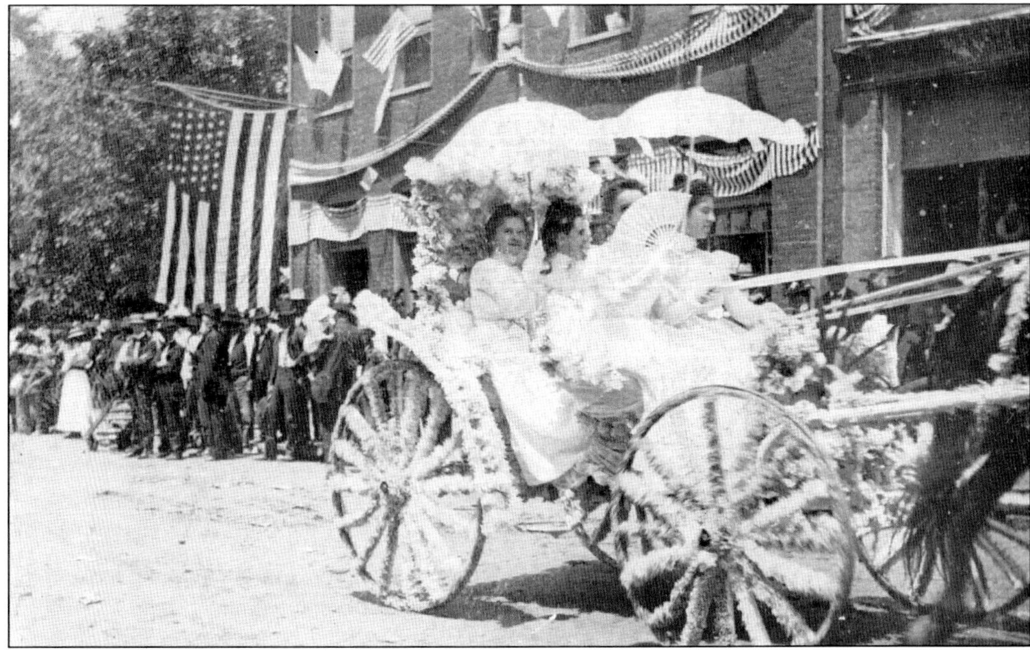

Fourth of July Parade. Since the early 1800s, July Fourth celebrations were commonplace in downtown Rogersville. The socialites from the Synodical College were paraded through the streets in horse and buggies decorated with flowers. Riding in the buggy are Maggie and Mary Pierce, Margaret and Lillie Walker, and Mary Parrott. (Photograph by Andrew Jackson Huffmaster.)

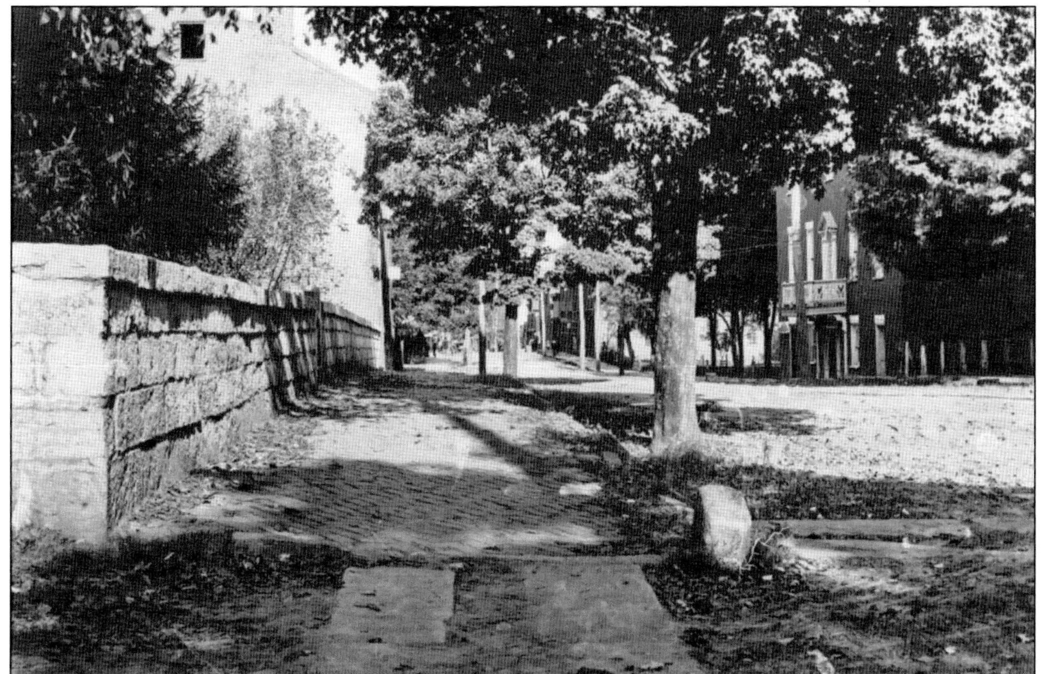

MAIN STREET, 1901. This view is looking east down Main Street long before the streets were paved in town. In the rainy season, the roads could be very muddy and hard to maneuver. On the left is the old Simpson home (presently the Kyle House), and on the right is the Hale Springs Hotel.

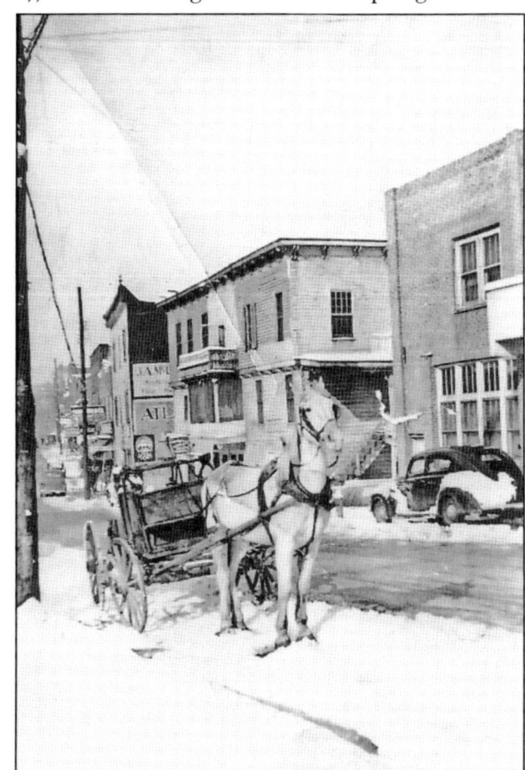

CHRISTMAS EVE. This view is looking west down Main Street in the 1930s shortly before the automobile completely replaced the horse. This photograph was taken in front of where the Rogersville Review building is presently located. (Courtesy of Stella Grudger.)

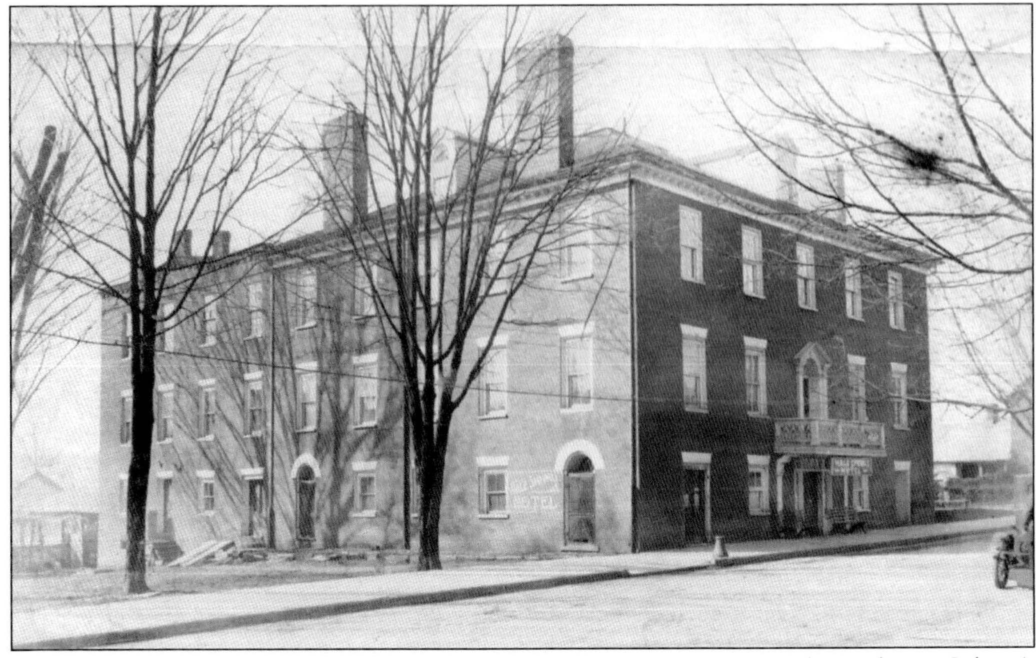

Hale Springs Inn. The majestic Hale Springs Inn was built in 1824 by Irishmen John A McKinney, a prominent judge and lawyer. It was known for many years as McKinney's Tavern. Three U.S. presidents have stayed there: Andrew Jackson, James Polk, and Andrew Johnson. In the late 1800s, it was used as an overnight stagecoach stop for the Hale Springs resort.

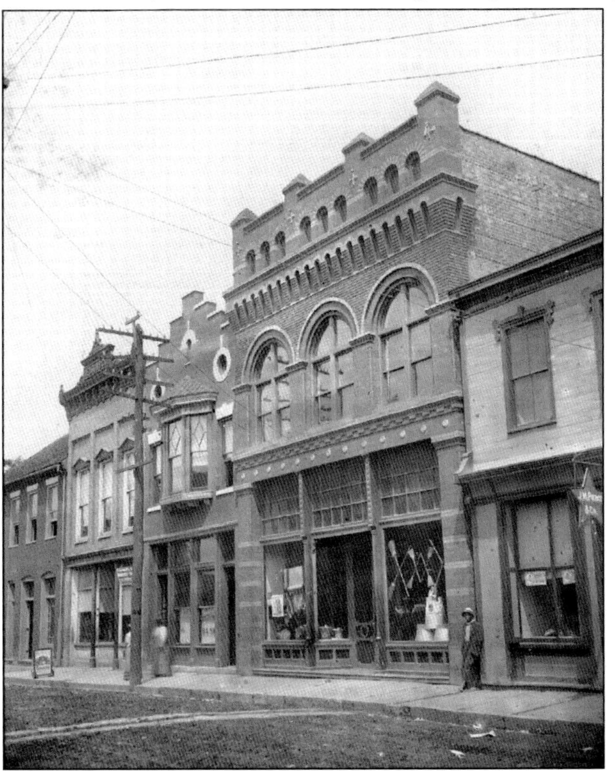

Rogan's. Rogans Hardware Store in downtown Rogersville was founded by James Woods Rogan in 1873 and was passed onto succeeding family members A. B. Rogan, Robert McKinney Rogan, Robert Moore Rogan, and Lance W. Rogan; it closed in 1947.

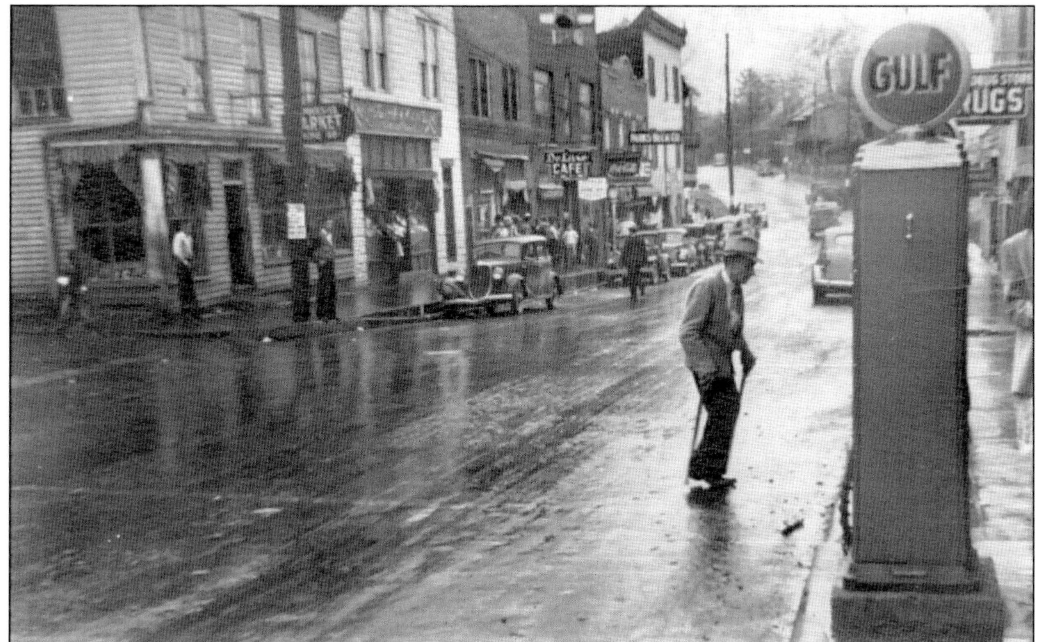

RAINY SATURDAY. This view is looking east down Main Street on a Saturday in 1940. Testerman Motor Company is on the right, and the L. L. Poates Grocery Store is on the left. Rogersville businessman William Kyle Armstrong is crossing the street.

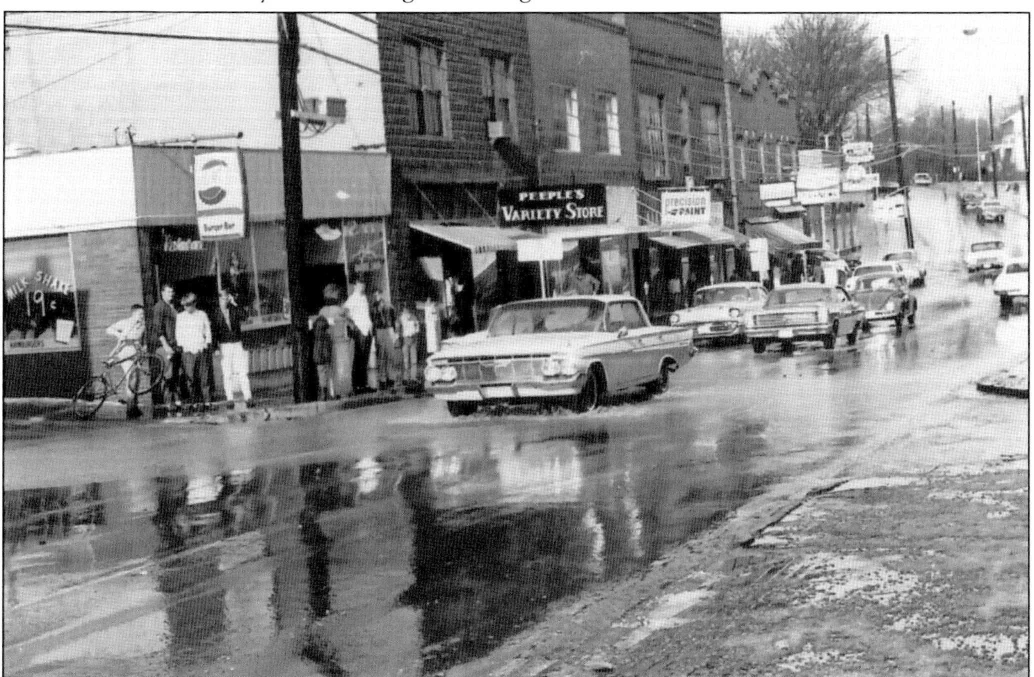

RAINY MONDAY. Here is the same view taken 20 years later; it features a rainy Monday in downtown Rogersville in March 1965. For over 40 years, the Burger Bar was known for having the best hamburgers in town. Peeples Variety Store on the right had the best bargains this side of Knoxville.

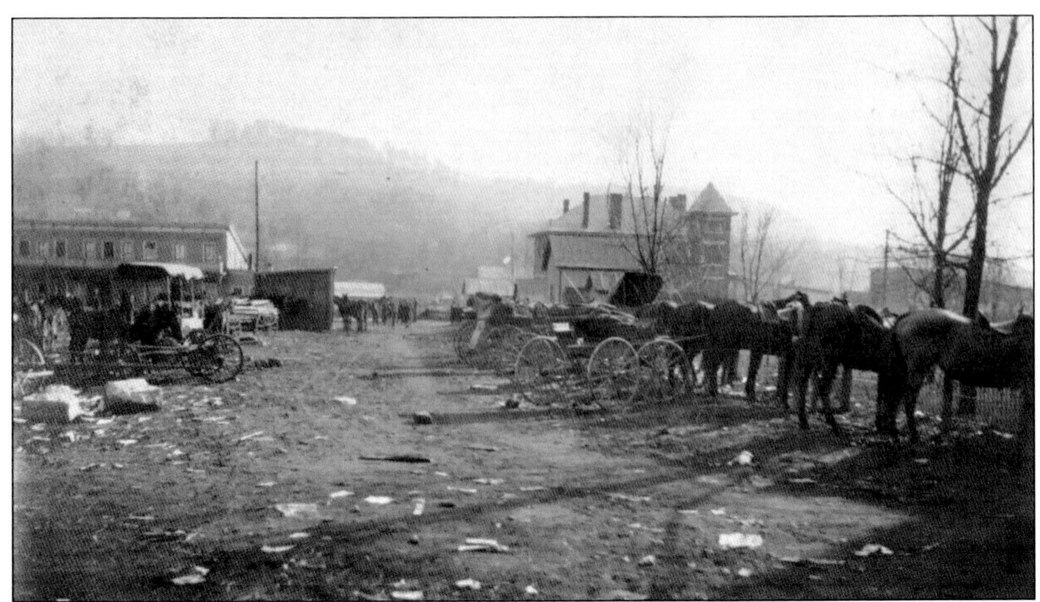

LIVERY YARD. This view is looking out from the door of the old Rogersville livery stable in 1900. The jailhouse is in the background. This photograph was taken directly behind the Hawkins County Courthouse.

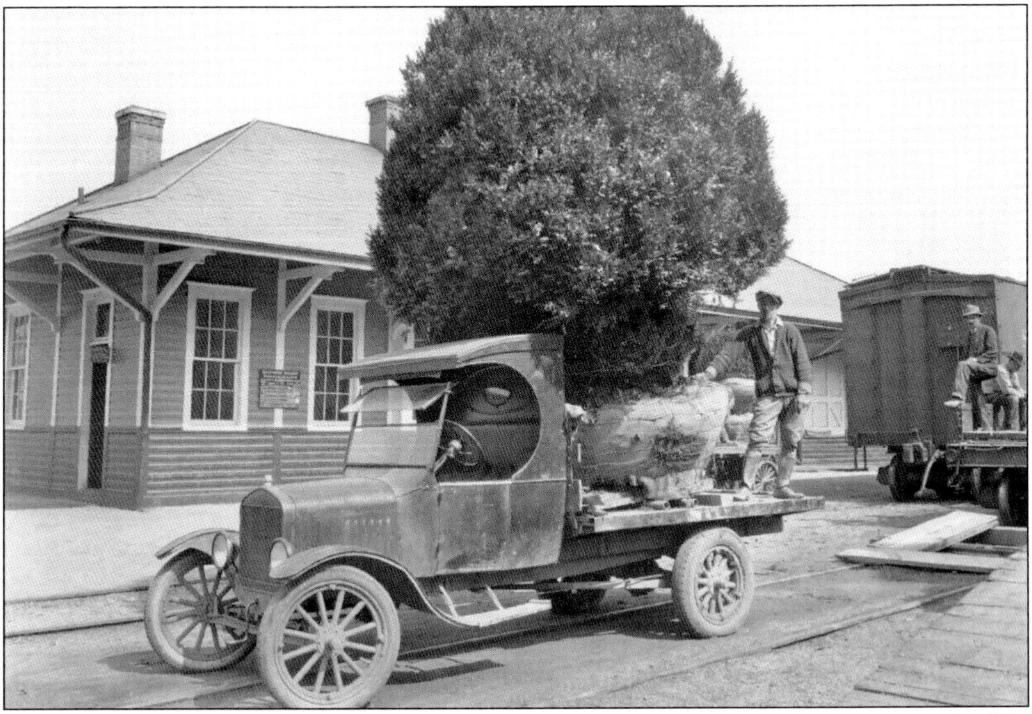

BOXWOODS. The first boxwood transplants were brought to Hawkins County from Scotland by William Young in 1760. These boxwoods from the home of Joseph Wright are being shipped to Washington, D.C., for planting around the U.S. Supreme Court building. At one time, boxwoods were collected from all over the county and shipped east. This photograph was taken at the Rogersville Train Depot.

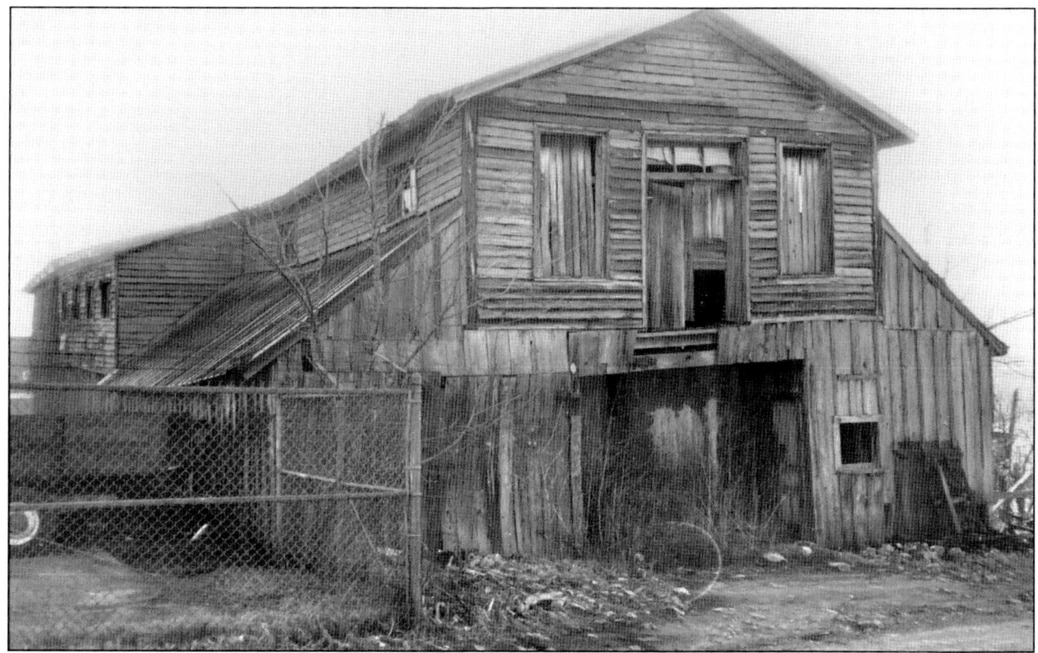

Hop Cross Theater. Formerly located on Church Street, the old Hop Cross Theater was built around 1866 shortly after the Civil War. Over the years, the structure served as a theater, saloon, boardinghouse, livery stable, and a garage. The building was condemned and torn down in the 1950s.

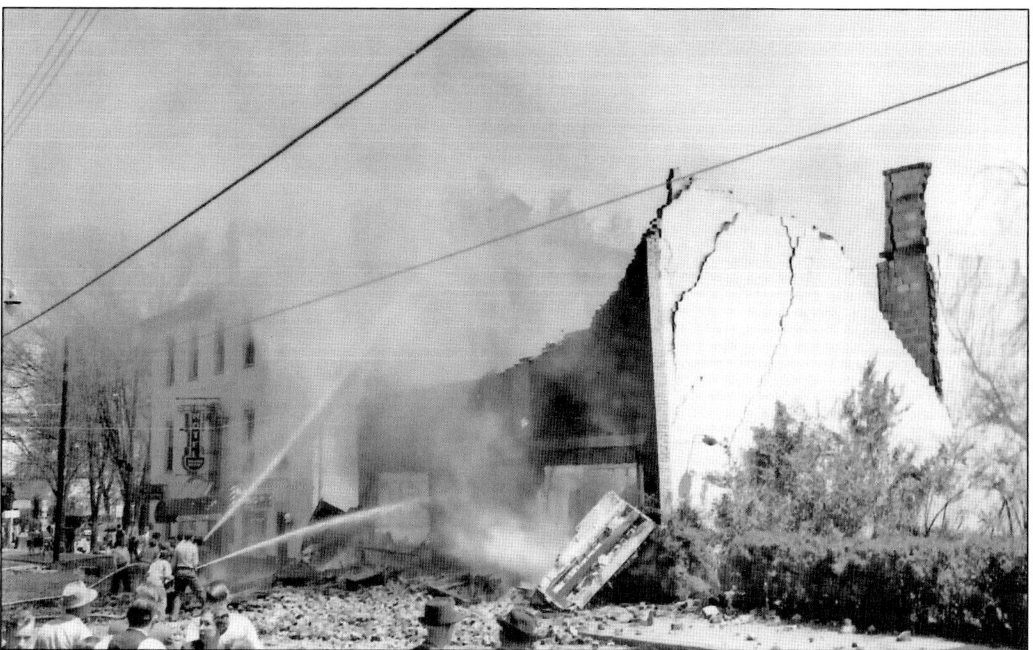

Theater Fire. The Rogersville Theater was built in 1936. The moving picture was managed by the Miller family. The building had stores on the east and west sides. The structure burned in 1946 and was rebuilt the same year. The nearby Hale Springs Hotel was almost destroyed by the same fire. The new theater was renamed the Roxy Theater.

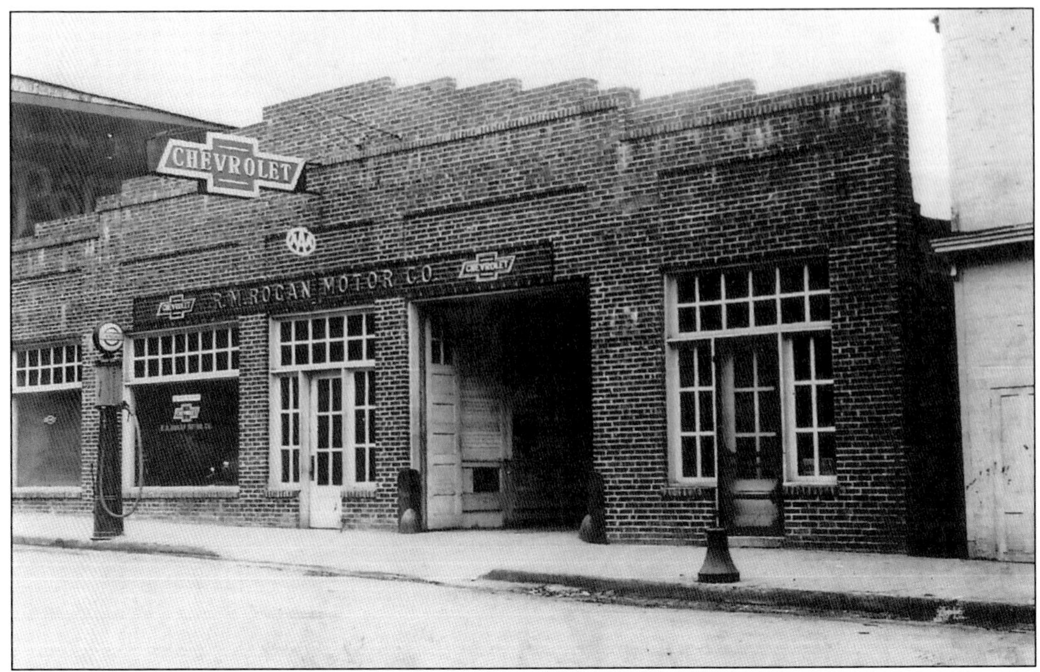

CHEVROLET DEALERSHIP. The former Chevrolet Garage building was constructed by the Rogan family in the 1930s. The car dealership was later run by the Livesay family. The structure was torn down in the 1960s. The property is now part of the U.S. Bank parking lot. (Courtesy of Barbara Beets Combs.)

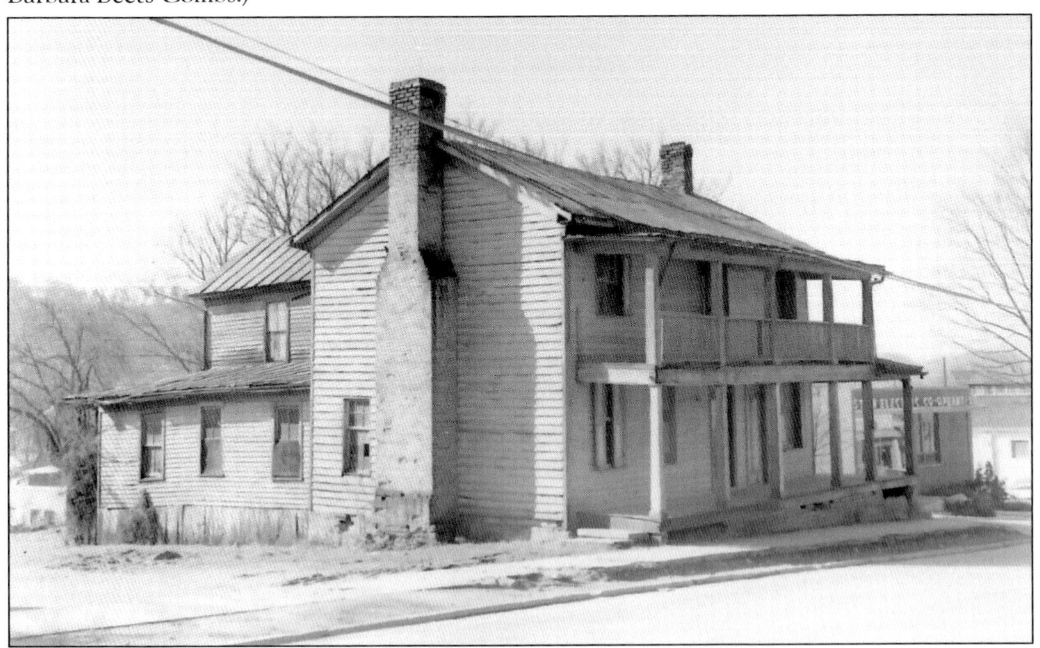

WILLIAMS BOARDING HOUSE. Located on East Main Street in Rogersville was the old Williams Boarding House. Built around the turn of the 20th century, the large structure was torn down in the 1960s—a victim of urban renewal. Its removal furnished the location for other buildings, including Bill Terry Motors, the Quick and Easy Market, and a pawnshop.

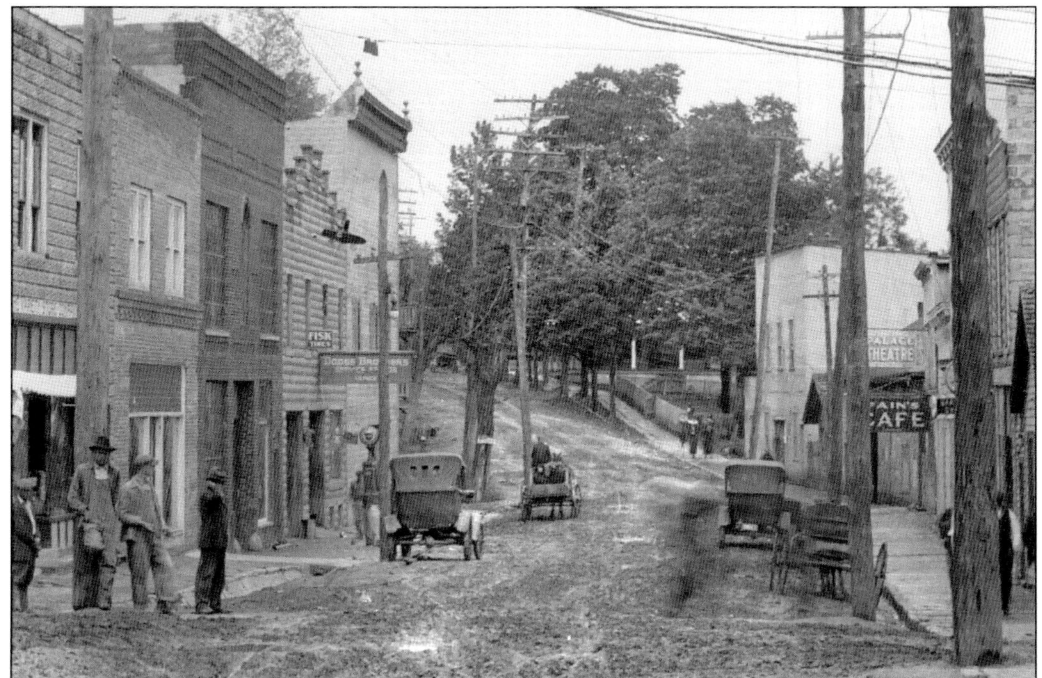

DOWNTOWN, 1924. This depicts a lazy summer afternoon in downtown Rogersville. The dirt streets were hard to pass over when they were dry, but during rainy periods, they turned into 6 inches of mud. The streets were finally paved in the late 1920s.

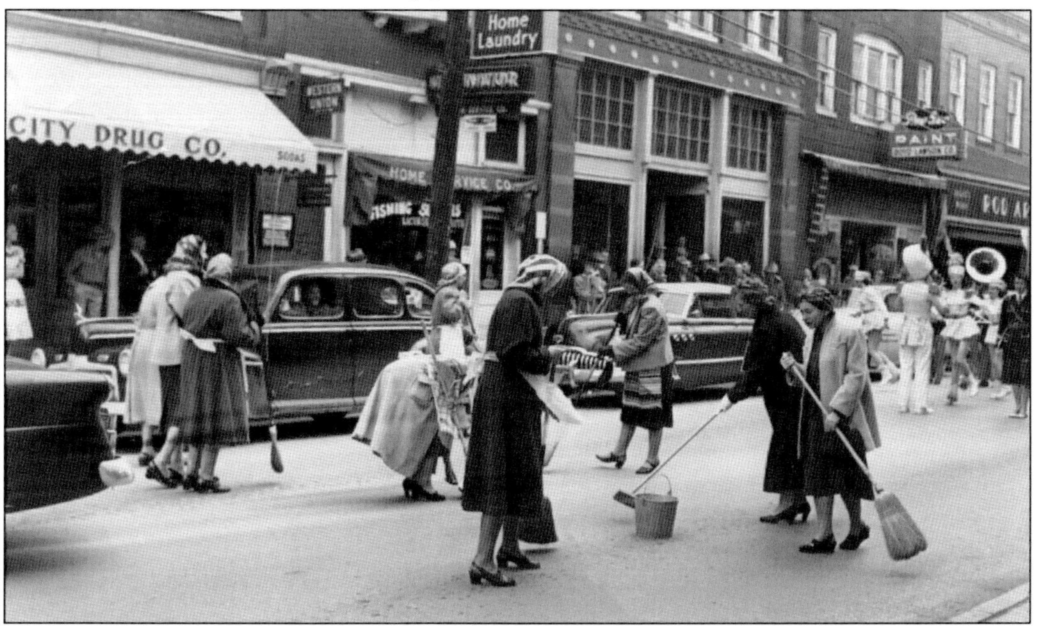

STREET CLEANERS. Members of the Hawkins County chapter of the Association for the Preservation of Tennessee Antiquities sweep the streets during a July Fourth parade in downtown Rogersville. In the old days, women went out early in the morning to sweep the streets. Members include Katherine Armstrong, Christine Armstrong, Josephine Peeples, Mary Clay Lewis, Mary Beal, and Jane Armstrong.

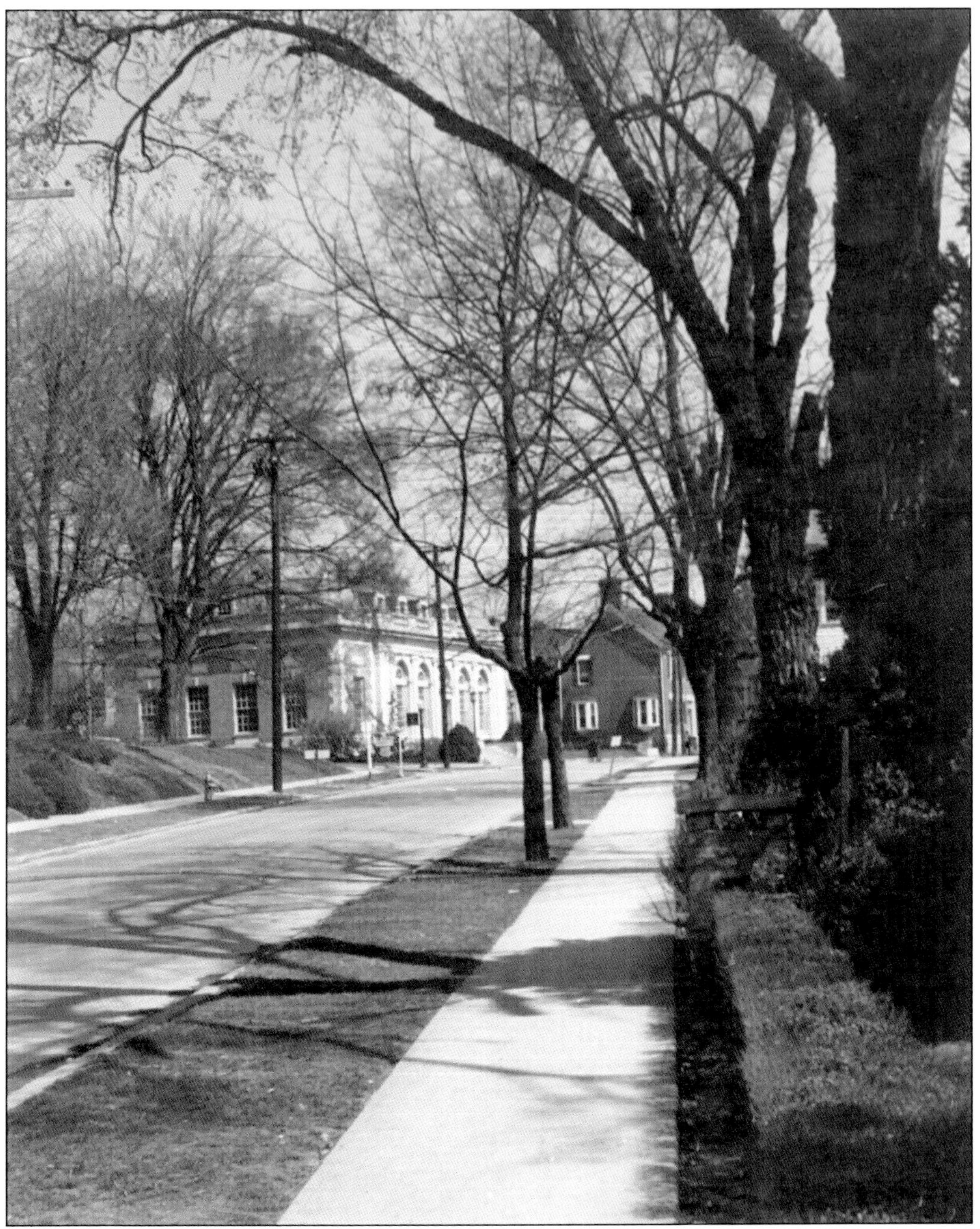

MARCH, 1937. This view is looking east toward the post office built in 1936. In the background is the Neil house, later known as the Rogan home. This photograph was taken by photographer William Phipps, a former mayor of Rogersville.

Two

Big Creek and the Holston River

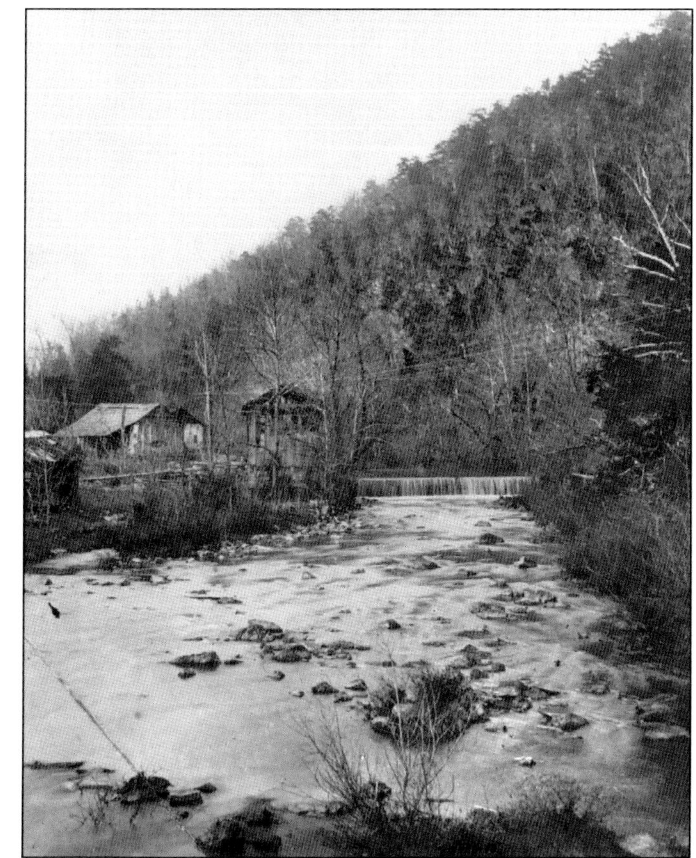

Big Creek. Running vertically through Hawkins County is a small-scale river called Big Creek. It was named Holly Creek by early explorer Dr. Thomas Walker in 1756. The fast moving stream has drawn Native Americans, millers, and early settlers for many years. A fort was built near the mouth of Big Creek in the late 1700s to protect settlers from the onslaught of Chickamauga raids. During the Civil War, the Battle of Big Creek was fought nearby, on the banks of the Holston River. This photograph shows the old Amis Mill.

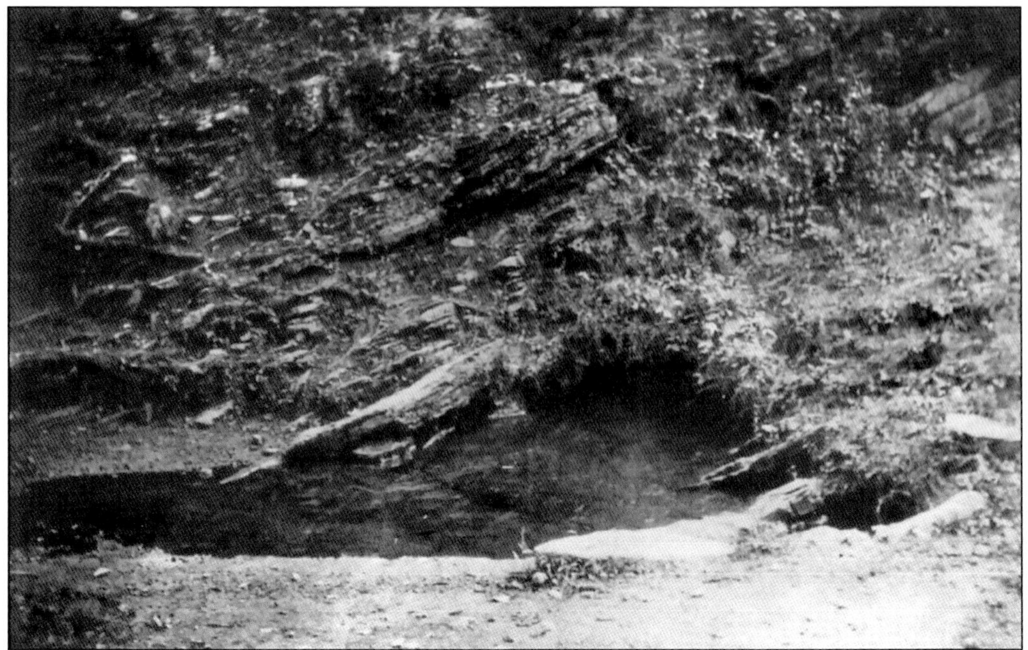

Ebbing and Flowing Spring. Ebbing and Flowing Spring is one of two such springs in the world—the other being in France. Located 3 miles east of Rogersville near Big Creek, the unusual spring is a source of wonder and much speculation. It ebbs and flows at fairly regular intervals of 2 hours and 40 minutes and has done so for centuries. (Courtesy of Mary Beal Doty.)

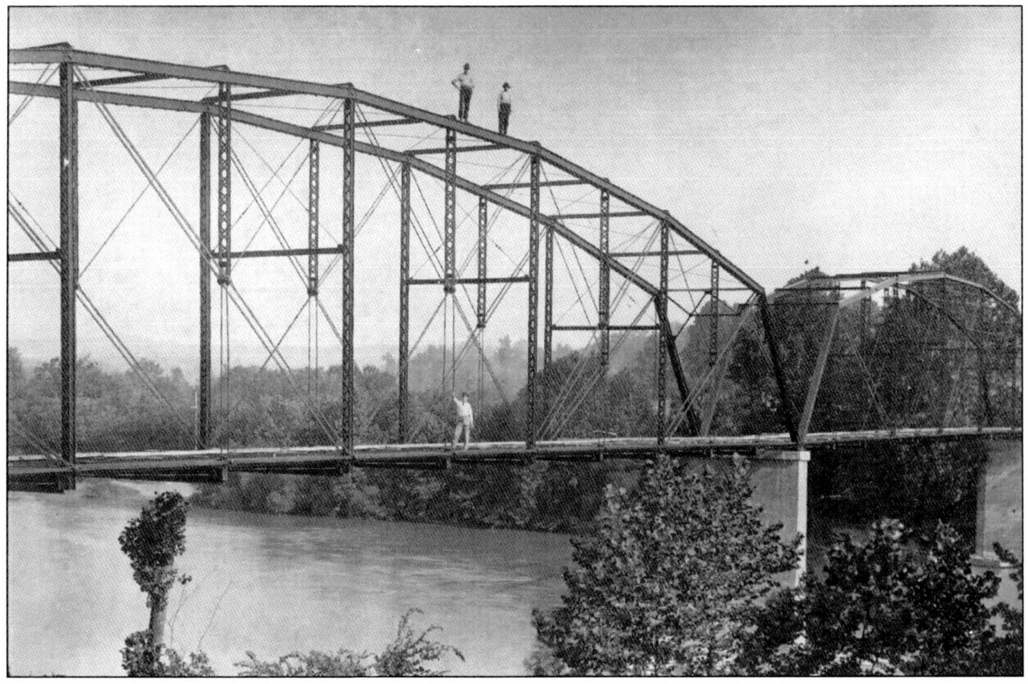

Burem Bridge. Located 2 miles from the mouth of Big Creek was the old Burem Bridge. Built in the 1920s, the large structure was torn down in the 1960s. A new bridge was built in its place and named the William H. Jenkins Bridge.

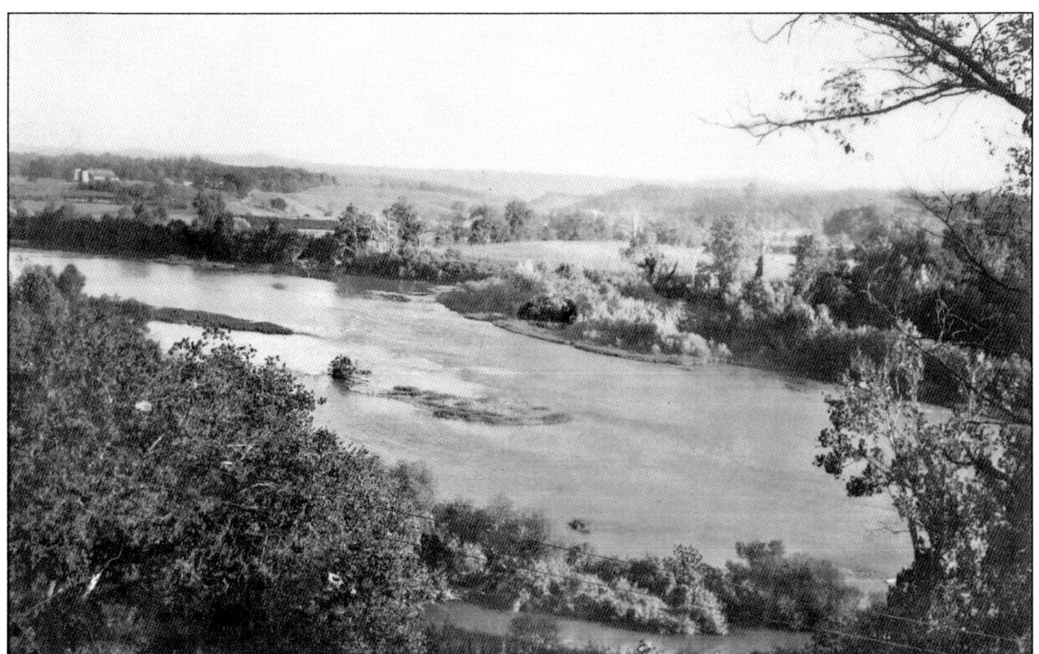

HOLSTON RIVER. The historic Holston River slowly winds its way through the entire length of Hawkins County. The waterway was named for Stephen Holston, who settled at its headwaters in 1758. The Cherokee Indians called it the Hogenogee. Several ancient American Indian villages have been found along the banks of the Holston River.

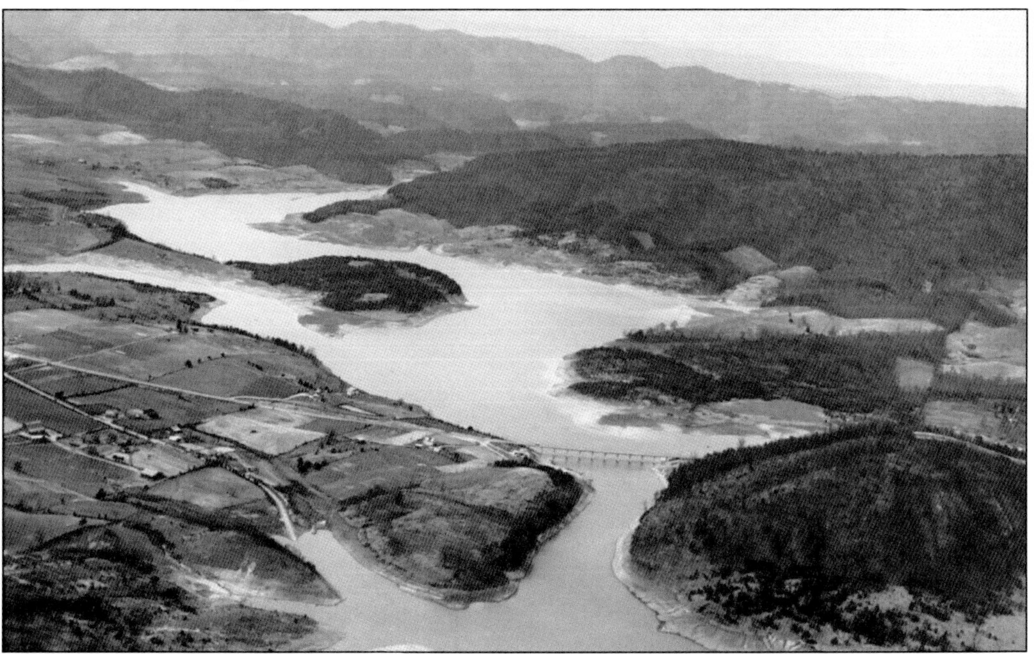

AERIAL VIEW. This photograph of the Holston River was taken from an airplane in 1961. Highway 66 and the Hugh B. Day Bridge are shown in the center. The Tennessee Valley Authority built a dam just a few miles north at the John Sevier Steam Plant. Today the Holston River is a fisherman's and boater's paradise.

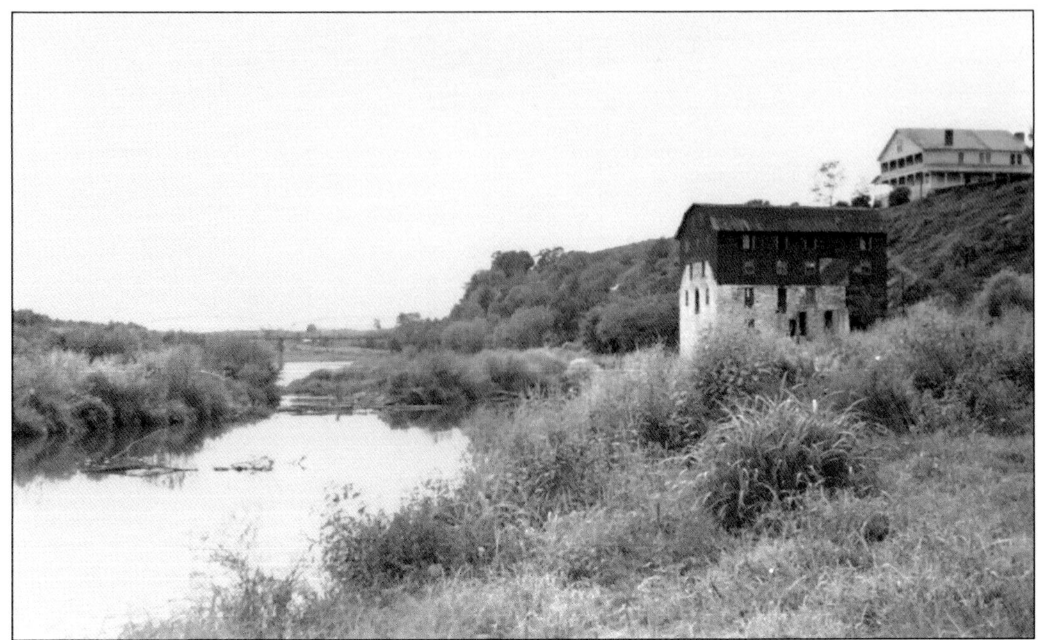

McDonalds Mill. The old McDonalds Mill, formerly the Austin Mill, was built in 1810 by Thomas Jackson. The McDonald house is shown upon the right, and the Austin Mill railroad bridge is in the background. Today the area is called McKinney's Chapel Road. This photograph was taken in 1936. The mill was sold to the Tennessee Valley Authority (TVA) in 1942 and razed in 1967. Its site is now part of the John Sevier Steam Plant.

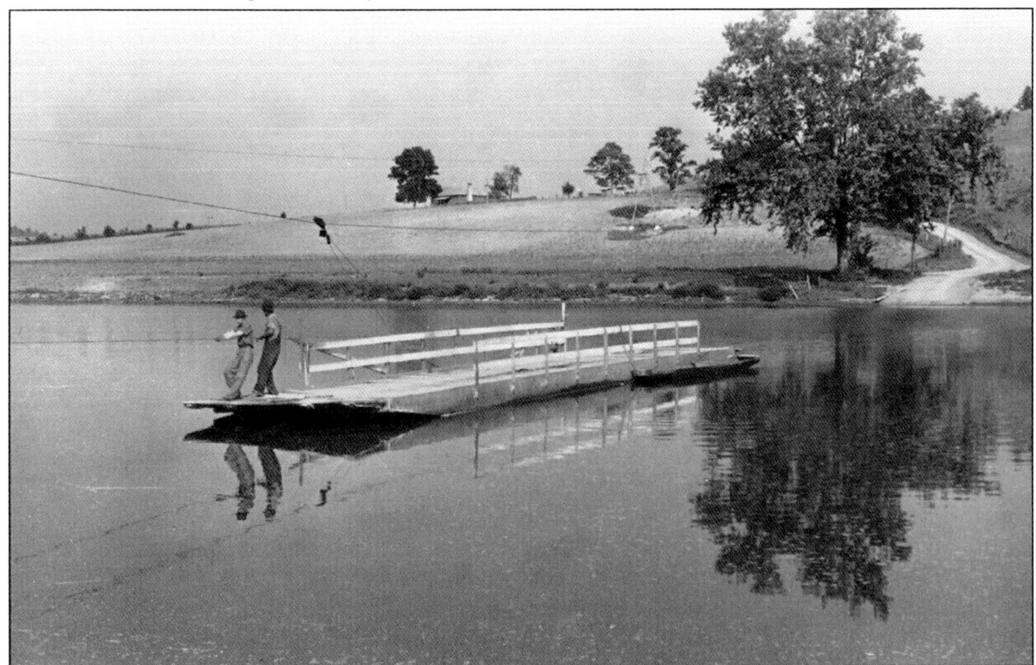

Old Ferry. One of the last ferries to operate in the state of Tennessee was the Surgoinsville Ferry. Situated on the Holston River, the wooden boat transported man and beast for nearly 100 years until it was discontinued in 1954. A large steel and stone bridge was built in its place.

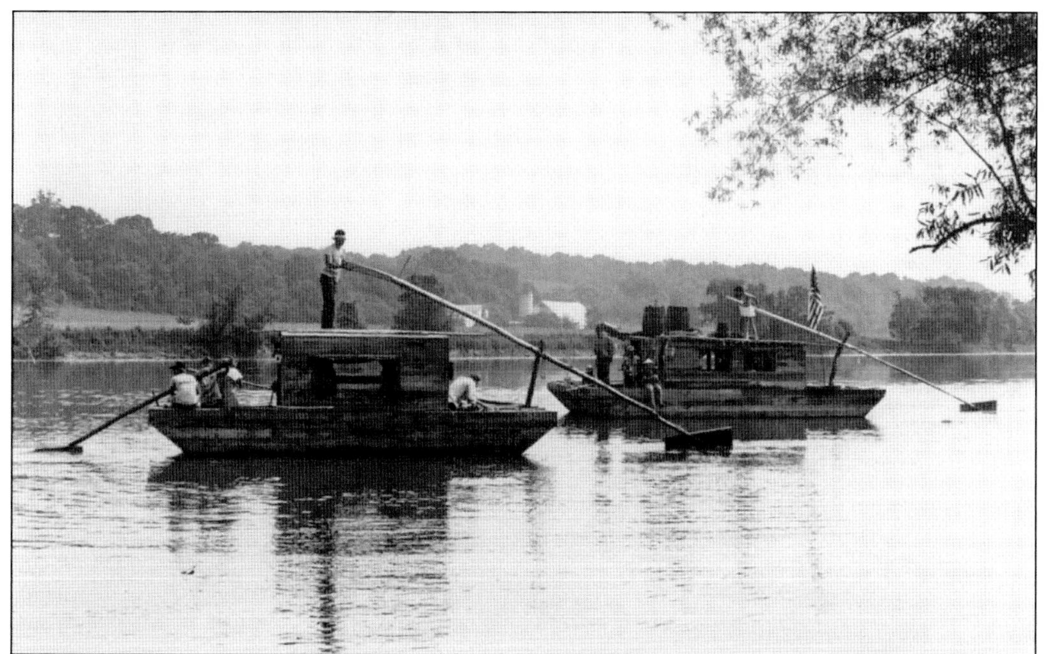

Flat Boat Trip. Col. John Donnellson's trip down the Holston River departing from Fort Patrick Henry in Kingsport and continuing to the French Lick in Nashville was reenacted in 1976 as a part of the bicentennial celebration. This photograph was taken by John Rowan as the entourage passed through Hawkins County.

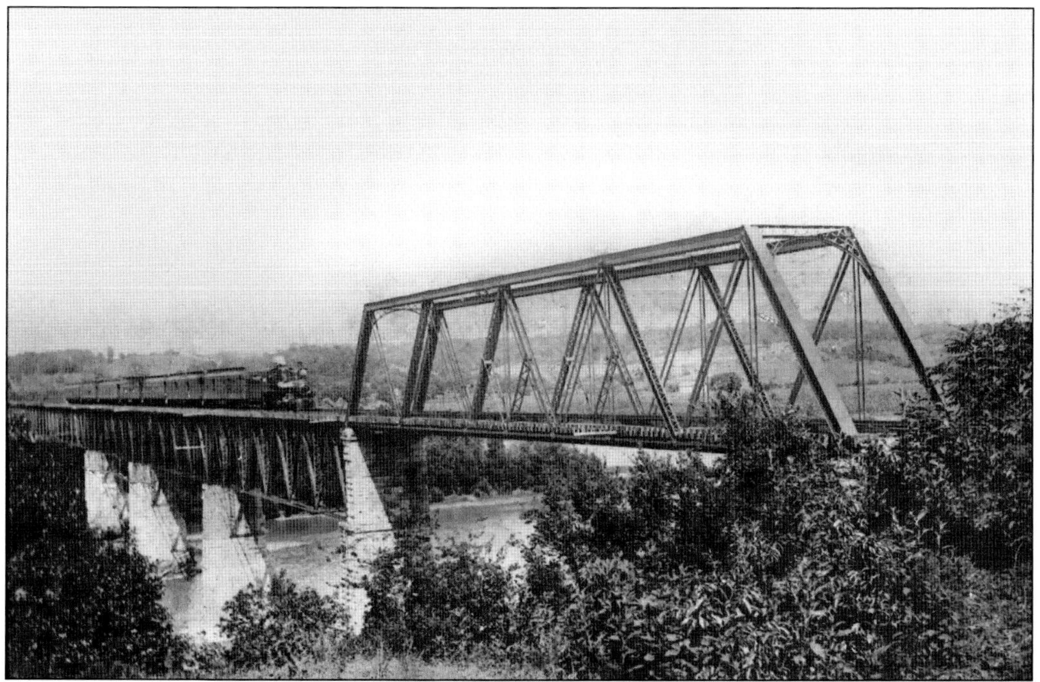

Railroad Bridge. Here is the No. 003 train crossing the Holston River on the Austin Mill Railway Bridge. The date of this photograph is August 16, 1931. The train is bringing passengers from Bulls Gap to the Rogersville Depot.

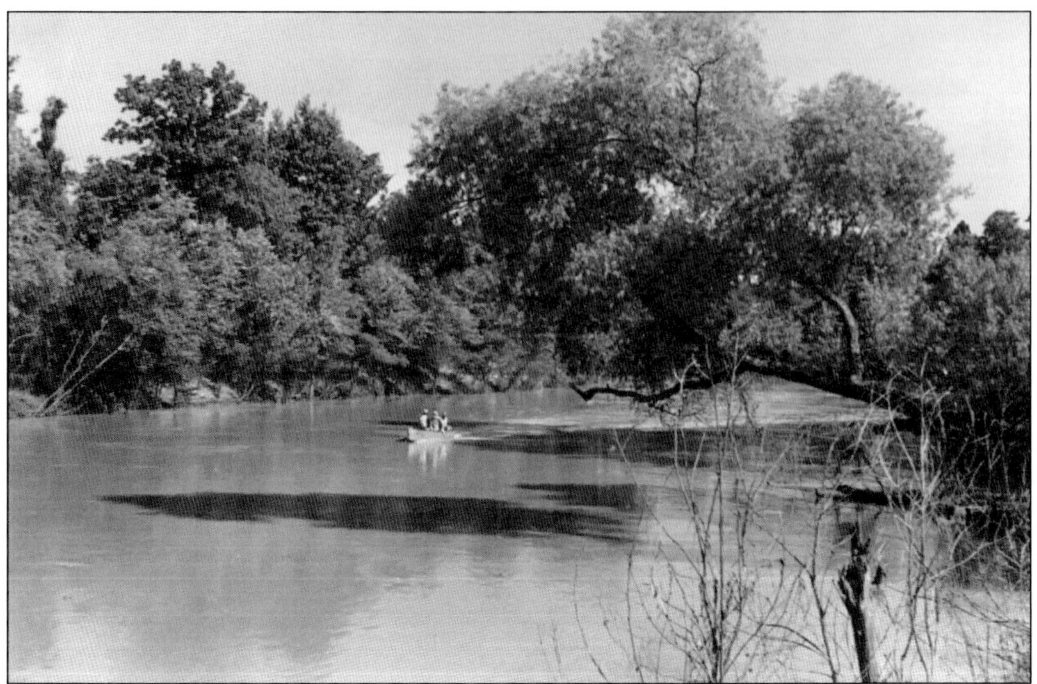

Summer Canoeing. This image depicts canoeing on the Holston River in the early 1940s. The Chickamauga and Creek Indians used the waterway for travel in hollowed-out tree canoes. The Holston River is a very easy flowing river and suitable for all kinds of boating.

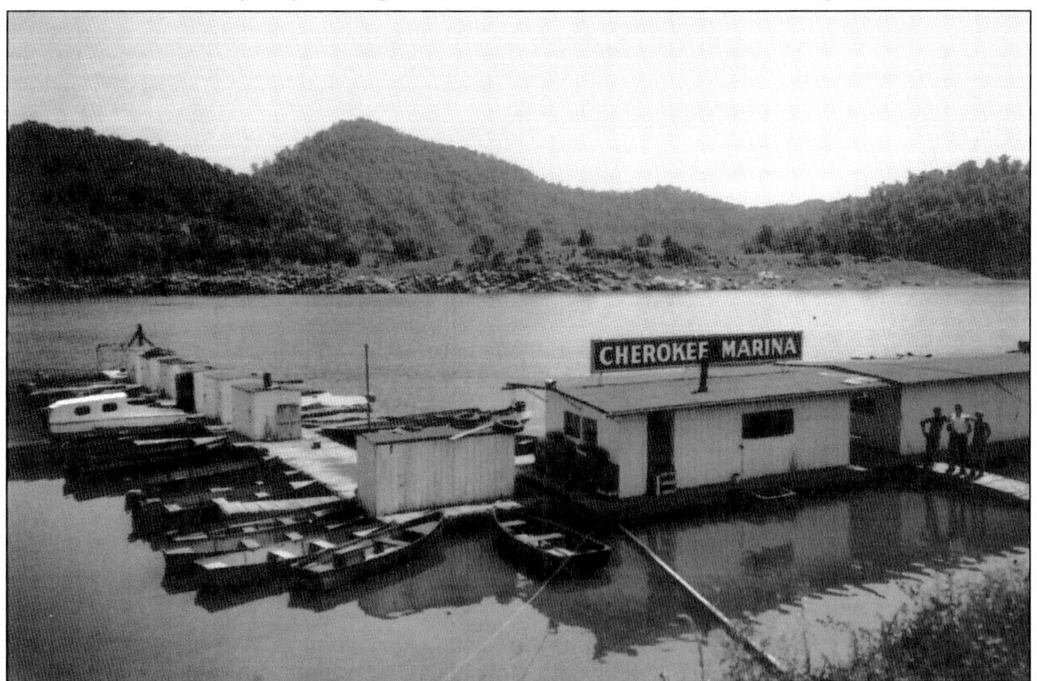

Cherokee Marina. Located 5 miles west of Rogersville on Highway 11 West, the Cherokee Marina was opened in the 1950s. In a 50-year span, the marina equipment that patrons brought in or rented went from simple canoes to high-tech speed and fishing boats.

Three

Various Schools

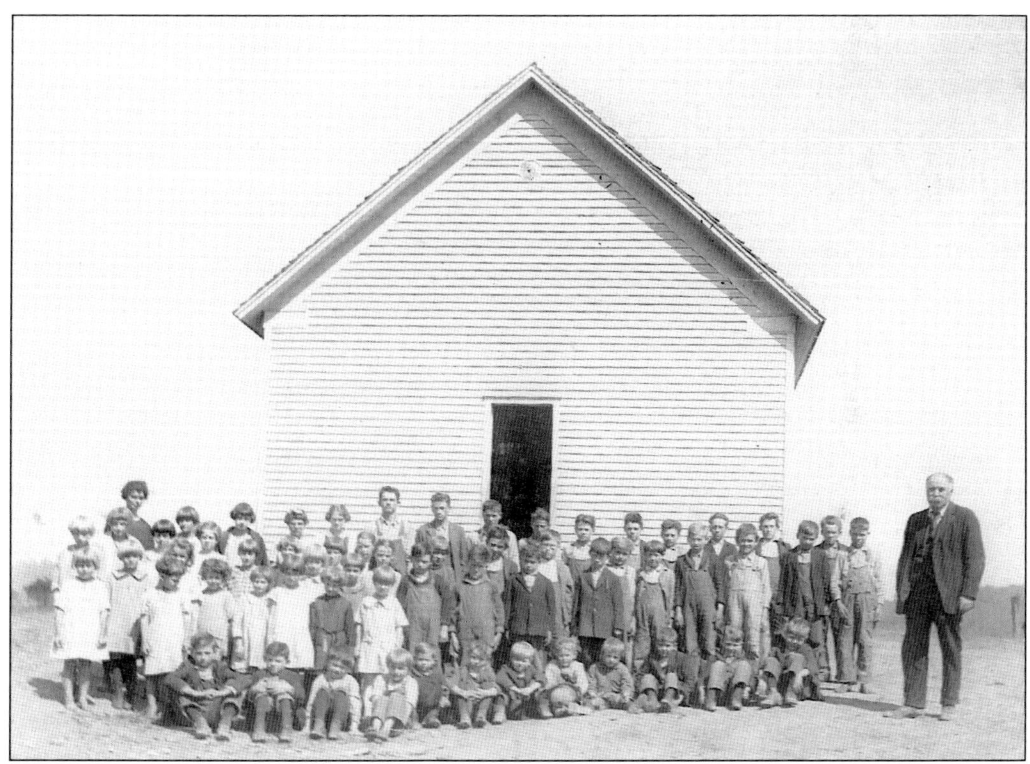

High Point School. Once located in the Stanley Valley section of Hawkins County, the old High Point School building burned down on February 10, 1926. This photograph was taken in 1924. Families who attended the school included the Christian, Jenkins, Edens, Mcpeek, Looney, Fields, Thacker, Allen, Charles, Horne, Kersey, and Ward families among others. Teachers were Grace Owen and Melvin Thurman.

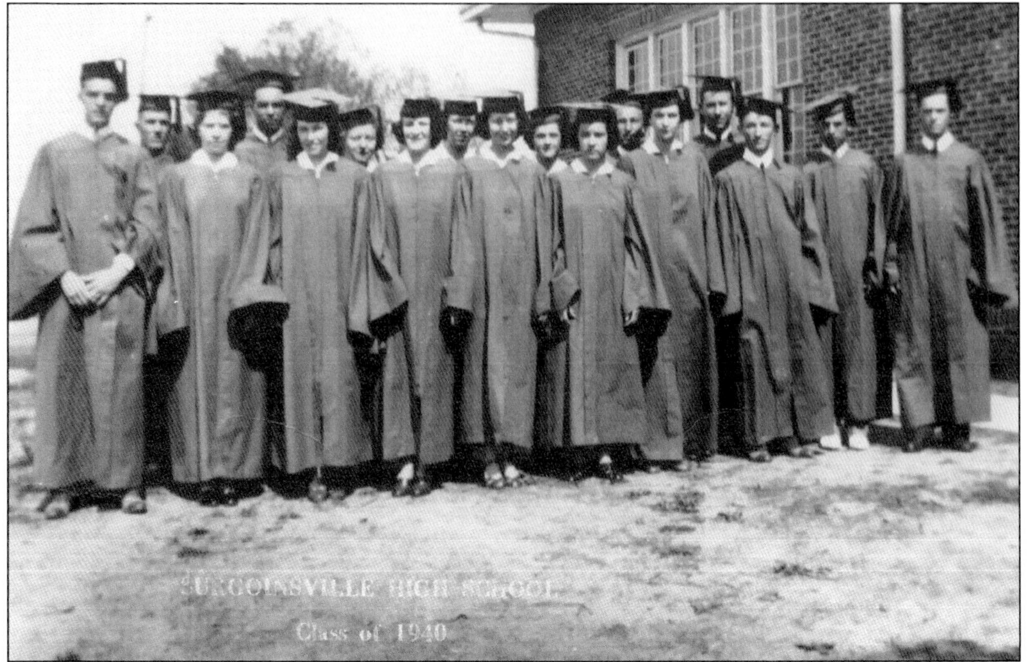

SURGOINSVILLE HIGH SCHOOL. Here is the 1940 graduating class at the old Surgoinsville High School. Among those pictured, in no particular order, are Herman Gatewood, Leonard C. McConnell, Al and Elizabeth Collins, Jane F. Cole, Ada Pearl Boyd, Ruby Ferrell, Bert Hyder Jr., Kenneth and Nora Roller, Charles Jones, Dennis Christian, and Blaine and Ruth Bowery. (Courtesy of Jane Fudge Cole.)

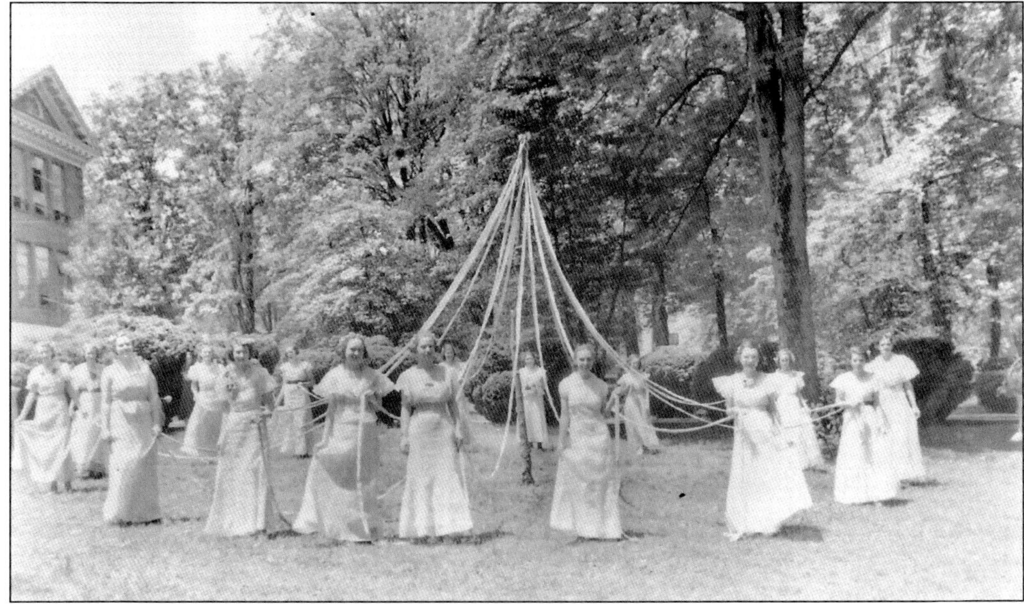

MAY DAY DANCE. The campus of the Rogersville City School is over 150 years old and dates back to when it was an all-female institute called the Rogersville Synodical College. This photograph was taken during a formal May dance in 1932, when the facility was used as the Rogersville High School.

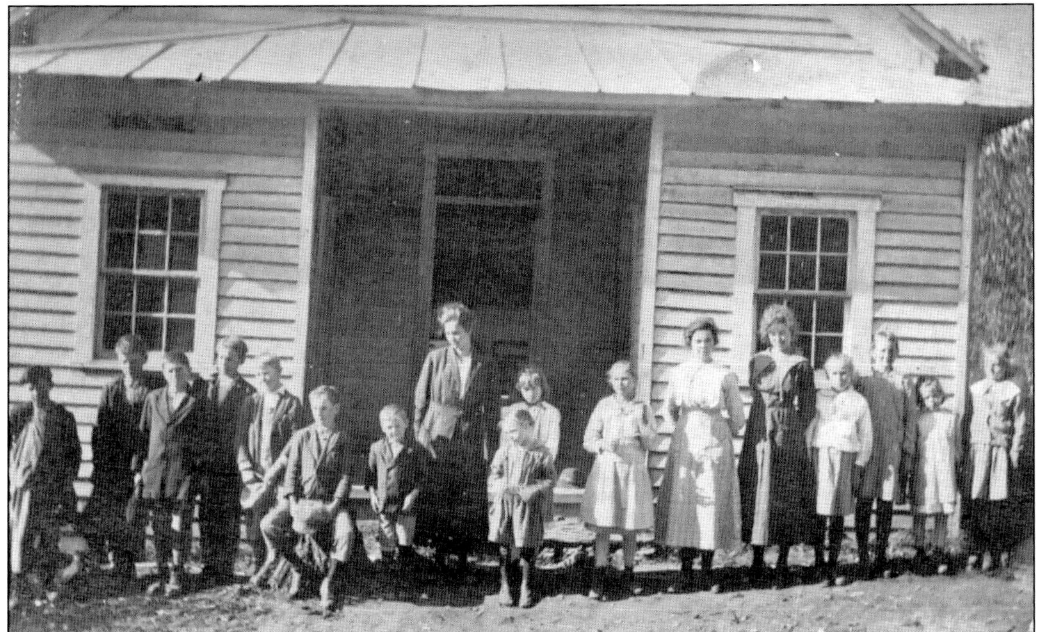

Caney Creek. Here is a 1930 school group photograph at Caney Creek School. Matilda Greene was the teacher at the time. Once located in the Striggersville community on Highway 70, the Caney Creek School served the area for many years. The old clapboard school was torn down after Hawkins County schools consolidated in 1950.

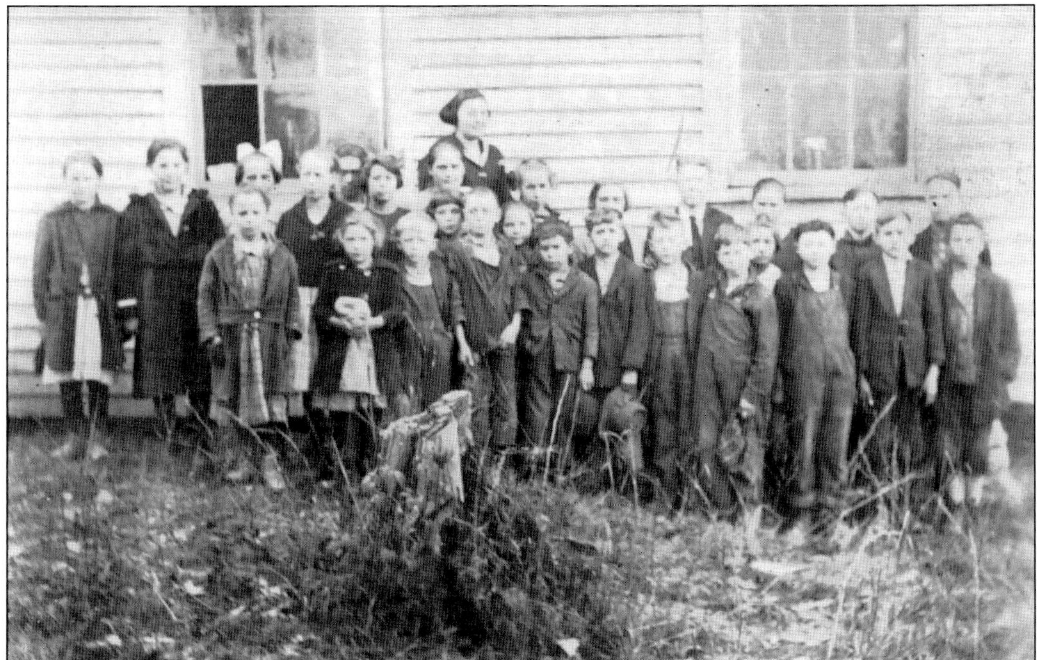

Spires Chapel School. Spires Chapel was founded in 1849 on land donated by Andrew Spires. The first church was a log structure until a wooden building was erected around the turn of the 20th century. The church was used as a school for over 100 years. This old photograph shows a 1919 school group at the side of the church. Blanche Morgan was the teacher.

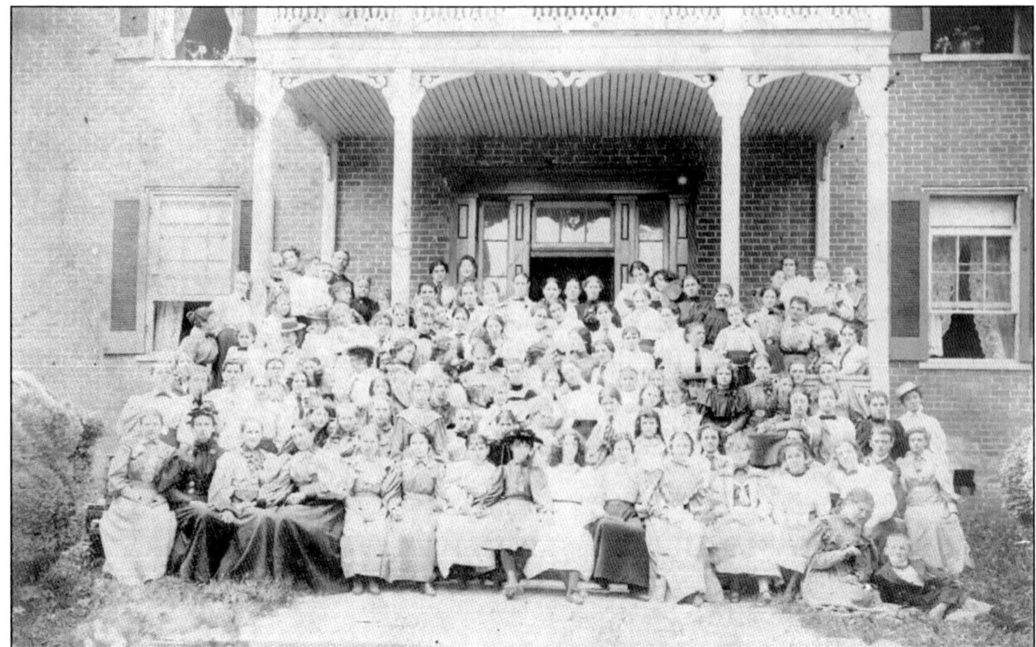

SYNODICAL COLLEGE. The original Rogersville Synodical College building was erected in 1850. Over the years, it has been the Rogersville High School and it is currently the Rogersville City School. This student body photograph was taken in 1902 in front of the old building. (Courtesy of Jane Fudge Cole.)

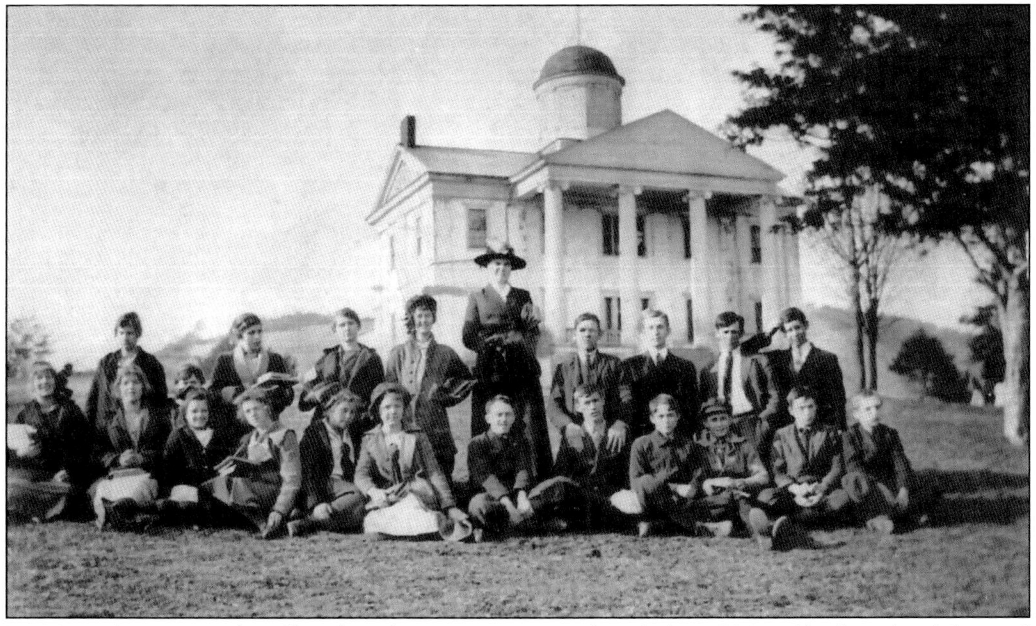

MCMINN ACADEMY. This all-male military institute was founded in 1806 and built on land donated by Joseph and Mary Rogers. It was named for early Tennessee governor Joseph McMinn. Located on present-day Holston Street, it operated as a private school until the 1920s when the building fell into a bad state of repair and was torn down a few years later. The people in this photograph are visitors from the Hale Springs resort.

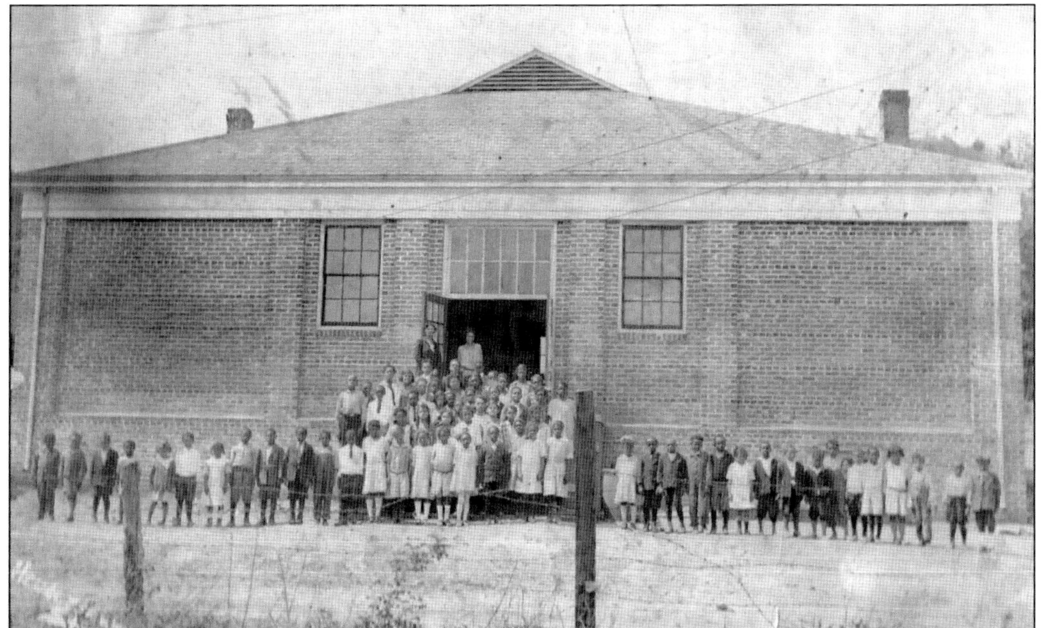

Price Public. Located on the corner of Hasson and Spring Streets is Price Public School. It was founded on March 17, 1868, by Alexander Fain, Jordan Netherland, Albert Jones, and Nathaniel Mitchell for the purpose of educating African American children. In the early 1990s, Stella Gudger was one of the driving forces behind the historical preservation of the school. (Courtesy of Stella Gudger.)

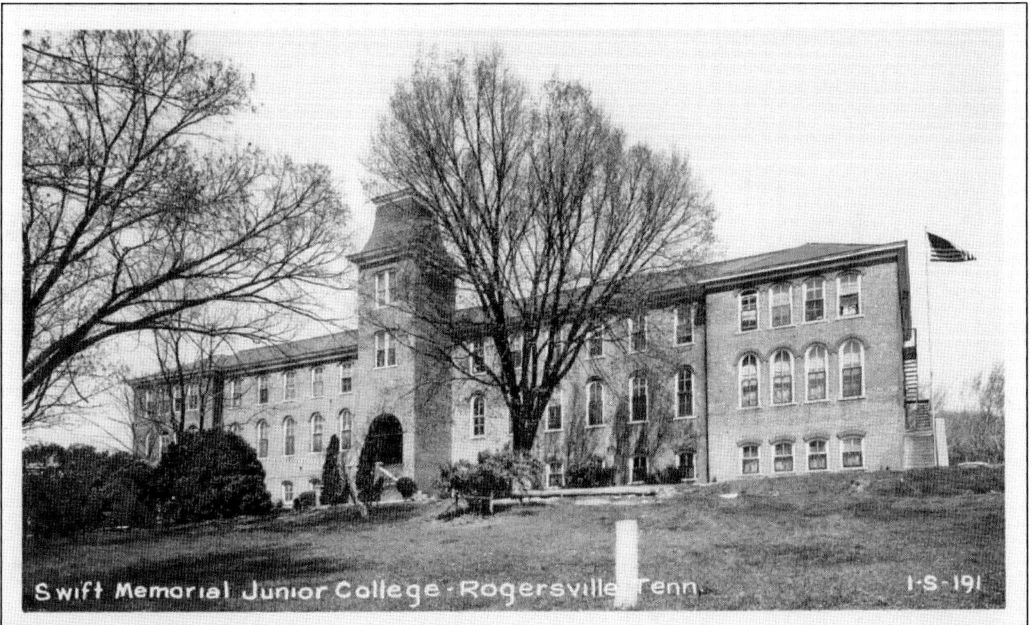

Swift Memorial. This institute for higher learning for the African American community was founded in 1883 by Dr. William H. Franklin, the first black graduate of Maryville College. The main three-story building was constructed in 1893. It housed the administrative offices, classrooms, library, dining hall, and women's dormitory.

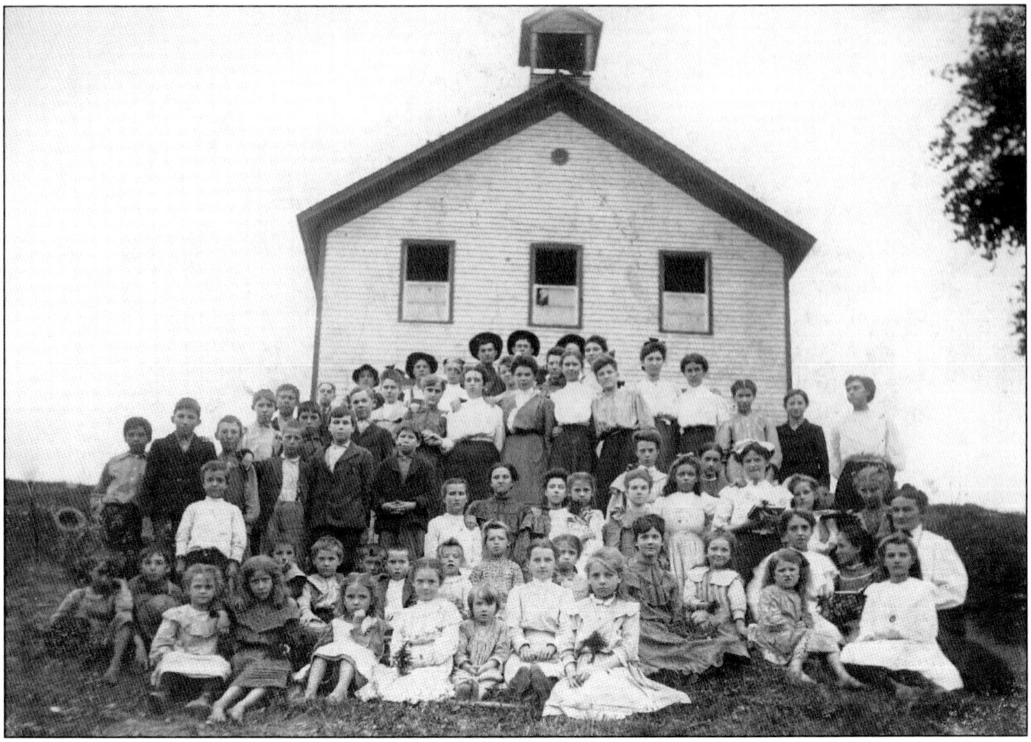

ALUM WELL ACADEMY. Here is the Alum Well Academy class of 1906 with Leila Jones as the teacher. The school was located on Wineager Road in the Hickory Cove community. Looney, Klepper, Ward, Bray, Brooks, Brice, and Anderson were just a few of the families who attended the school.

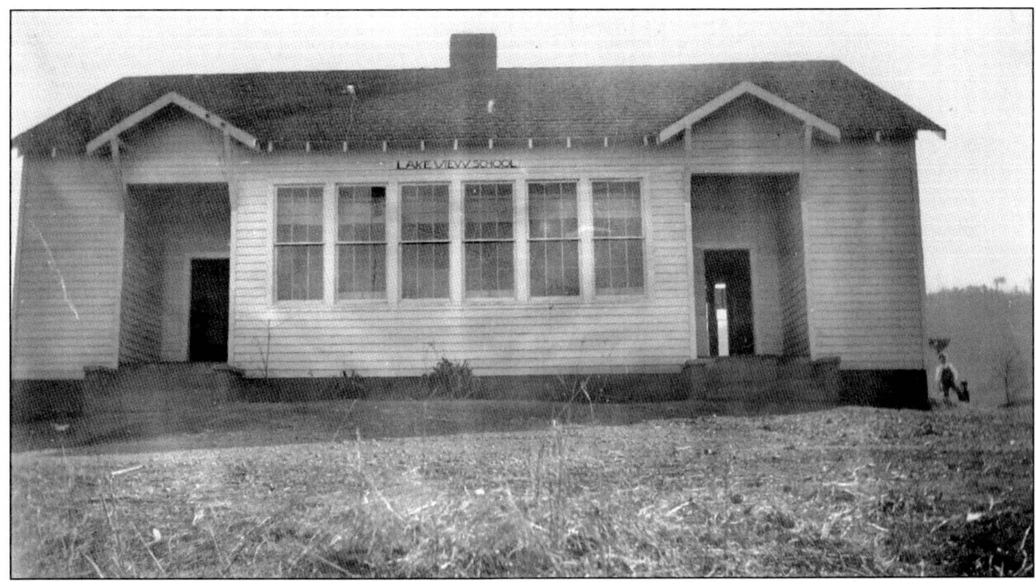

LAKEVIEW SCHOOL. This schoolhouse was located in the Mooresburg community. Before the waters of Cherokee Lake flooded the valley, the school was moved up to higher ground, but it was eventually torn down in the 1960s.

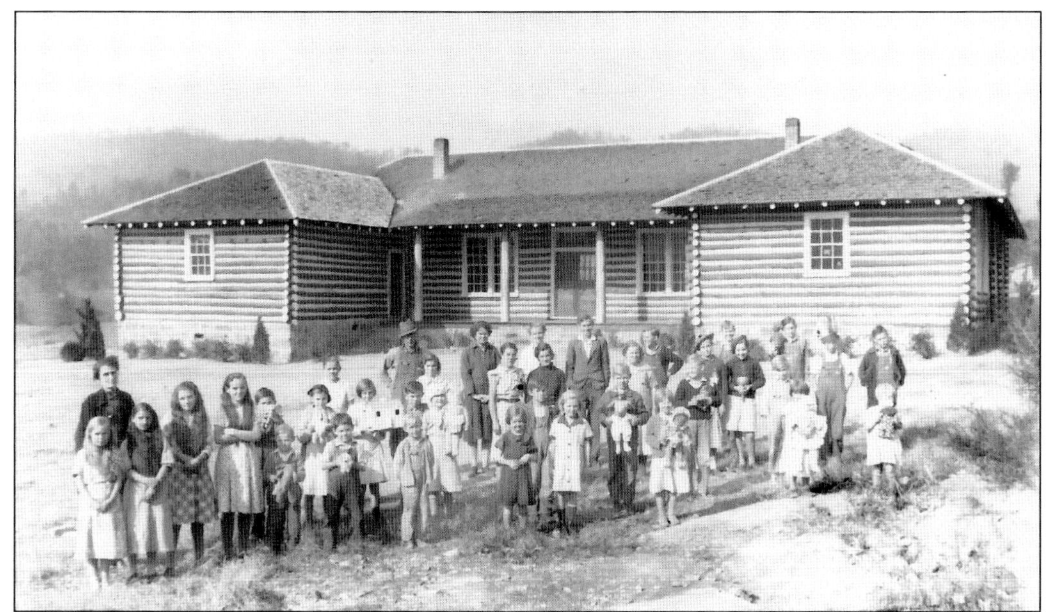

STONE MOUNTAIN SCHOOL. Located in the Poor Valley region of Hawkins County, this log structure was built in 1921. It was organized by George and Marie Berry for the purpose of educating the underprivileged children from nearby Pressmen's Home and surrounding areas. Famous journalist Ernie Pyle wrote an article about the school in the 1930s.

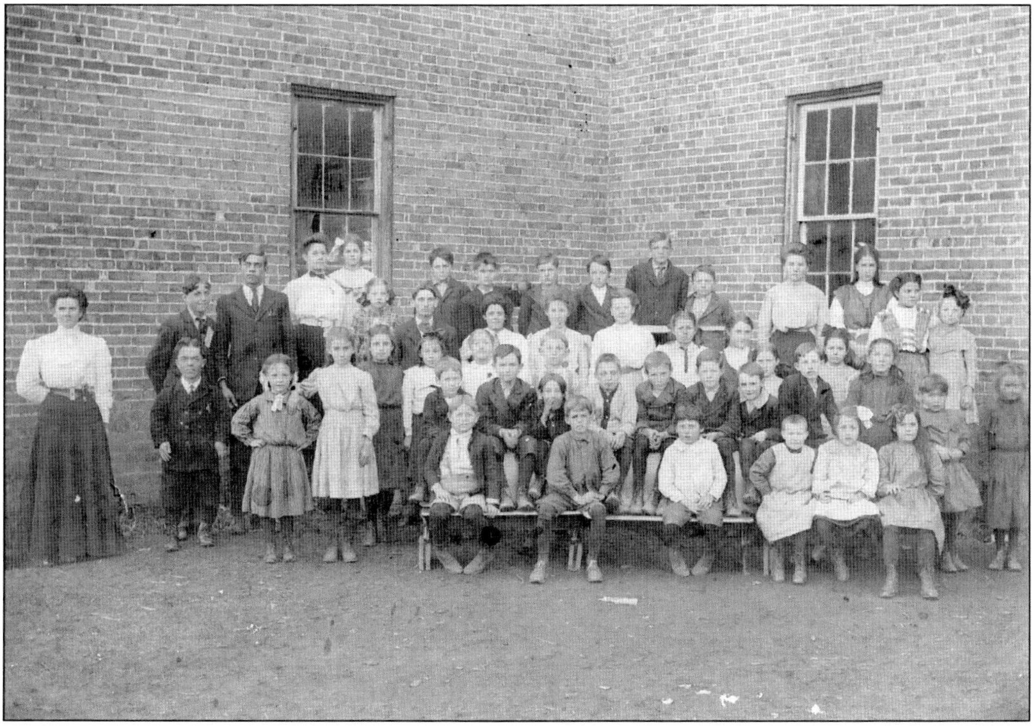

CHURCH HILL HIGH SCHOOL. Here is an unidentified school group at Church Hill High School in 1909. The town had one of the finest high schools in East Tennessee.

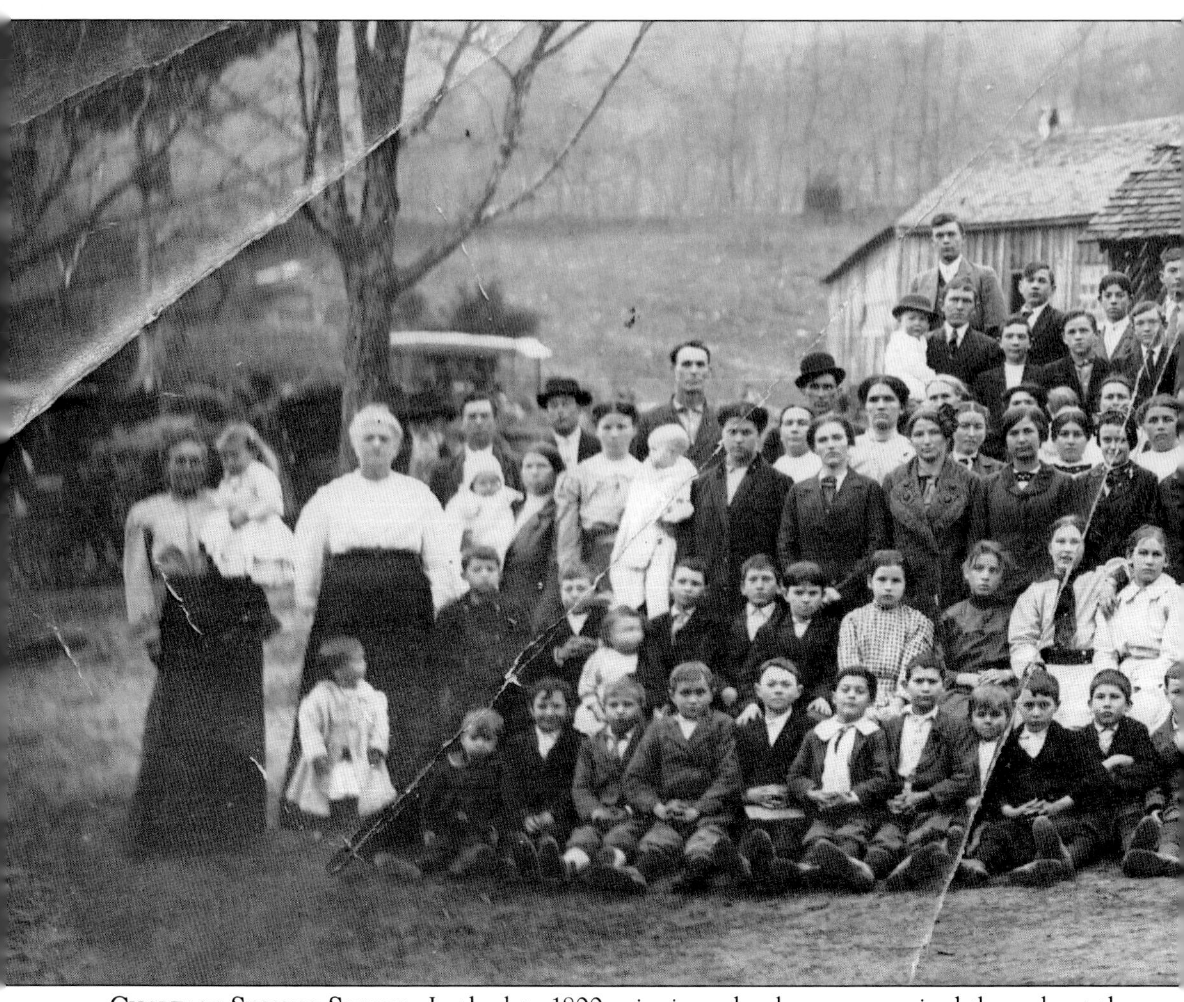

CHOPTACK SINGING SCHOOL. In the late 1800s, singing schools were organized throughout the South. A traveling teacher would be brought in to teach the students shape-note harmony. Huge

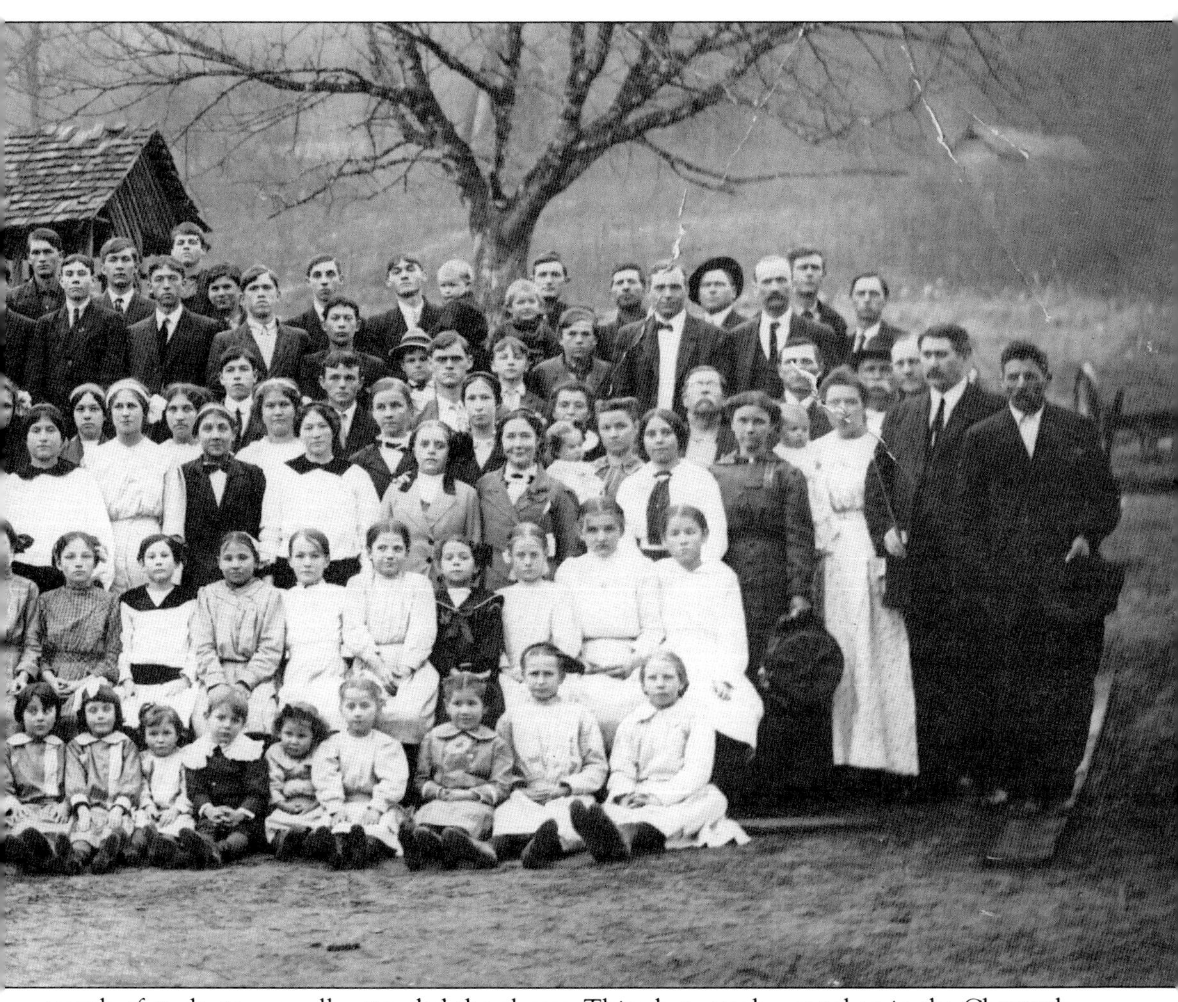

crowds of students normally attended the classes. This photograph was taken in the Choptack community in 1905.

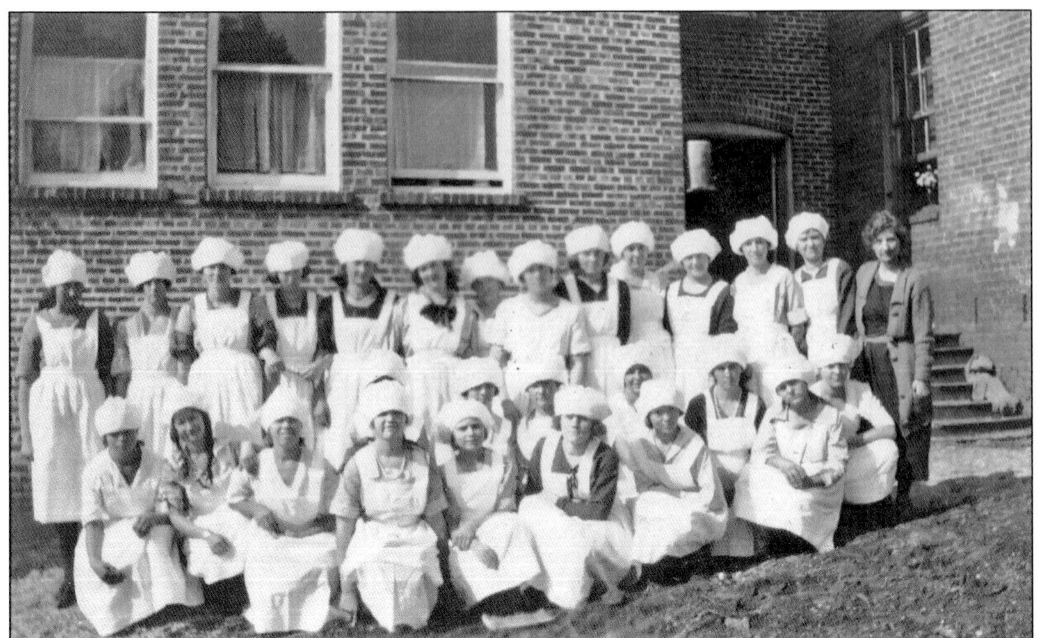

Economics Class. Here is the 1922 home economics class of Church Hill High School. The old high school building served the community for many years until it was abandoned in the 1960s when Hawkins County consolidated its high schools.

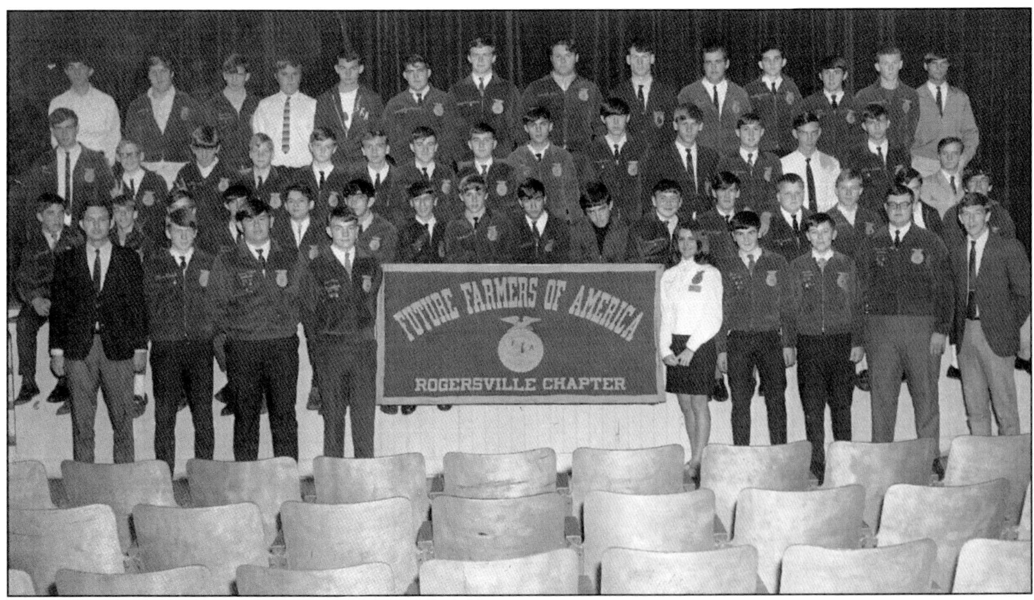

Future Farmers. Here is the Rogersville High School association of Future Farmers of America and their sweetheart. At one time, agriculture was the backbone of the Hawkins County economy. The FFA turned out farmers who could use modern farming technology to their advantage.

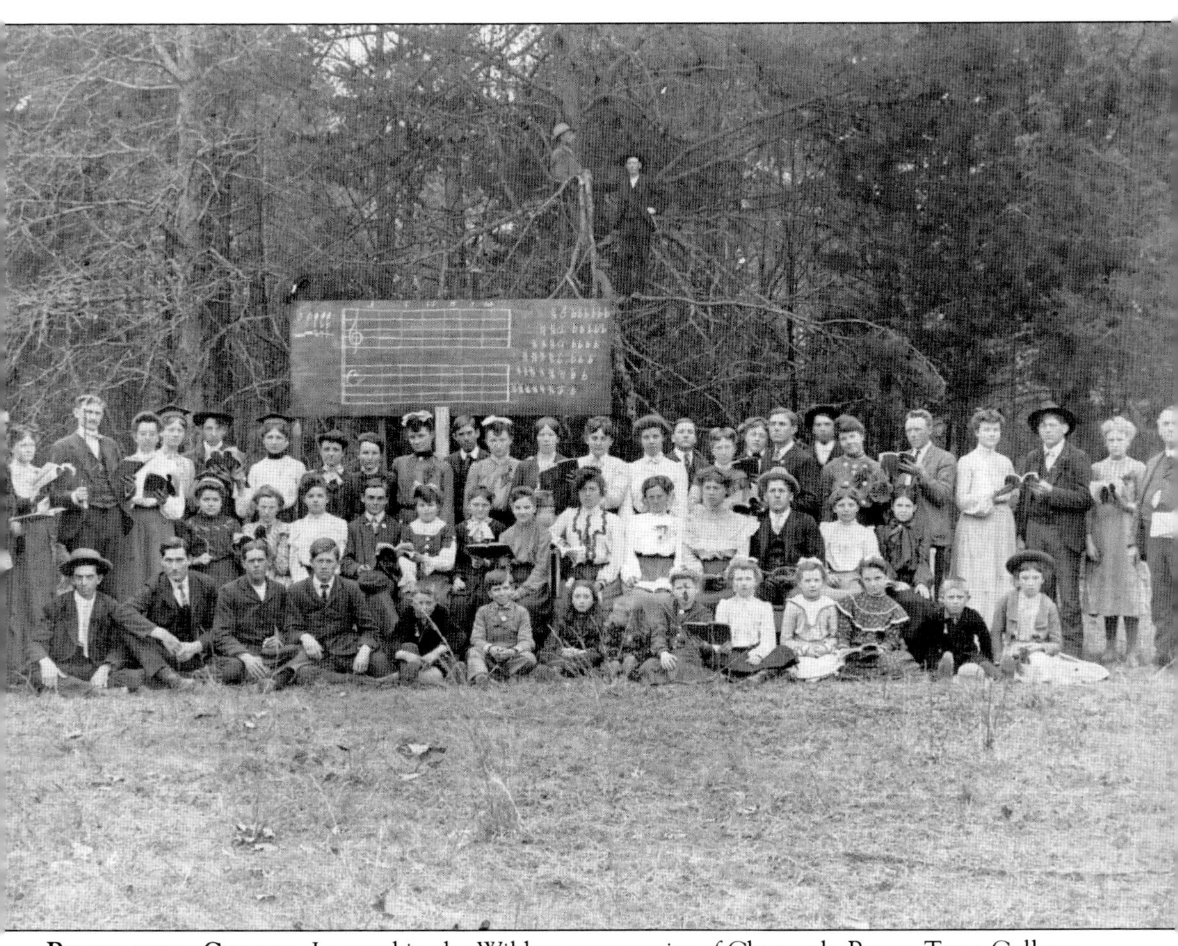

Brown town College. Located in the Wildcat community of Choptack, Brown Town College was founded in the 1860s. This photograph was taken in 1905 at a summer singing school.

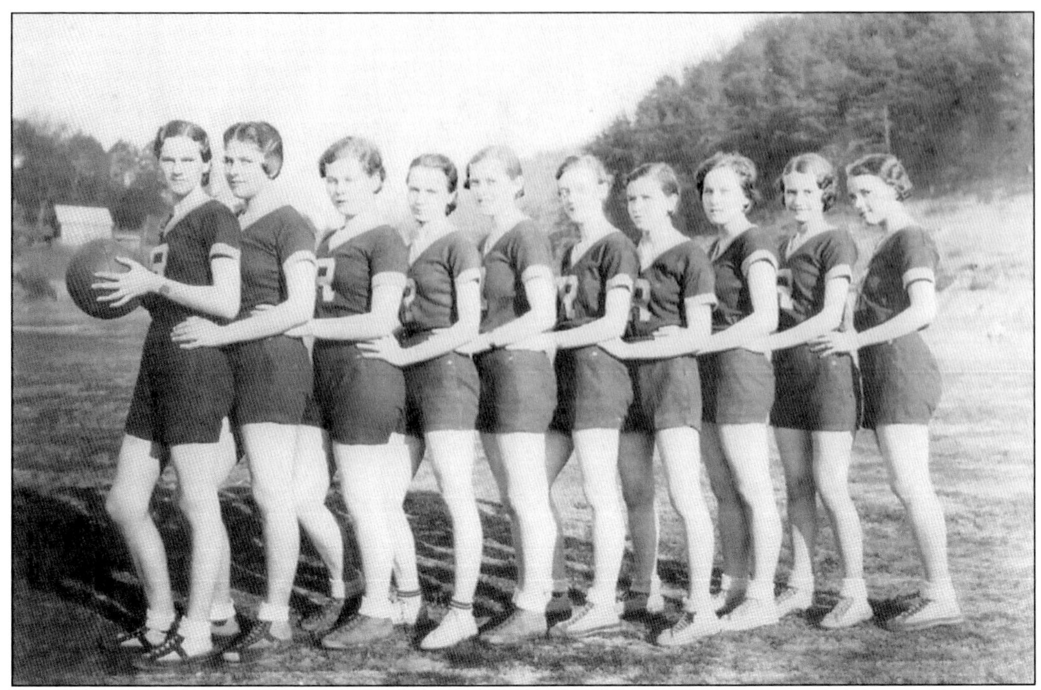

Girls' Basketball. Here is the Rogersville High School girls' basketball team of 1932. From left to right are Gladys Haynes, Kate Kyle, Josephine Miller, Ruth Wheeler, Virginia Carson, Ann Armstrong, Irene Neale, Gladys Cooper, Bea Miner, and Pauline Anderson.

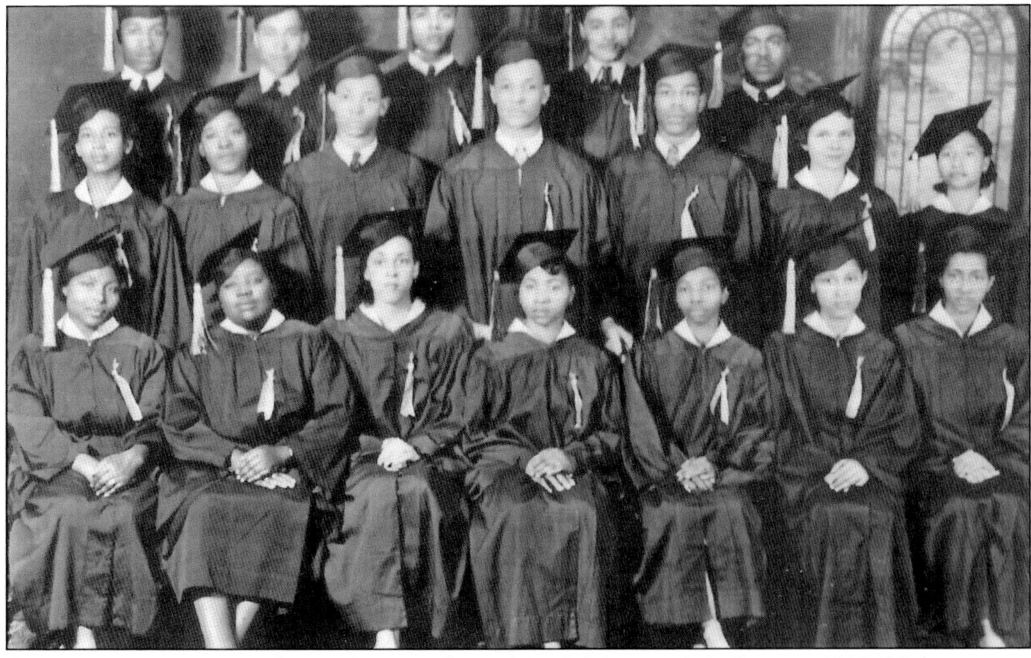

Class of 1919. Here is the graduating class of Swift Memorial College in 1919. This institute for higher learning for African Americans was one of the finest in the country. Graduates from the school went on to be doctors, lawyers, journalists, and athletes. (Courtesy of the Swift Museum.)

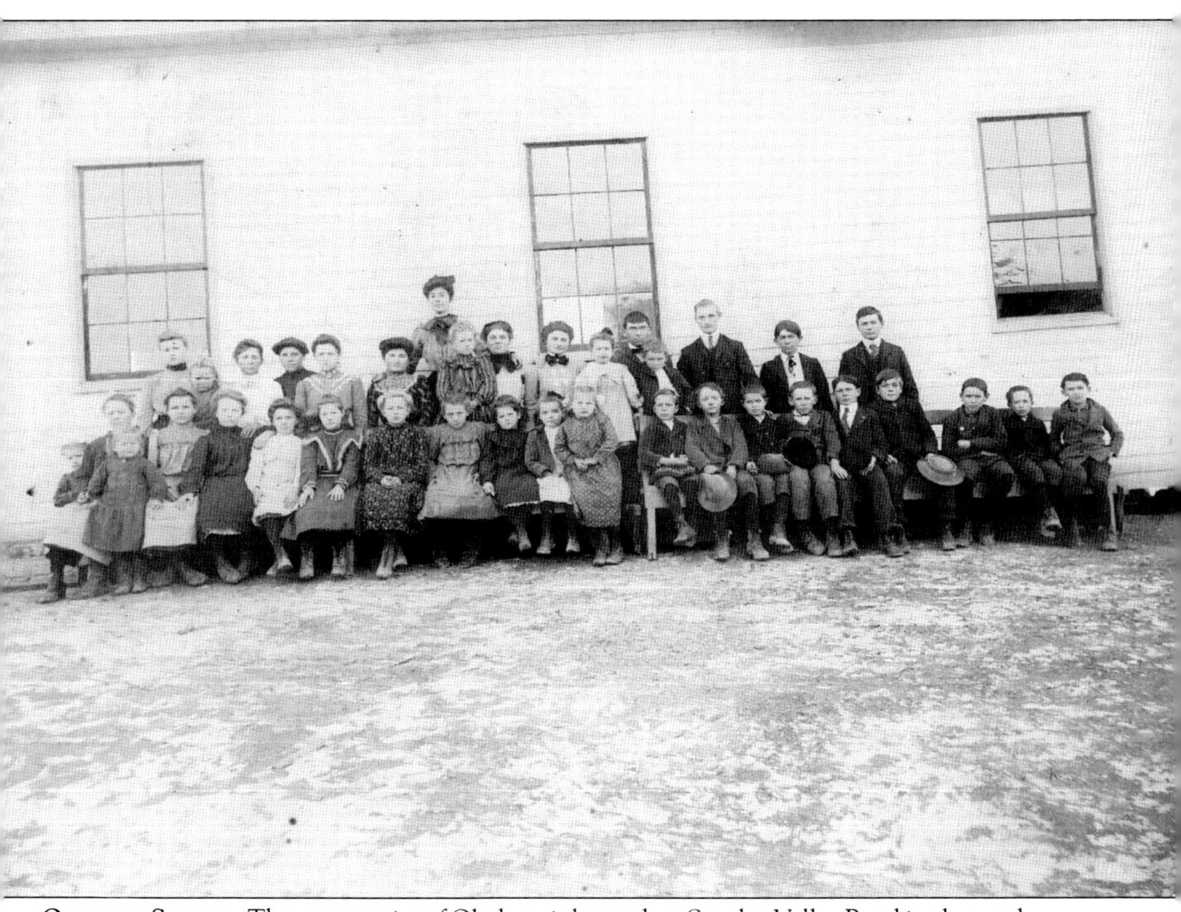

Okolona School. The community of Okolona is located on Stanley Valley Road in the northern section of Hawkins County. This class photograph was taken in 1898. Alice Mitchell was the teacher.

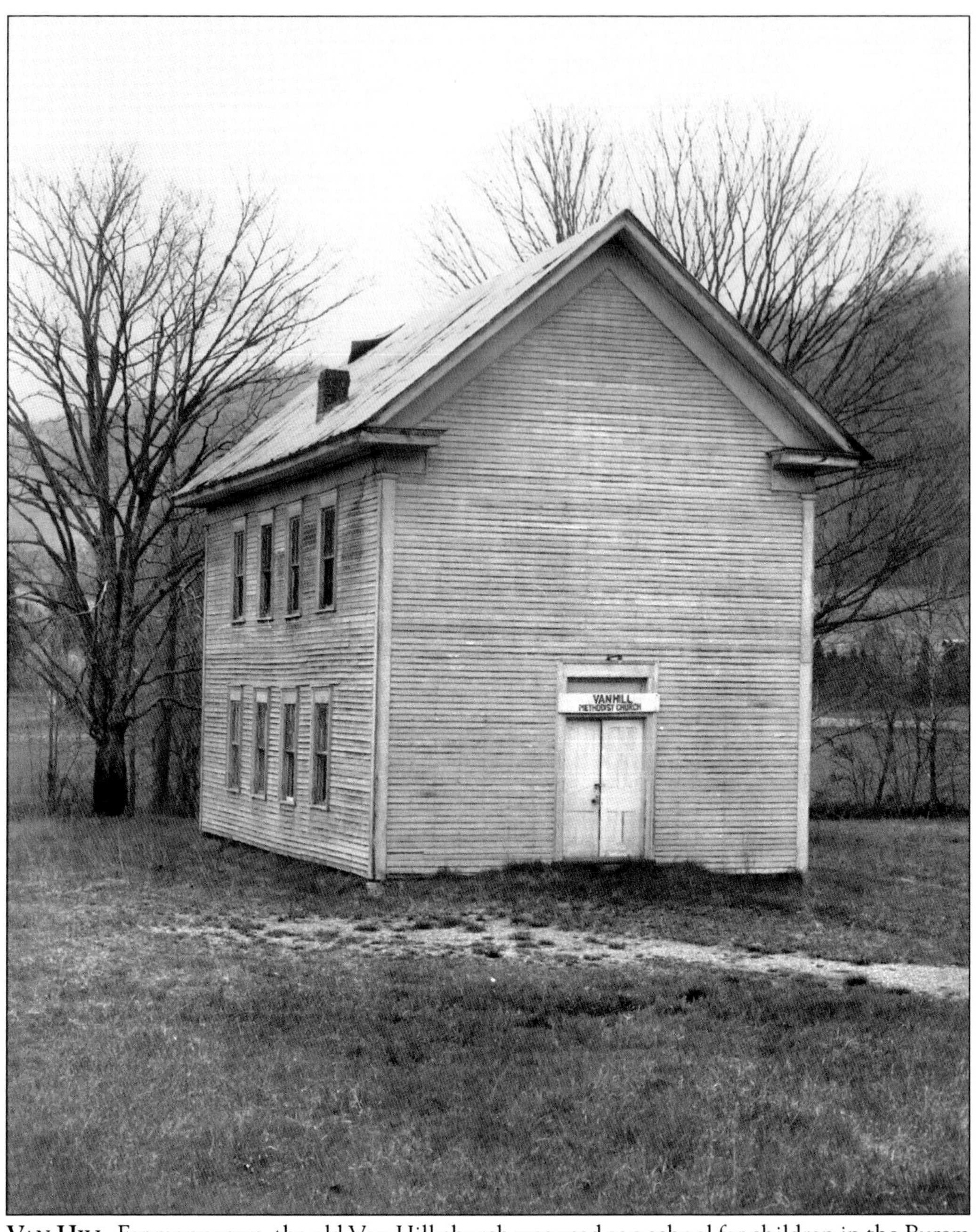

VAN HILL. For many years, the old Van Hill church was used as a school for children in the Burem community. It was founded in the 1800s.

Four

People and Places

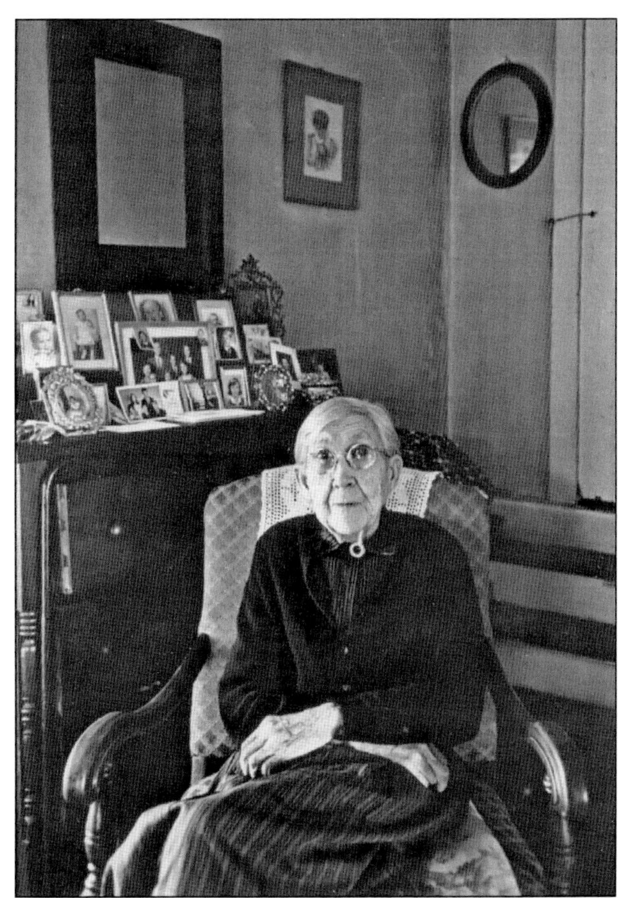

Anne Amis. A direct descendant of early settler Thomas Amis (pronounced Aim-ee), Anne Amis was a marvelous raconteur, and she loved to regale visitors with stories of American Indians, Revolutionary and Civil War soldiers, and memories of an era long since vanished. This chapter is just a sampling of the diverse people and places of Hawkins County.

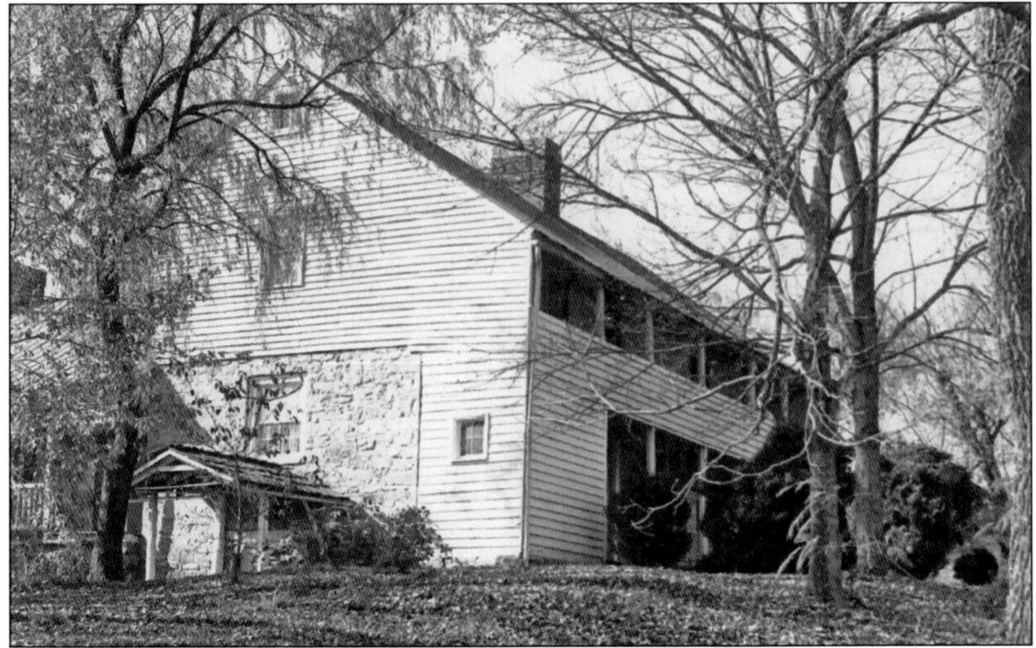

Amis House. Located 1.5 miles from the mouth Big Creek is the old Amis house. Built around 1780 by Thomas Amis, it was originally a stone fort with a log palisade surrounding it. Early settlers sought refuge here during the sporadic Creek Indian raids of the late 18th century. The homestead eventually included hay barns in addition to a distillery, tavern, gristmill, and trading post.

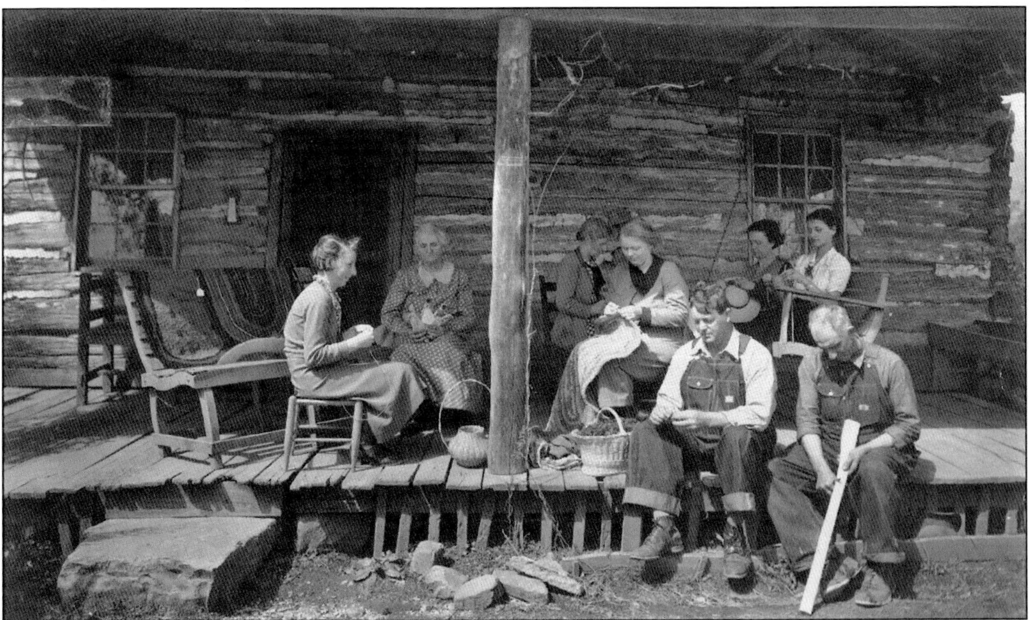

Front Porch Memories. These people are enjoying a Saturday afternoon at the Mollie Brooks cabin in Mooresburg just a few days before the waters of Cherokee Lake flooded the 200-year-old homestead. Pictured are, from left to right, Marion Slaughter, Mollie Rogers Brooks, Agnes Rogers, Mollie Payne, Grace Rogers, Frances Koger, Herbert Payne, and Ernest Rogers. (Courtesy of Regina Koger.)

MISSING LINKS. These local Hawkins County teenagers were members of a popular singing group in the 1960s. The Missing Links was made up of, from left to right, (first row) Harold Walker; (second row) Bill Rymer and Benny Wilson; (third row) David Hyder, Mike Pyne, and Steve Hyder.

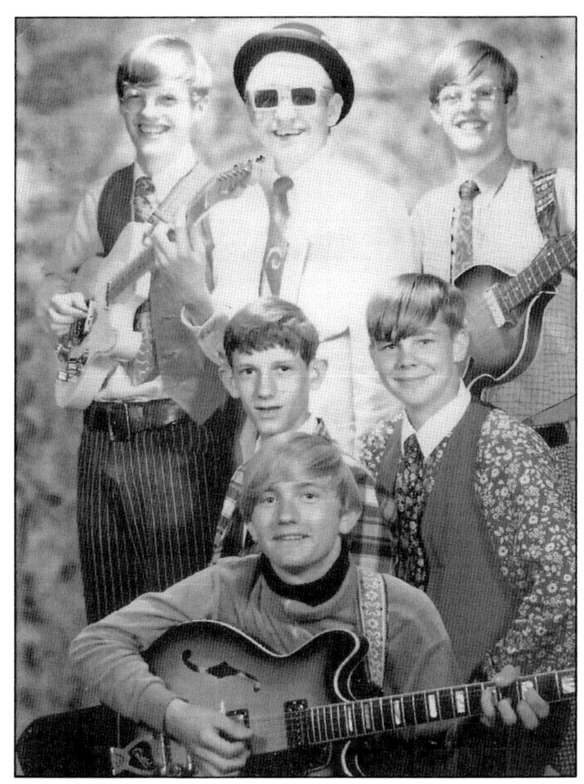

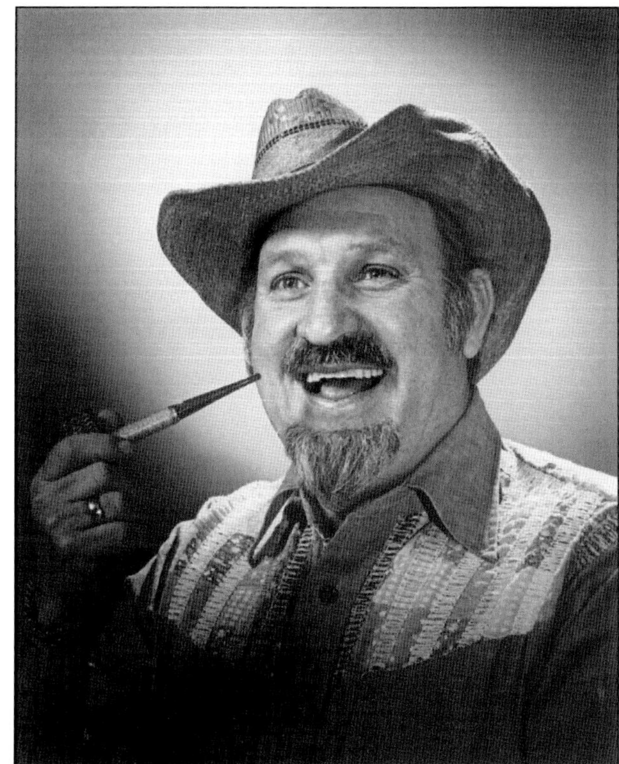

DOC MCCONNELL. Nationally known storyteller and Surgoinsville native Doc McConnell was one of the founders of the National Storytelling Festival in Jonesboro, Tennessee, and was a featured teller there for many years. Throughout an outstanding 50-year career, he entertained thousands of people who enjoyed his homespun stories and tall tales through television, radio, and live shows. (Courtesy of Guerry McConnell.)

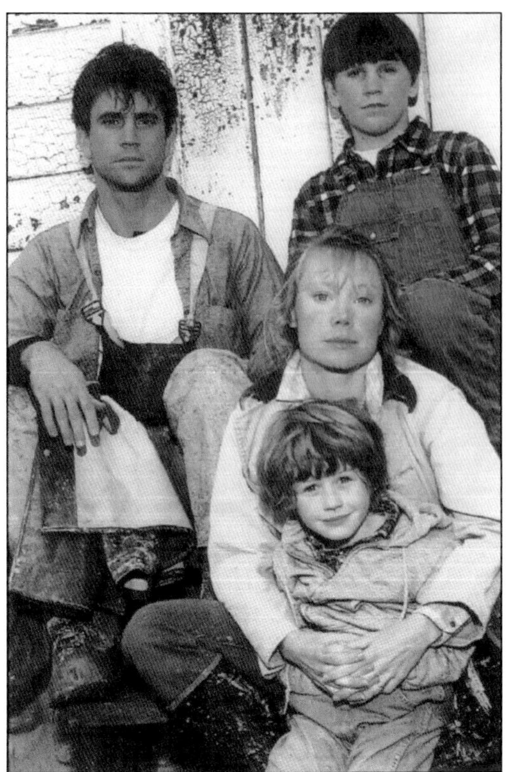

Shane Bailey. In 1983, Wayne Bailey read in a local newspaper where Mark Riddell was casting a movie called *The River* to be shot primarily in Hawkins County. He was sure that his 12-year-old son would be perfect in one of the roles. His hunch proved right. Shane's uncanny resemblance to Mel Gibson, one of the lead actors, secured him the role. (Courtesy of Universal Studios.)

The River. In 1983, Hollywood came calling to Hawkins County when the major motion picture *The River* was filmed at Laurel Run Park in Churchill. The movie starred Mel Gibson and Sissy Spacek and a supporting cast of local residents. This house, used as a movie set, burned down on Halloween in 1986. (Courtesy of Kathy Lawson.)

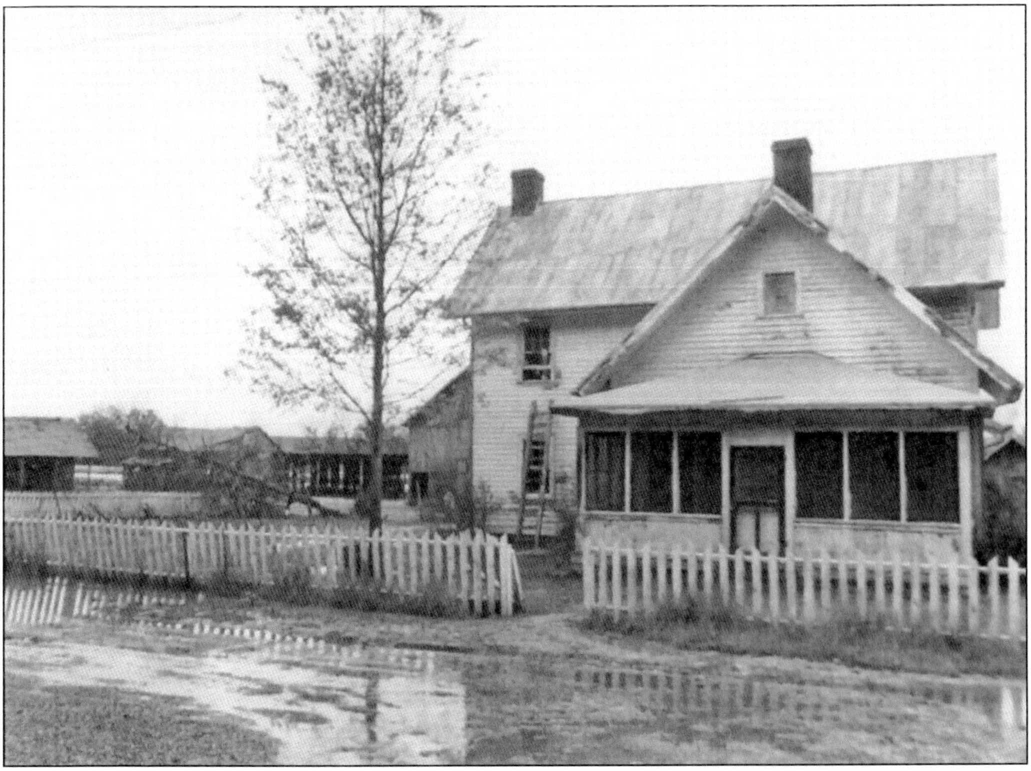

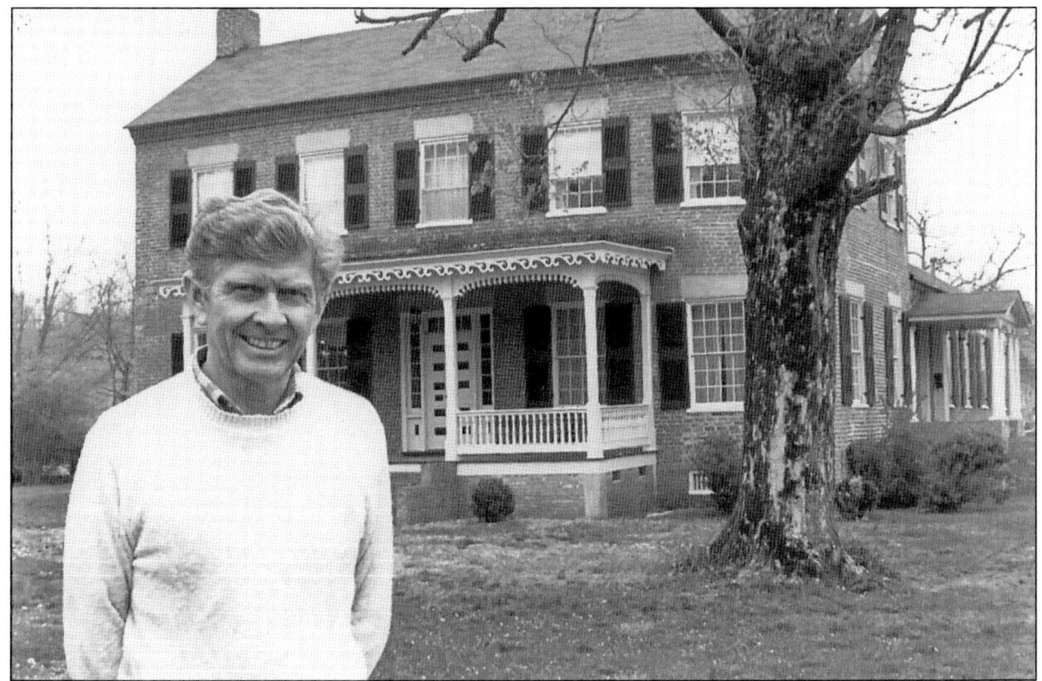

CAPTAIN BROWN. Capt. Carl Netherland Brown led the crusade for historic preservation in Hawkins County. He purchased Rosemont, his ancestral home (pictured in the background), as well as the Hale Springs Inn, the McKinney Law office, and several other historic landmarks.

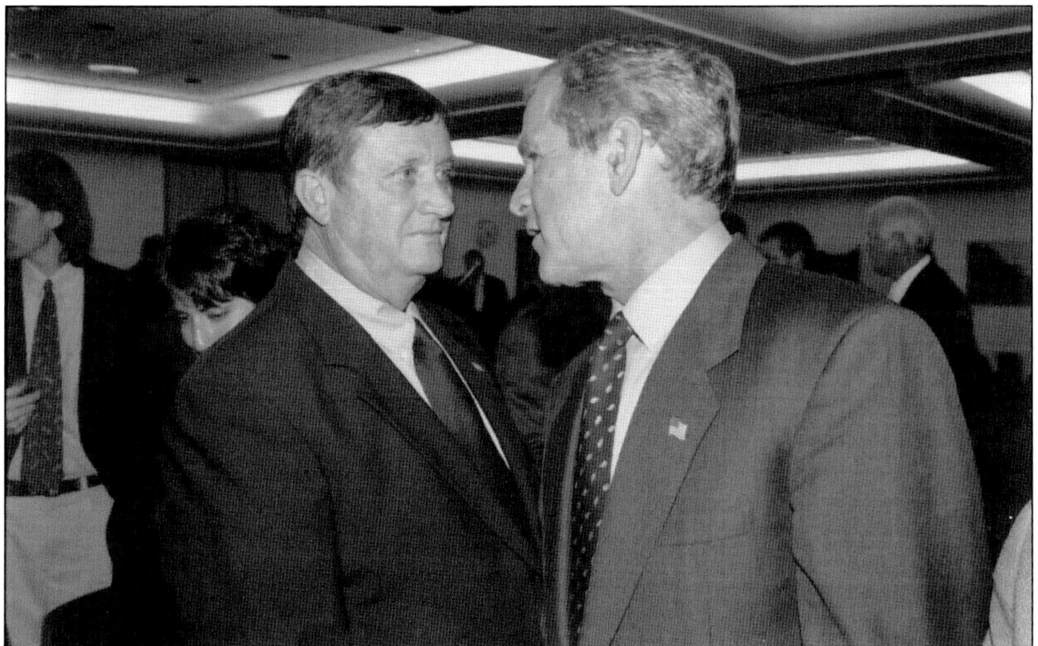

CONGRESSMAN JENKINS. William Jenkins is a seventh-generation Tennessean. Elected to the Tennessee General Assembly as a Republican in 1962, he served as Speaker of the Tennessee House from 1969 to 1971. He was the only Republican to serve as Speaker of the Tennessee House in the 20th century. Here he is shown with Pres. George W Bush. (Photograph by William Jenkins.)

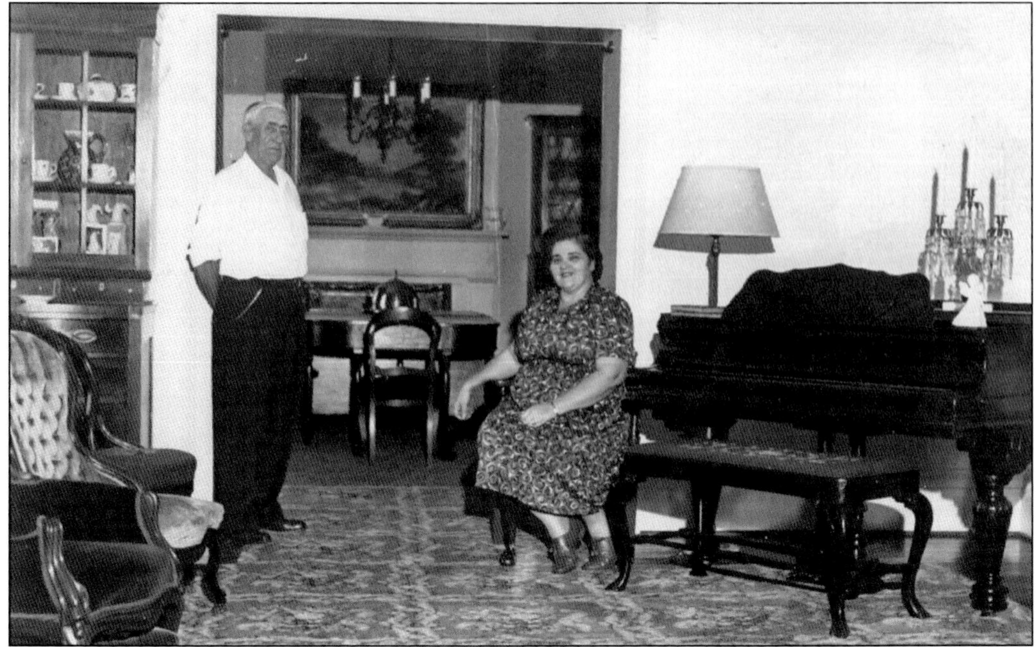

Innkeepers. This photograph is of Ellis Cary and his daughter, Mrs. Mike P. (Ella) Walker, in the parlor of their home, the Stage Coach Inn. Built in 1840, the old inn has entertained many prominent visitors over the years including Presidents Jackson and Polk. The old mansion was torn down in the 1970s to make way for the TRW plant.

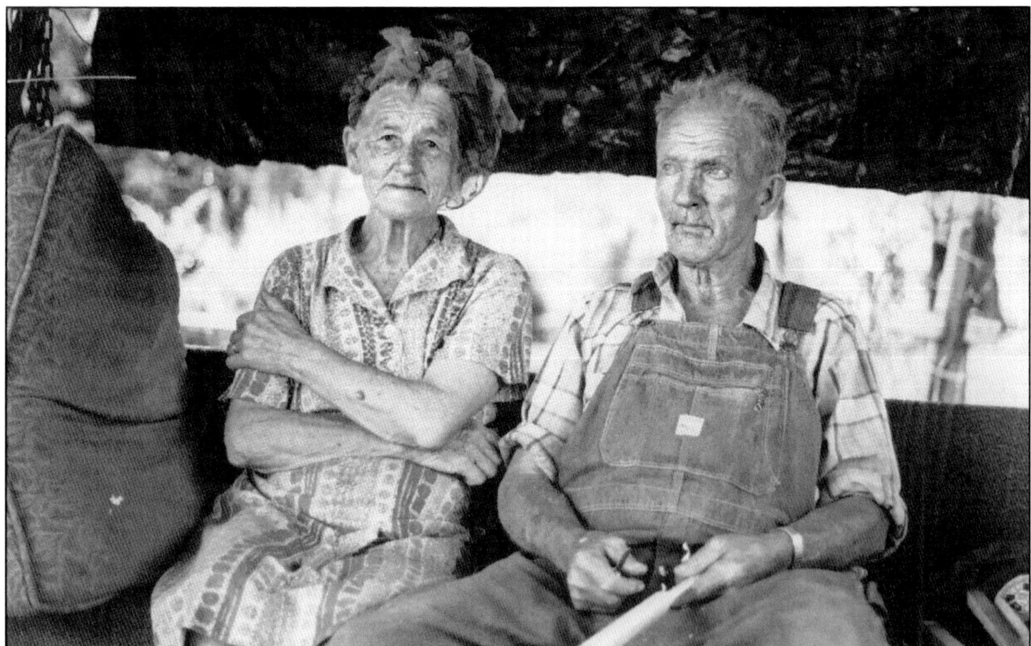

The Mauks. Luther and Ida Mauk lived a peaceful and simple life in their 200-year-old log cabin home in Stanley Valley. Their life was an Appalachian portrait set in another era. Ida cooked on a woodstove, and Luther raised chickens. Together they were the subjects for many traveling photographers. (Photograph by Randy Ball.)

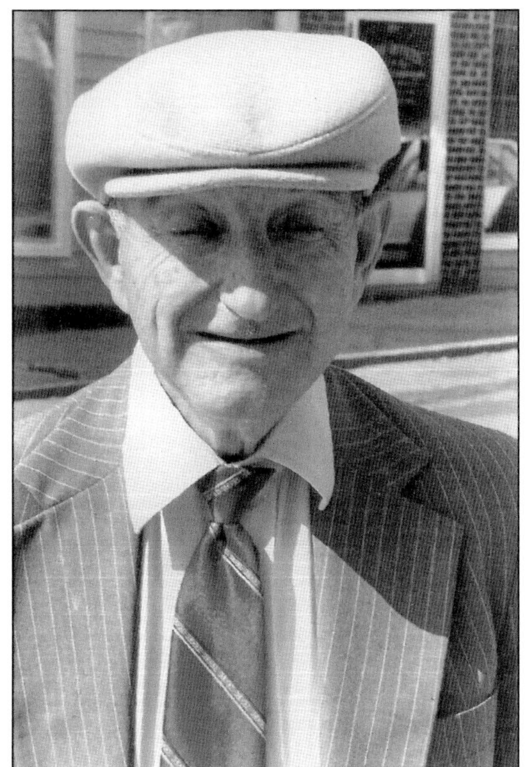

Hardrock Lovin. Everybody called him Hardrock, and he was one of Hawkins County's most unforgettable characters. His real name was Hobart Walter Lovin, and he was born June 30, 1930, in a cabin on Short Mountain. He hitchhiked all over the United States and was loved by everyone. (Photograph by Randy Ball.)

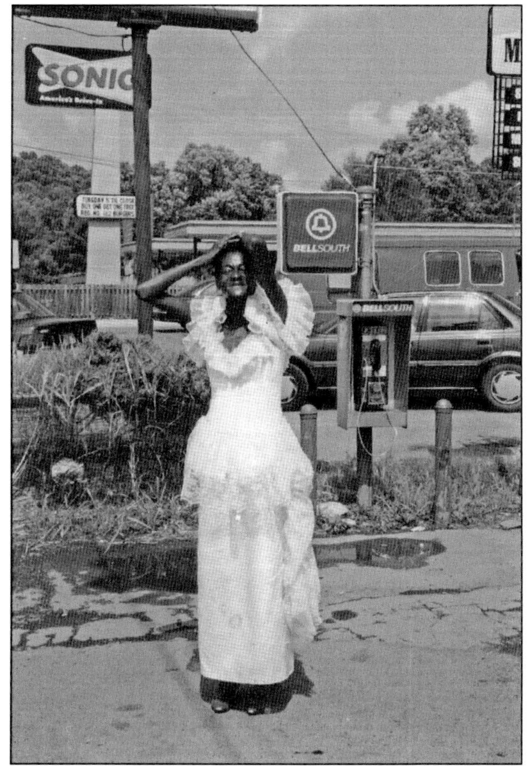

Janice Rogers. One of Hawkins County's most recognizable characters was born in the Petersburg community in 1948. She was known simply as "Detcie." Many remember her standing in front of the old Big John's Restaurant on Main Street always smiling and waving at passersby.

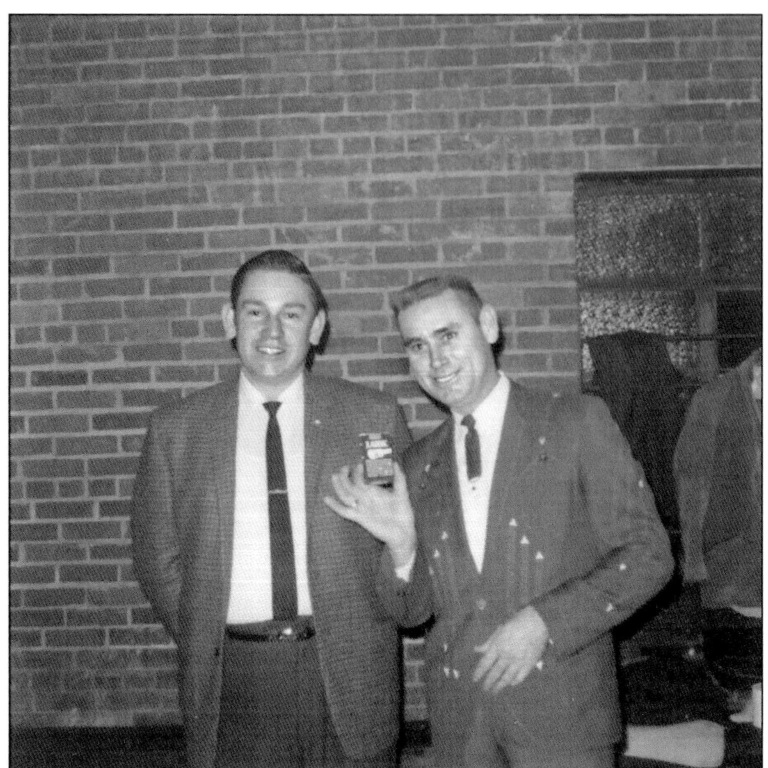

Gene Vance. A beloved and respected Hawkins County businessman, Gene Vance (left) has been responsible for bringing some of the most popular entertainers in country music to the East Tennessee area. Here he is pictured with the legendary music icon George Jones at Rogersville High School in 1967. (Courtesy of Hale Vance.)

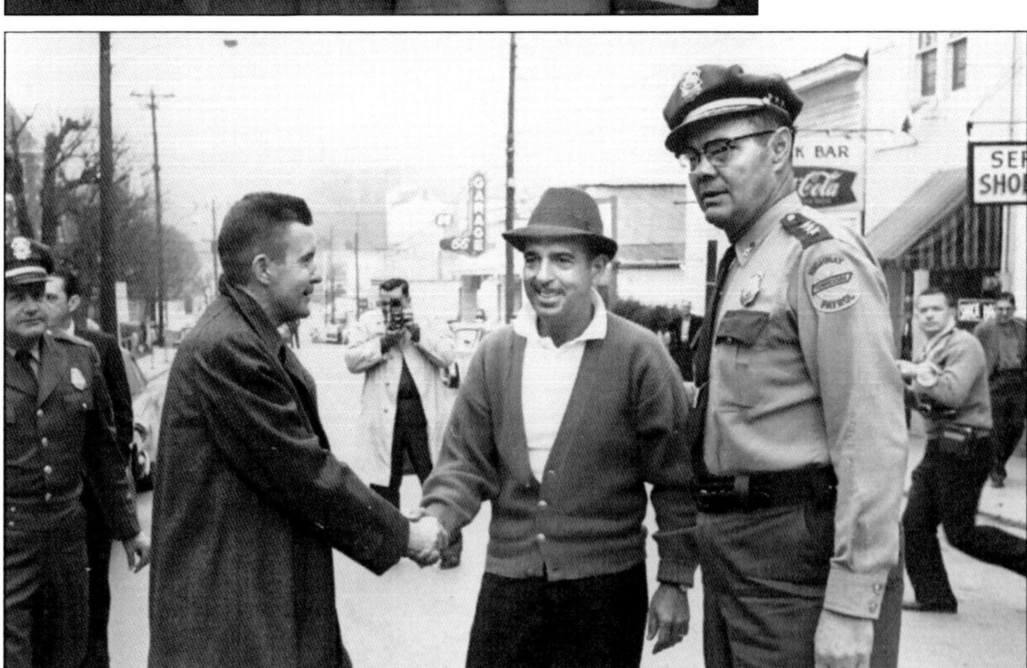

Ol' Pea Picker. Mayor Bill Phipps welcomes Grand Ole Opry star and Bristol native Tennessee Ernie Ford (center) to Rogersville in the 1960s. To the right of Ford is Sheriff Dan Anderson. This photograph was taken on the town square facing Depot Street. The Ol' Pea Picker was passing through on his way to Nashville.

BOXING BUDDIE. Hawkins County resident Buddie Russell began boxing when he was a teenager. In 1958, he competed in the National Golden Gloves championship in Chicago. Also competing that night was Cassius Clay, who would later change his name to Muhammad Ali. Russell has devoted his life to working with children in athletic circles. (Courtesy of Buddie Russell.)

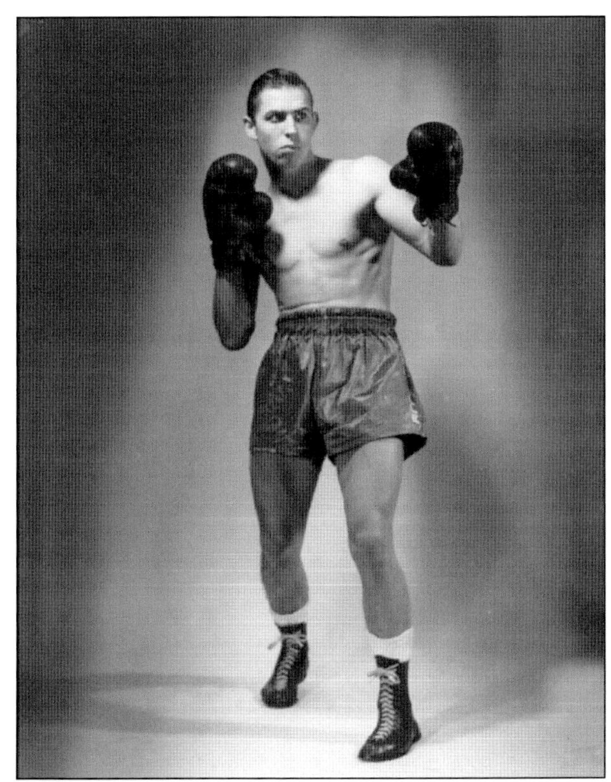

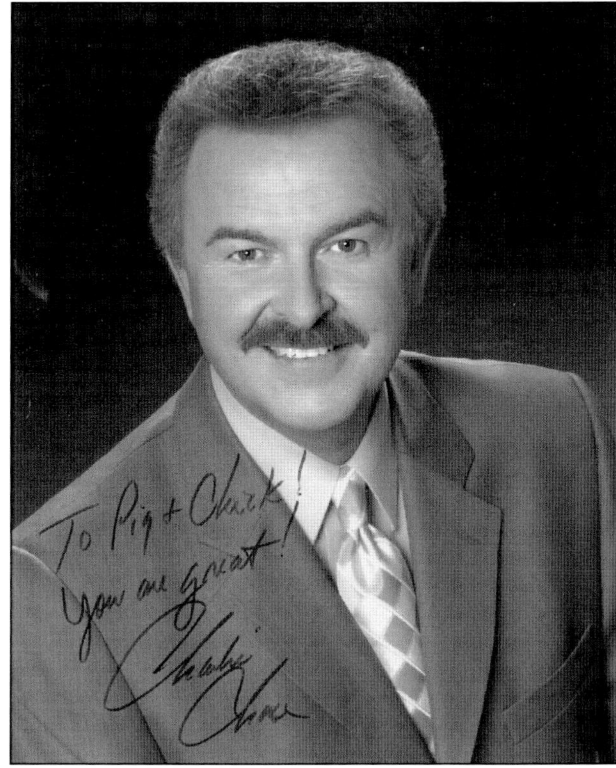

CHARLIE CHASE. Radio and television host Charlie Chase is best known for his work on the Nashville Network program *Crook and Chase*. Chase was born October 19, 1952, in Rogersville. He began his radio career at the age of 13 at WRGS Radio. (Courtesy of Richard Beets.)

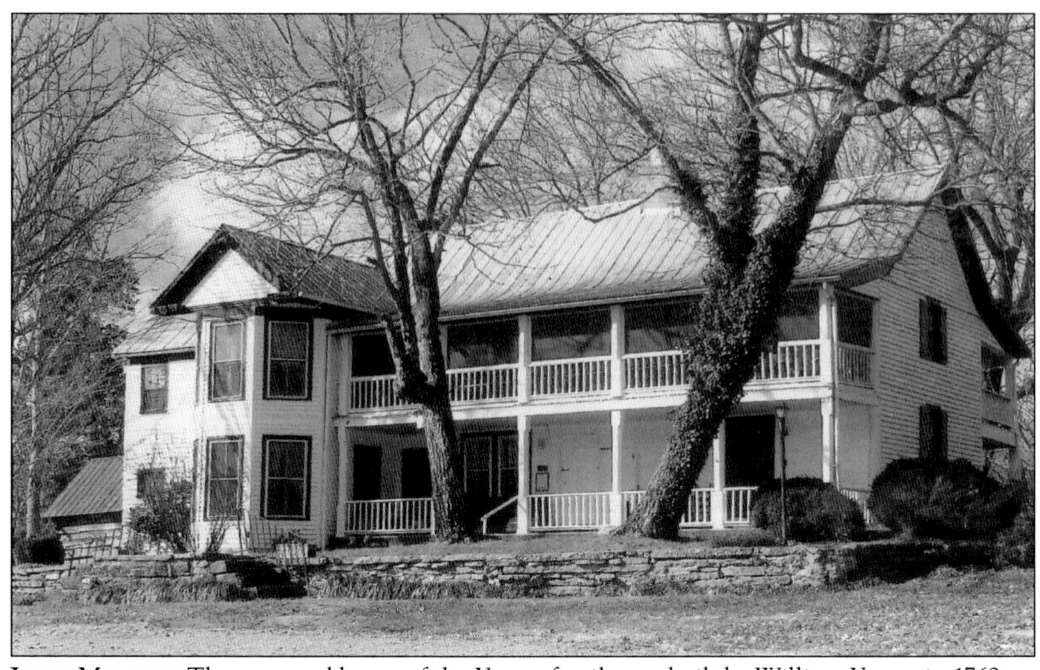

LONG MEADOW. The ancestral home of the Young family was built by William Young in 1762 on a land grant from King George III. The house also has a connection to Harry S. Truman, whose mother was a Young. Long Meadow is listed on the National Register of Historic Places and considered one of the oldest wooden structures in Tennessee. (Photograph by Randy Ball.)

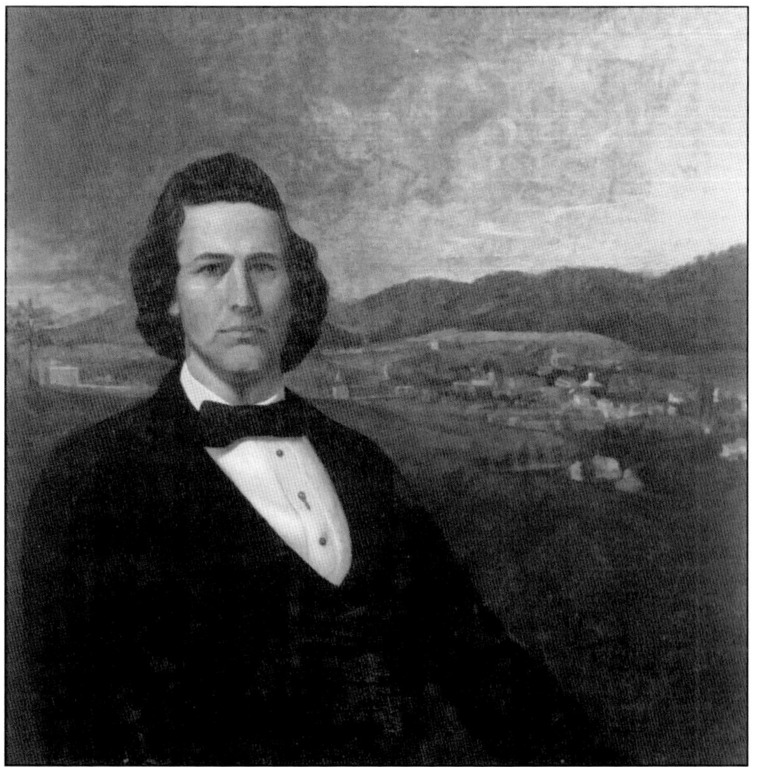

JOSEPH FOARD. Cornelia Young married a young Kentuckian, Maj. Joseph Foard, in 1858. The Confederate army major was captured on Christmas day in 1862 by General Stoneman's Union army Cavalry troops and forced to walk to Knoxville. This painting of Foard was done by Samuel Shaver in 1857 and shows Rogersville in the background.

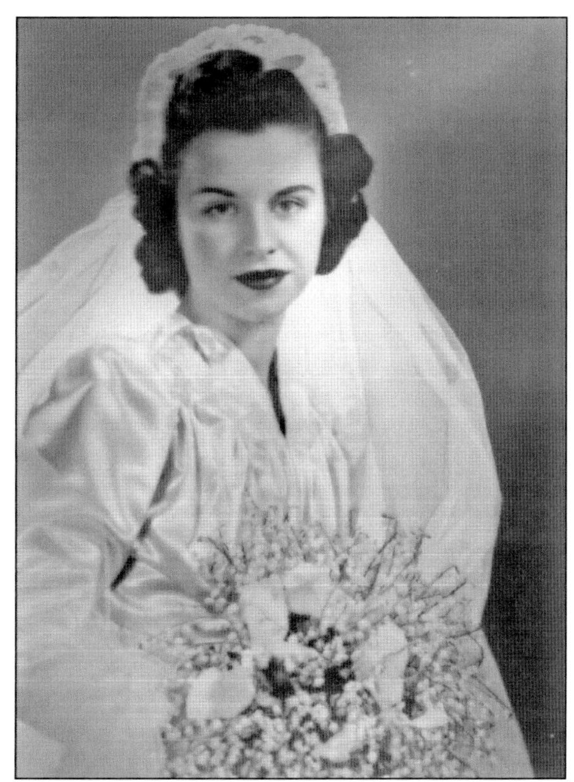

CAMAY BRIDE. In the 1940s, Procter and Gamble began an advertising campaign called the Camay Bride. Young newlywed brides were chosen from all over the United States. Jan Smith of Rogersville was one of the beautiful ladies chosen as a Camay Bride. (Courtesy of Jan Smith.)

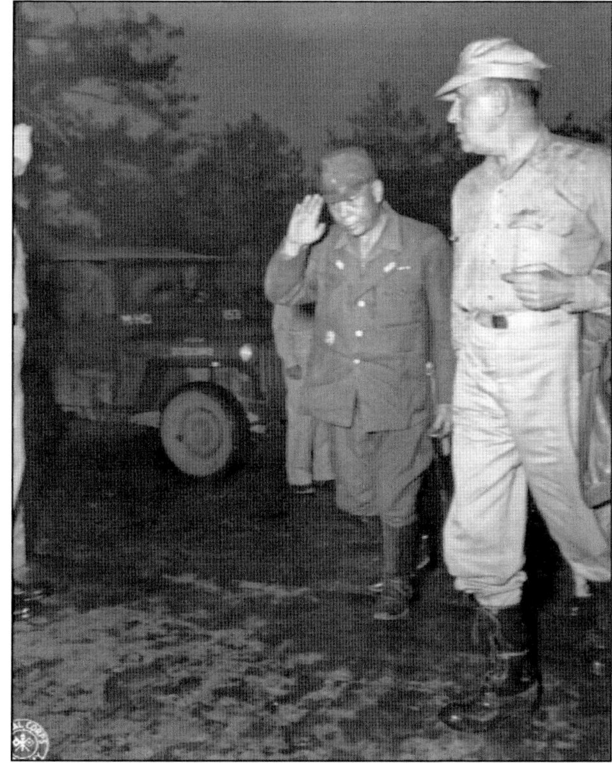

COL. FRANK SMITH. Col. Frank Smith served during World War I with Gen. John Pershing. He also served during World War II. Here he is shown with Gen. Tomoyuki Yamashita, highest commander, Imperial Japanese Army in the Philippines, at Camp John Hay. Colonel Smith received the informal surrender sword on September 2, 1945. (Courtesy of Jan Smith.)

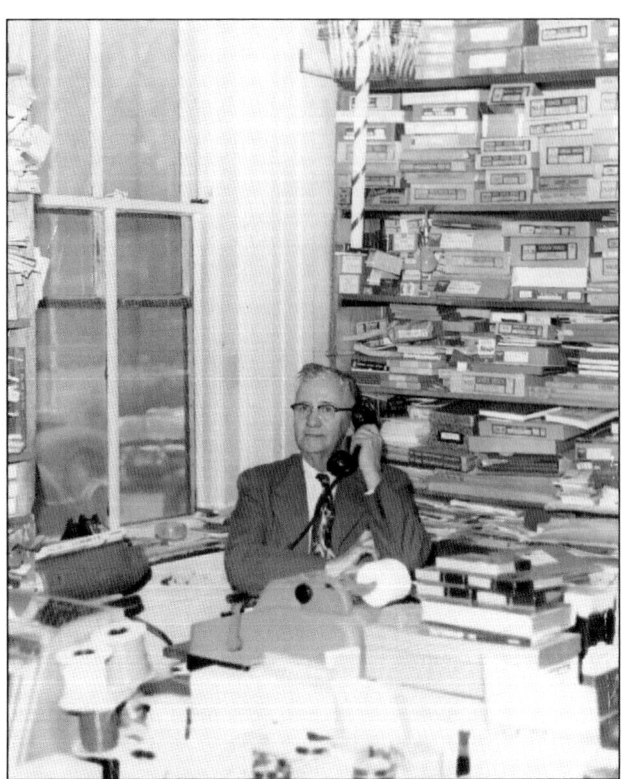

E. A. Cope. A descendant of one of Tennessee's earliest families, E. A. Cope was a much-respected member of the Rogersville community. He opened up a school and office supply store in the old Miller Hospital building in 1948. He also served on the Hawkins County School Board.

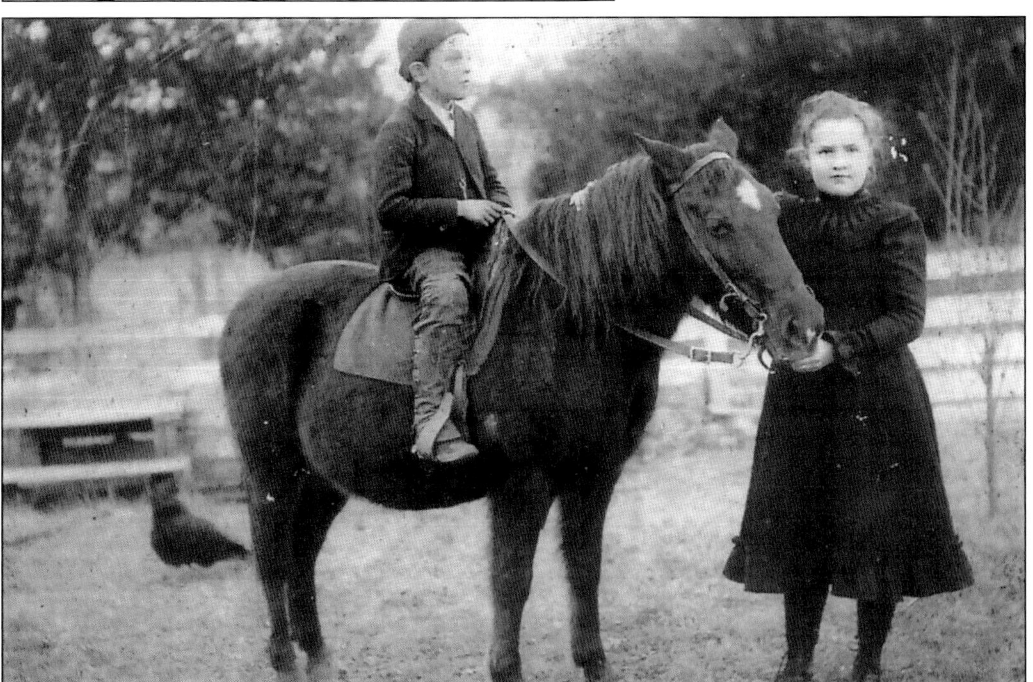

Lyons Children. Here is a very young Dr. Connor Lyons and his sister Willie Lyons Westmoreland playing with the pony they rode to Maxwell Academy at Stony Point. Dr. Connor would later become mayor of Surgoinsville. (Courtesy of Jesse Lyons Brown.)

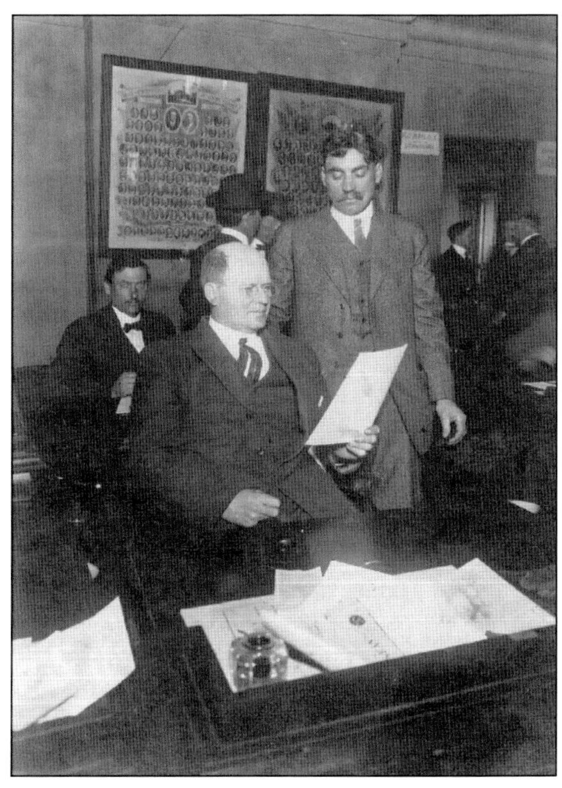

CONGRESSMAN MITCHELL. Samuel Howard Mitchell was born in Rogersville in 1868. He moved from Hawkins to Grainger County in 1907 and served two terms as member of the Republican Executive Committee for the third Congressional District. Mitchell died December 4, 1945.

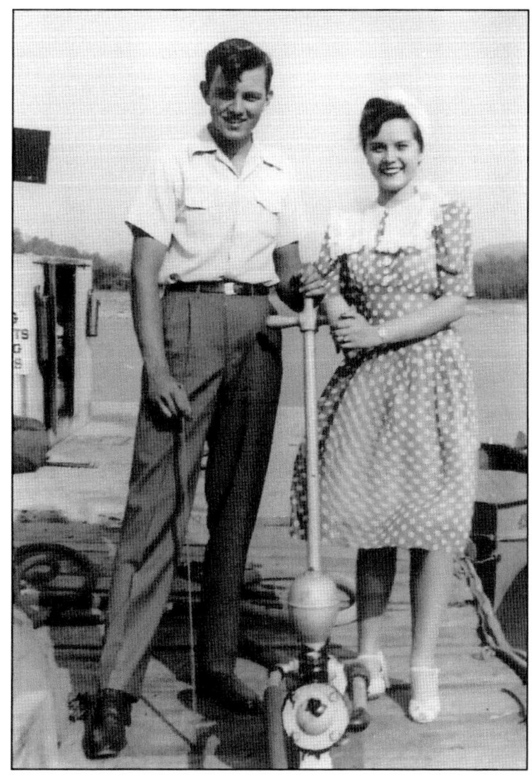

THE BEETS. Harold and Irene Livesay Beets were well known in Hawkins County social circles. The Livesay family ran a Chevrolet dealership in Rogersville for many years. (Courtesy of Barbara Combs.)

First Historian. James Woods Rogan was Hawkins County's first official historian. He researched and documented the earliest periods of East Tennessee's past. Without his diligent preservation efforts and precise records, much of the county's history would have been lost.

Socially Speaking. Bea Cope was a columnist for the *Rogersville Review* for over 50 years. Her column "Socially Speaking with Bea Cope" was not only popular with the African American community but was loved by readers from all backgrounds. (Courtesy of Norma Bowers.)

DR. JAMES J. KOGER. Dr. Koger practiced medicine in Hawkins County for nearly 40 years. A direct descendant of legendary hero Davy Crockett and Rogersville founder Joseph Rogers, he was a true pioneer doctor. He rode his faithful horse, Tom, on nearly every call. (Courtesy of Regina Koger.)

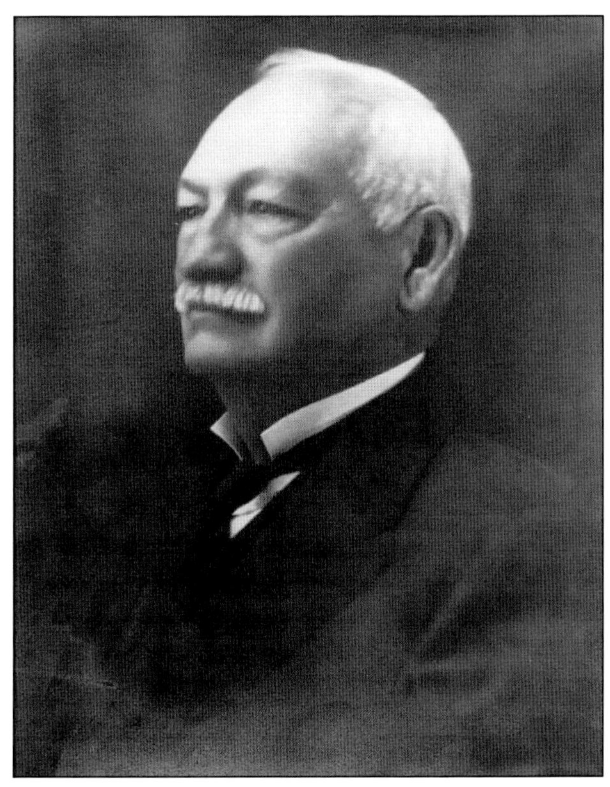

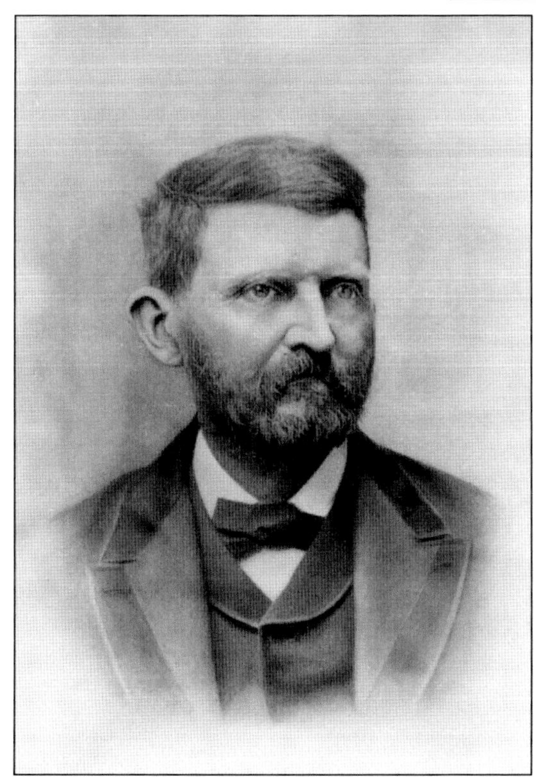

COUNTRY DOCTOR. Dr. Joseph Rogers Walker, grandson of Joseph Rogers, was a graduate of Jefferson Medical College in Philadelphia and practiced medicine in Rogersville for over 60 years. For many years, he was the only trained physician in the county. As a small boy, he remembered hearing Andrew Jackson speak on the town square. His 100 years of living enriched the entire area.

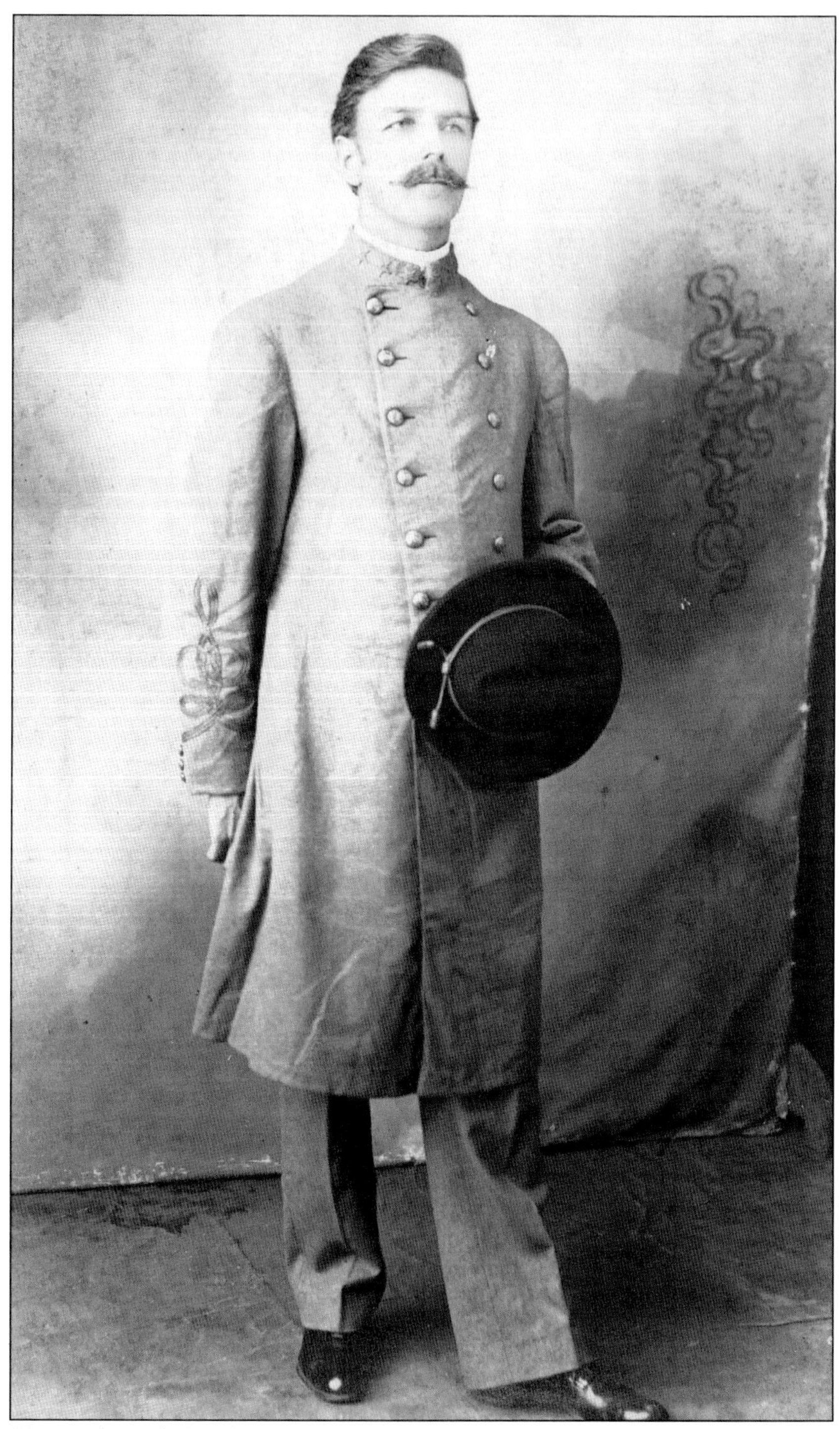

CAPTAIN KYLE. The Kyle family is one of Hawkins County's oldest and most prominent families. Capt. Gale P. Kyle is pictured here in his Confederate army reunion uniform. The Kyle family residence was occupied by Confederate army soldiers during the Civil War while the Hale Springs Inn across the street was held by Union army soldiers.

CAPTAIN CLAY. Henry Boyle Clay (1840–1919) was born in Kentucky. Captain Clay was the grandson of the famous statesmen Henry Clay. The captain was a Confederate army soldier and was with General Morgan when Morgan was killed in Greenville. Captain Clay first came to Hawkins County at the start of the Civil War.

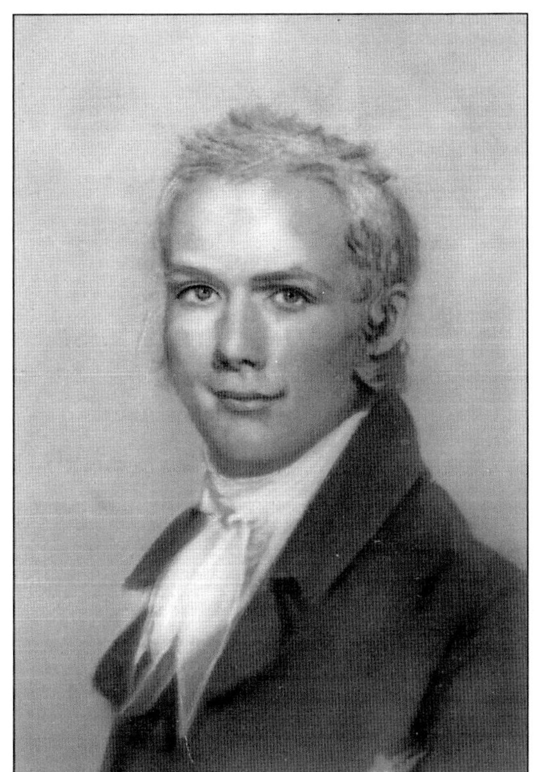

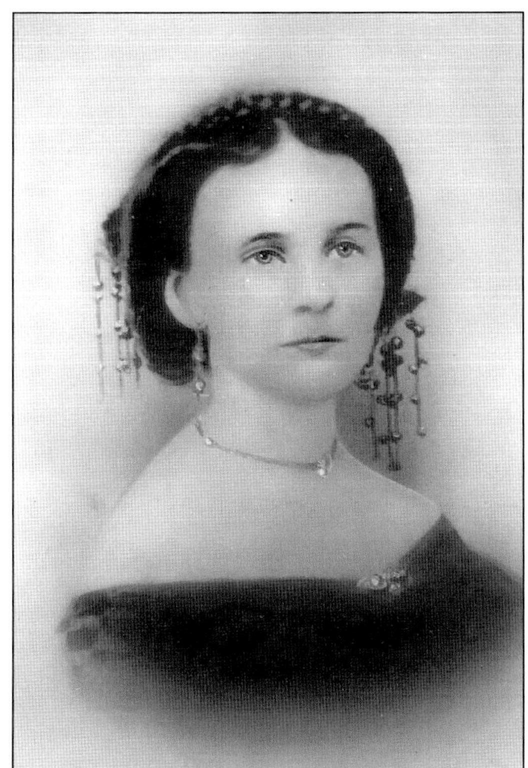

NANCY. Nancy Bynum Clay was the daughter of East Tennessee land magnate Joshua Phipps. After the murder of her first husband, Gen. John Bynum, Nancy married Capt. Henry B Clay. The couple met while Clay's troops were passing through Rogersville. Clay ran a successful cattle and farming operation. At one time, he was known as the cattle king of East Tennessee.

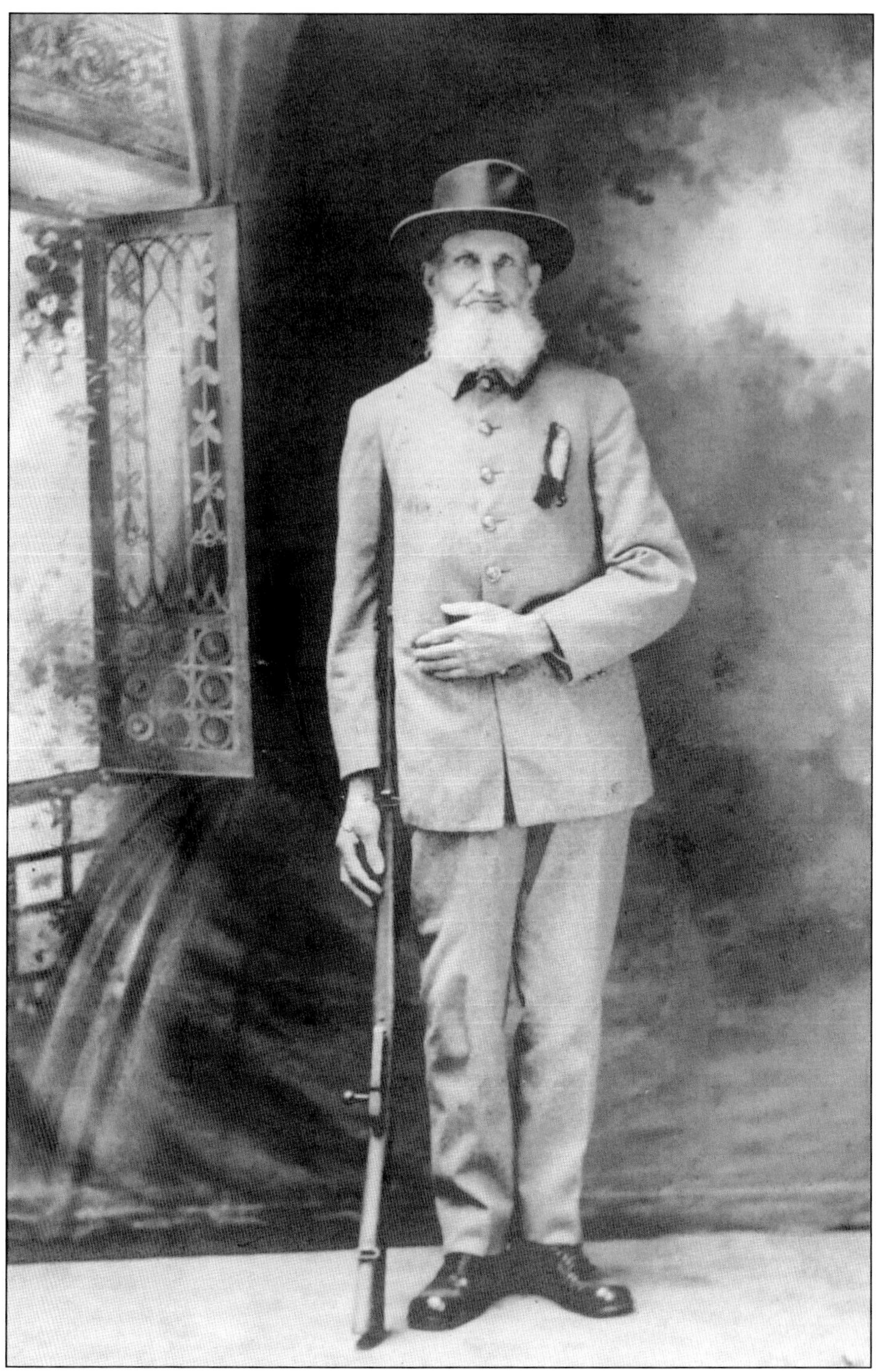

Oldest Veteran. Surgoinsville resident Samuel Grubb (1838–1938) claimed he was the last Confederate army soldier to die in Hawkins County. Grubb came to Hawkins County in 1861 and enlisted in the 63rd Tennessee Company C in 1862. Grubb was wounded at Brury's Bluff, Virginia, in 1865 and sent to prison at Point Look Out, Maryland, and was released after the war.

Lazarus Spears and Sister. Lazarus and Rachel Spears were the children of Drury Alsbrook Spears. Lazarus was a Confederate soldier. While home on a furlough in 1862, he was captured by a band of Union army sympathizers led by Bill Sizemore and murdered in front of his family home.

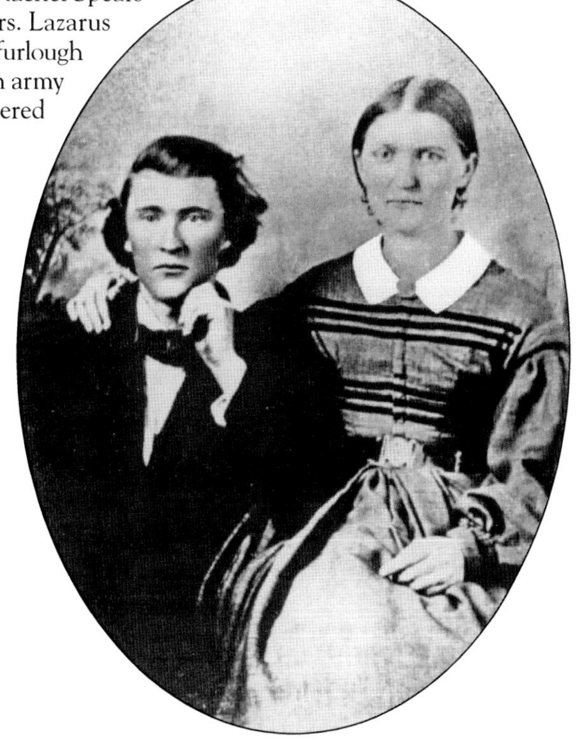

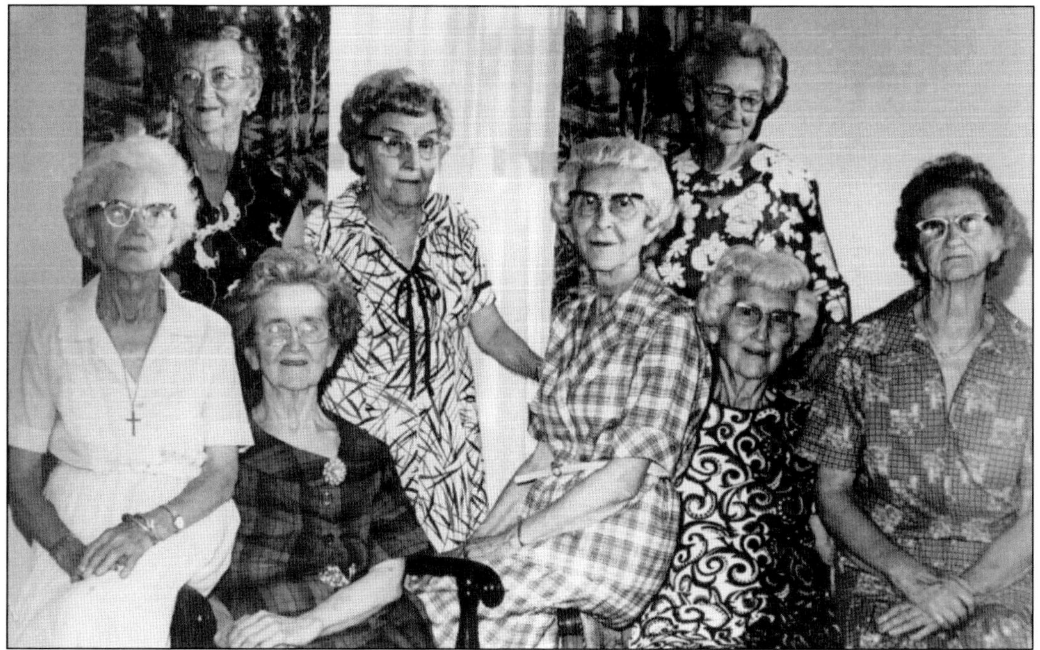

Grigsby Girls. The Grigsby girls gather for a family reunion in 1965. All of the ladies were born in the 19th century. Pictured are, from left to right, Mildred Grigsby, Gladys Grigsby, Lucille Grigbsy, Juno Grigsby Altom, Blanche Grigsby, Clara Headrick, Lois Grigsby, and Minnie Kathryn Grigsby.

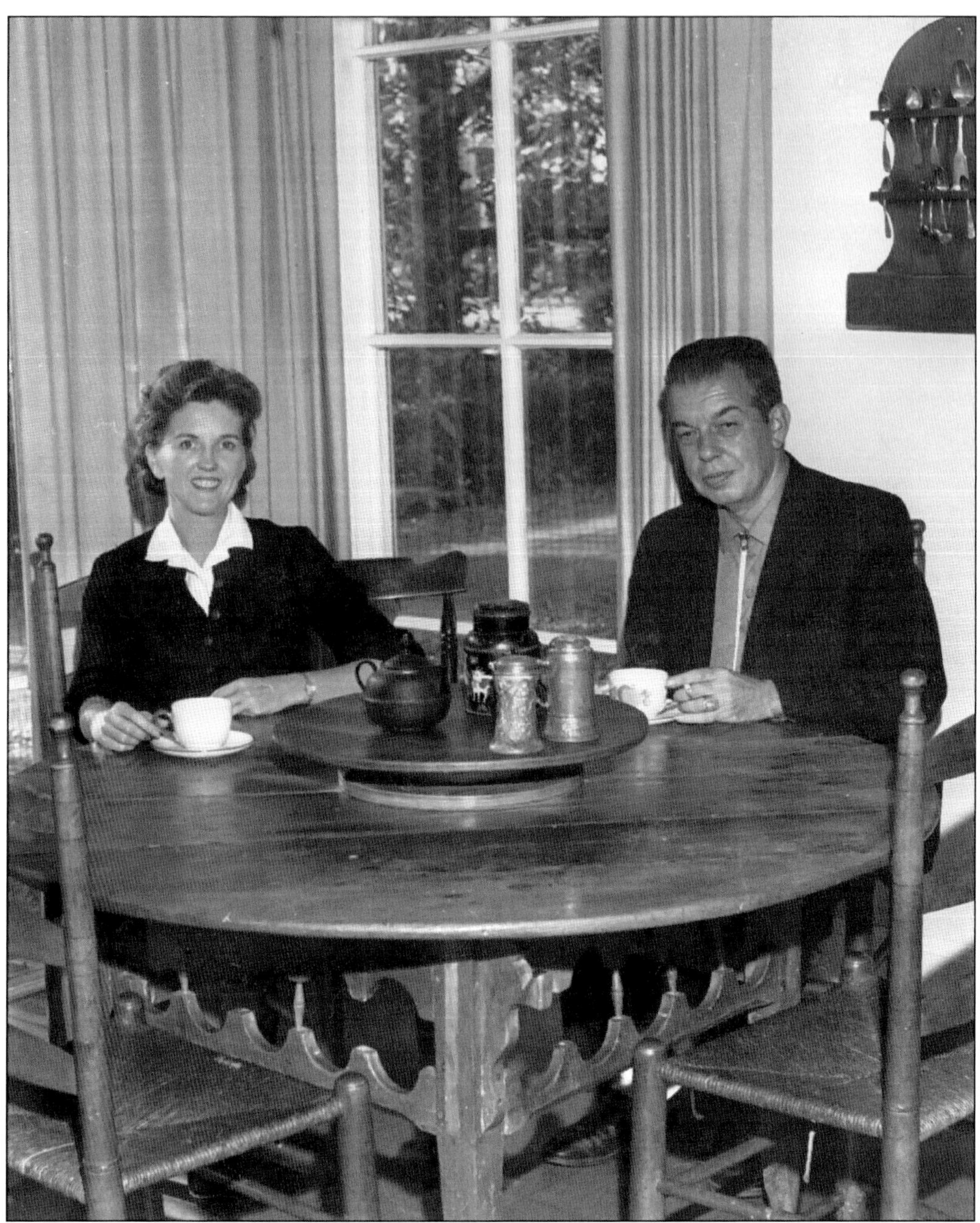

TEATIME. Alice Summers Hale and Hawkins County historian Prentiss Price discuss historical matters over a cup of coffee. Hale has been instrumental in the preservation of many East Tennessee antiquities. Price was widely known in library and genealogical circles.

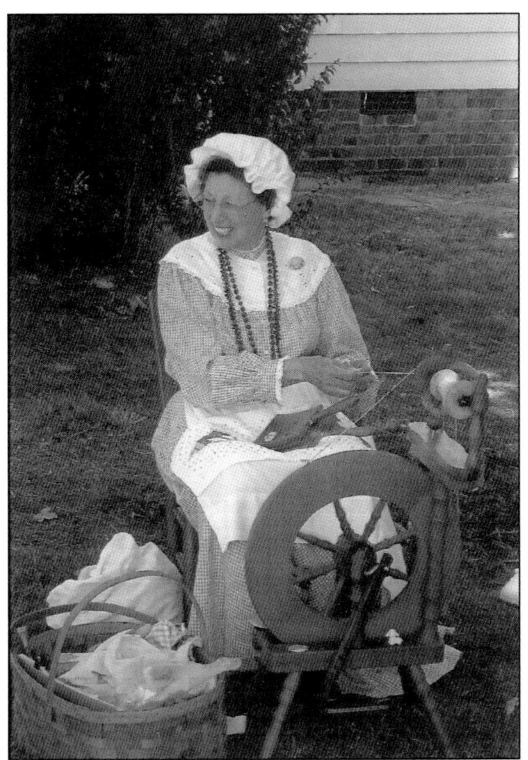

Wool Spinner. Mary Jo Shanks of Rogersville demonstrates the pioneer process of spinning wool. This photograph was taken at a Civil War reenactment at the Fudge Farm in Stony Point. (Photograph by Mary Jo Shanks.)

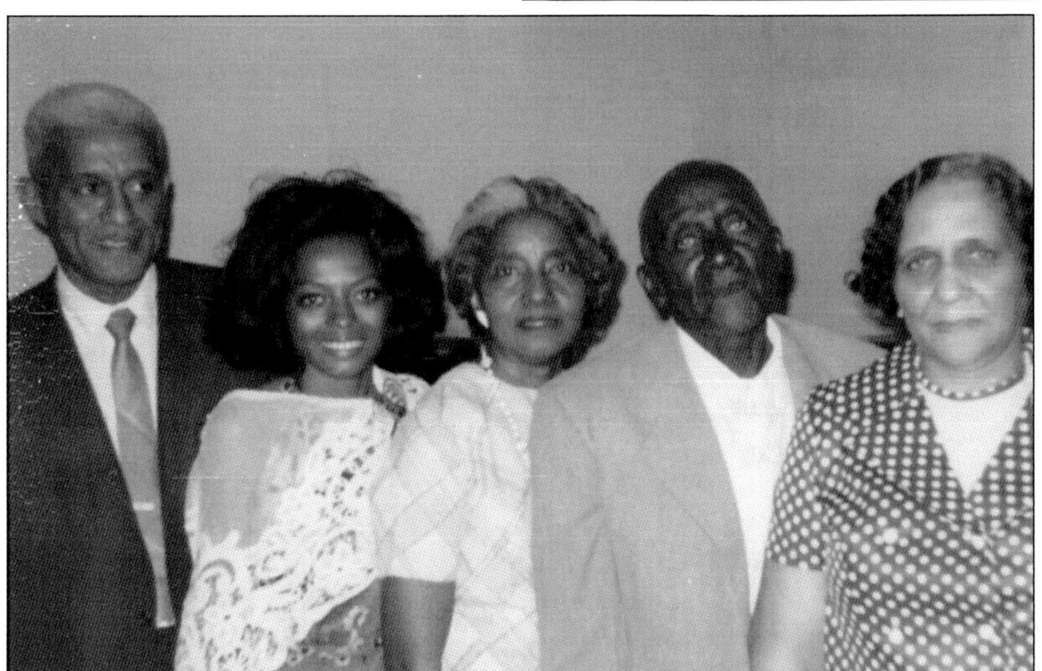

Diana's Visit. Motown legend Diana Ross has ancestral ties to Hawkins County. Her father, Fred Ross, was born in the Petersburg community and raised by his uncle George Cope. Diana Ross and her family visited Rogersville in 1970 and stayed at the Cope home. From left to right are Fred Ross, Diana Ross, Bea Cope, George Cope, and Edna Martin.

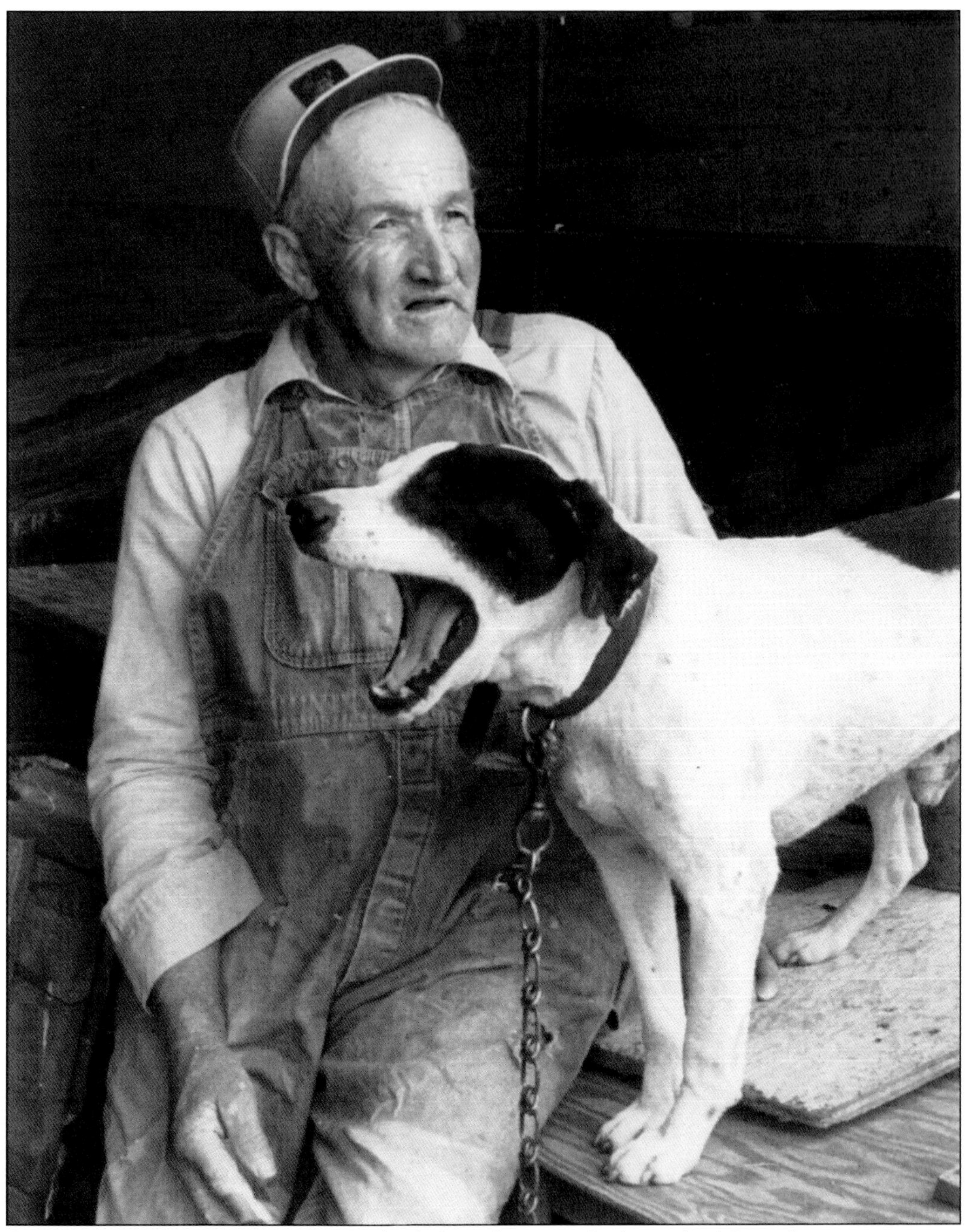

GOOD OL' BOAST. His name was Earl Gladson, but everybody in the Mooresburg community called him "Boast." He could outhunt and outfish anybody in Jim Town Hollow. (Photograph by William Jenkins.)

Big Haley. Mahala Mullins was considered one of the world's most famous Melungeons. She weighed between 500 to 700 pounds, and she made and sold moonshine for a living. Southern author Jesse Stuart wrote about her in his novel *Daughter of the Legend*. According to local stories, Mahala was so large that when she was arrested for moonshine, the sheriff could not get her out of her cabin.

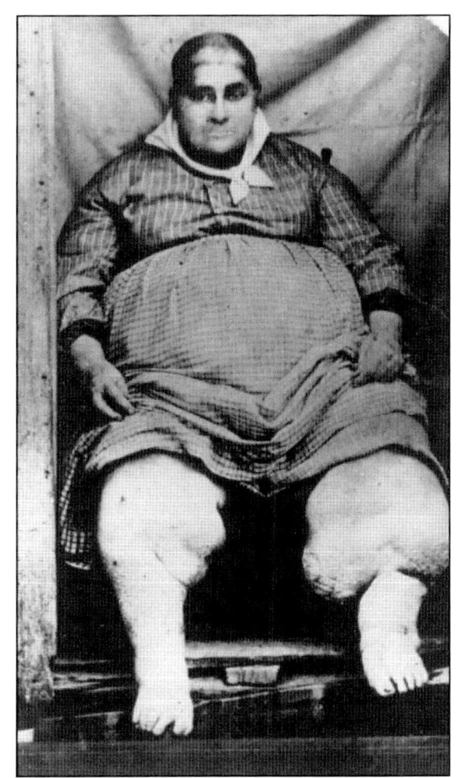

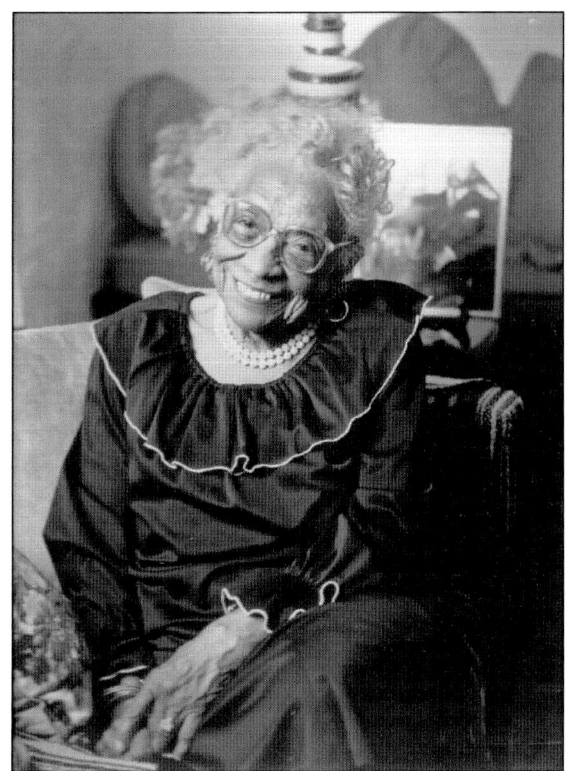

Ella. Ella Galbraith Miller was born in the Mooresburg community in 1880. In an incredible life that spanned 120 years, she enriched many lives and impressed Presidents Bush and Clinton, who found her zest for life enchanting. At the time of her death in 2000, she was considered the oldest living person in Virginia.

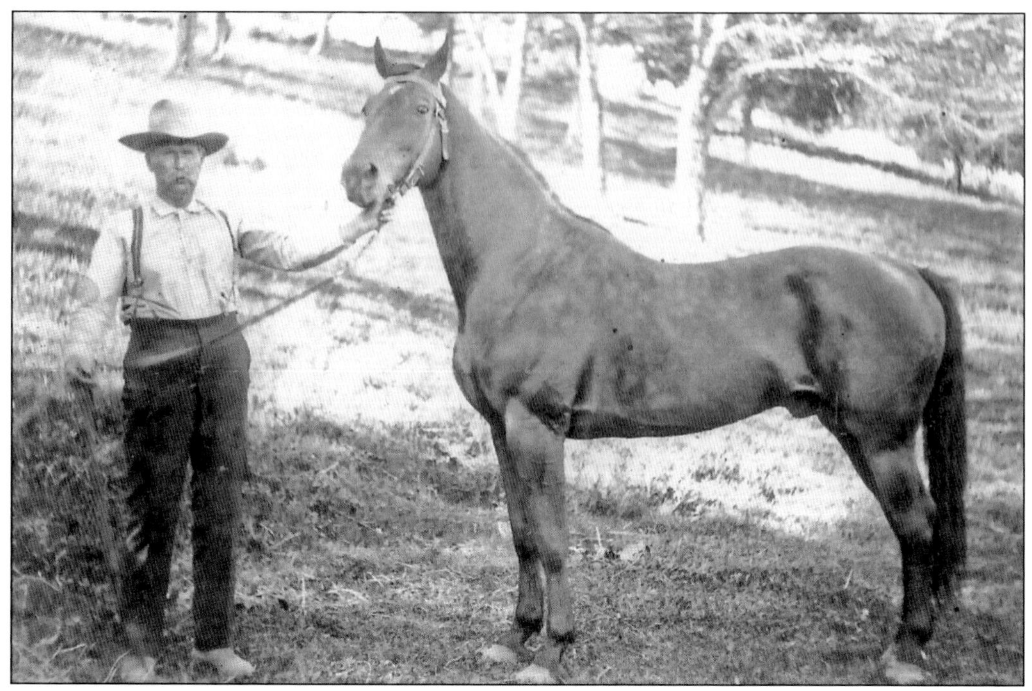

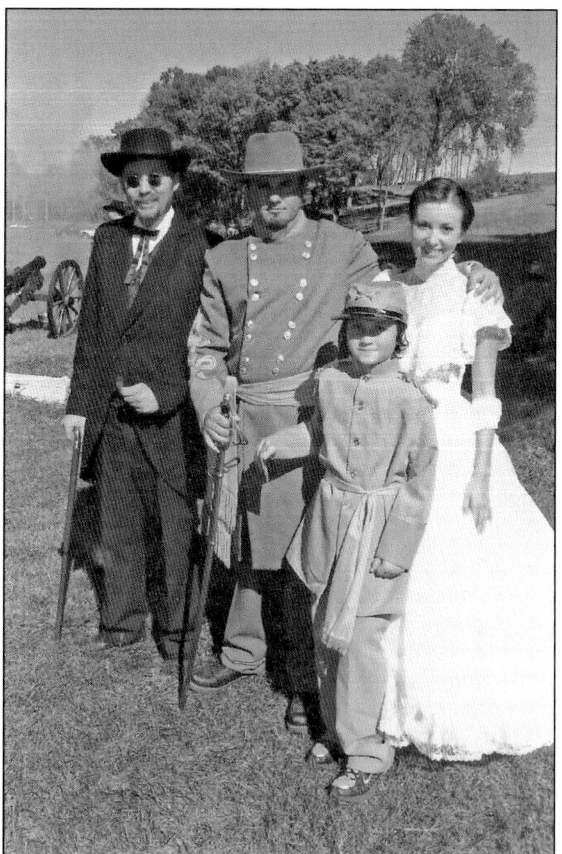

COUNTY AGENT. Marvin V. Koger was county agent for Hawkins County from 1916 to 1924. He instituted modern agricultural and conservation practices with dramatic results. He later served as county agent for Lee County, Virginia, and Hancock County, Tennessee.

REENACTORS. Hawkins County historian Rodney L. Ferrell, left, welcomes guests, from left to right, Mike Ringley, Crystal Adams, and Levi Ringley to the annual Civil War reenactment commemorating the Battle of Stony Point, an event held each September at the historic Fudge Farm in Surgoinsville. (Courtesy of Ellen Myatt.)

Five

Pressmen's Home

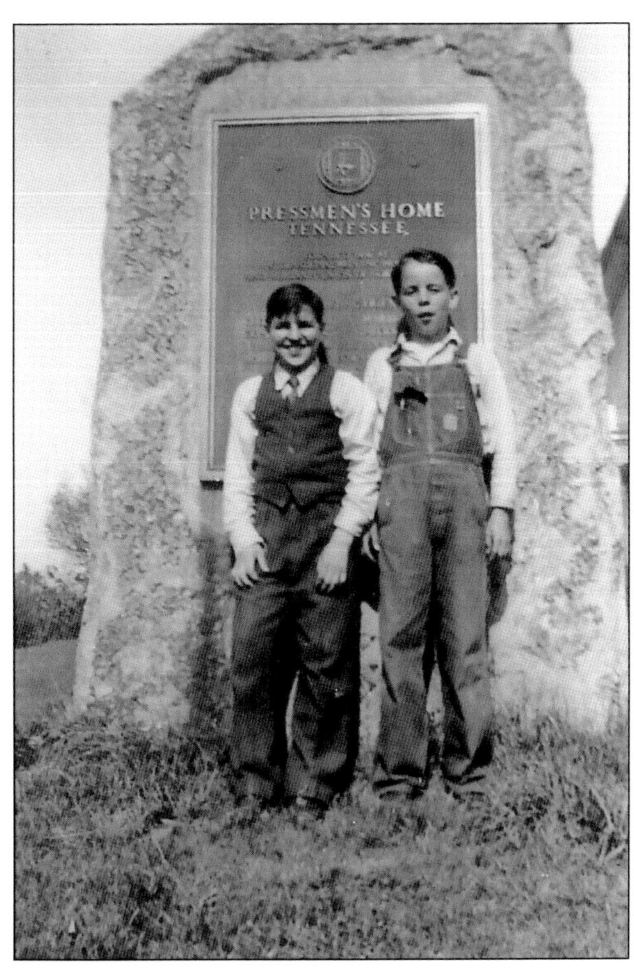

Pressmen's Home. Sammy Mallory (left) and Charles Barker are in front of the bronze plaque dedicated to Pressmen's Home in 1928. The International Printing Pressmen and Assistants' Union of North America (IPPAU) headquarters was relocated to the former Hale Springs resort in Hawkins County in 1909 under the leadership of IPPAU president George L Berry. Old-timers still call the place "Happy Valley." (Courtesy of Sammy Mallory.)

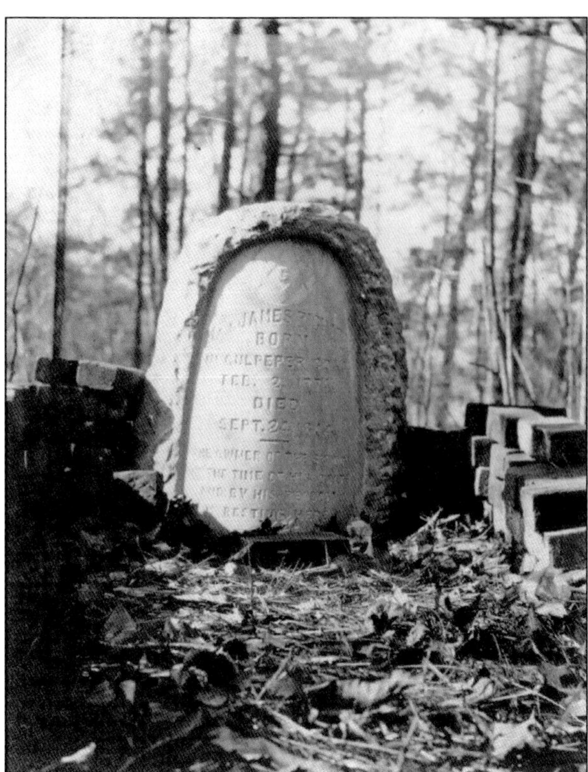

Colonel Richards's Grave. Col. James Richards was the first owner of the Pressmen's Home valley. He came to Hawkins County in 1825 and purchased the 800-acre property. He eventually built a resort there. The old colonel loved Happy Valley so much that his last request was to be buried on the ridge overlooking his vast property. His lofty grave is located behind the Memorial Chapel.

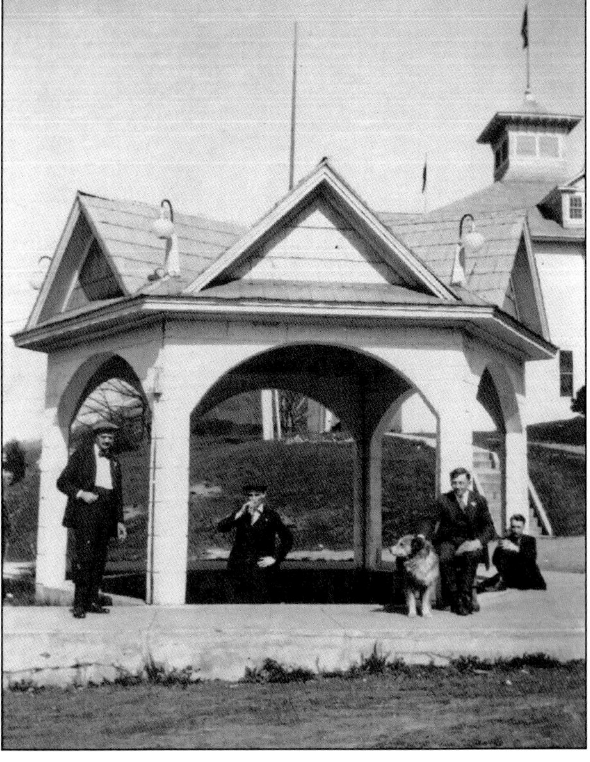

Resort Springs. The special red and white mineral springs in Happy Valley were prized very early on: first by the American Indians and later by tourists from around the world. The waters were thought to have medicinal qualities. There were also iron and Epsom salt springs. This stone and tile gazebo was built over the main springs in 1910.

Richards Plantation. The old Richards plantation house was later turned into a resort hotel by the colonel's daughter, Harriet Hale, and her husband, Phillip. Over the years, additional cottages were built. The finest furnishings were used at Hale Springs, and a special stage line was put in to transfer guests to and from Rogersville.

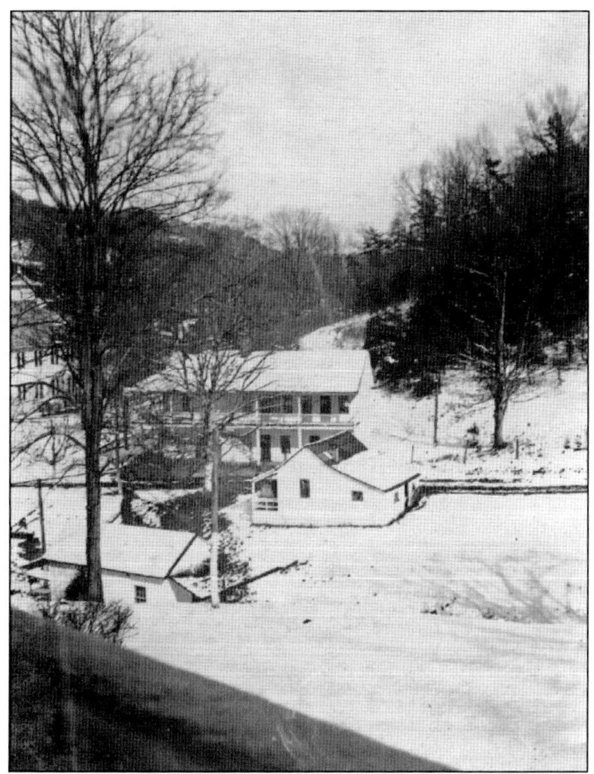

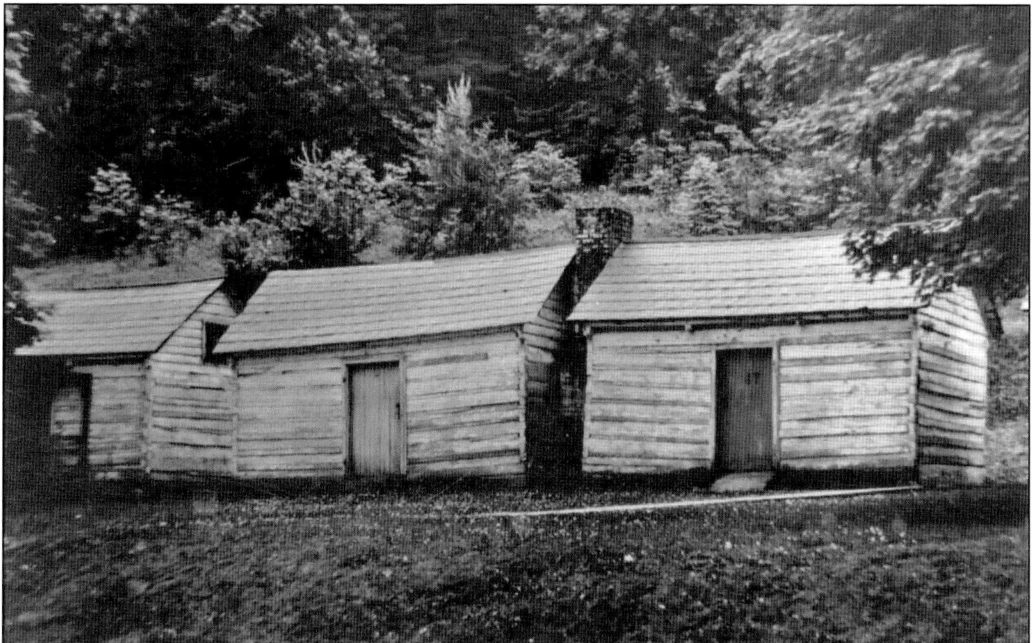

Slave Cabins. Twenty-seven log cabins were built for the Richards family's slaves in 1827. In the early days of the Hale Springs resort, the cabins were used for the servants' quarters. In the early days of Pressmen's Home, the cabins were used as segregated quarters for all visiting and residential blacks.

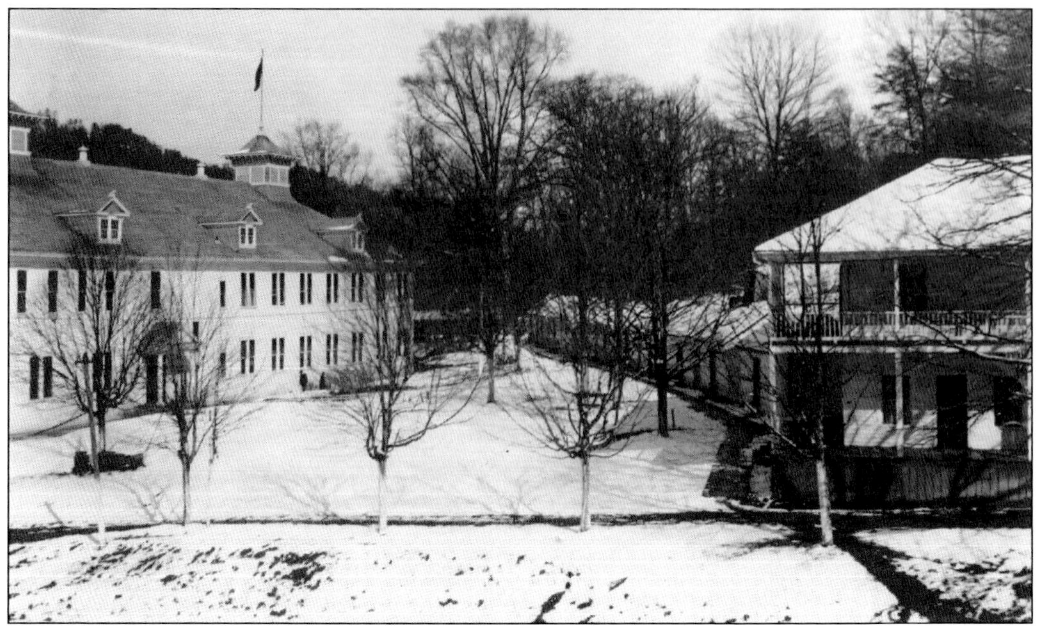

HALE SPRINGS. For many years, the Hale Springs resort flourished in Happy Valley. People from near and far came to Hawkins County to enjoy the therapeutic spring water and relaxing atmosphere. Most of the guests came by train to Rogersville and stayed overnight at the Hale Springs Inn. The next day they were transferred via stage to the resort springs to begin their visit. In 1909, the resort springs came up for sale.

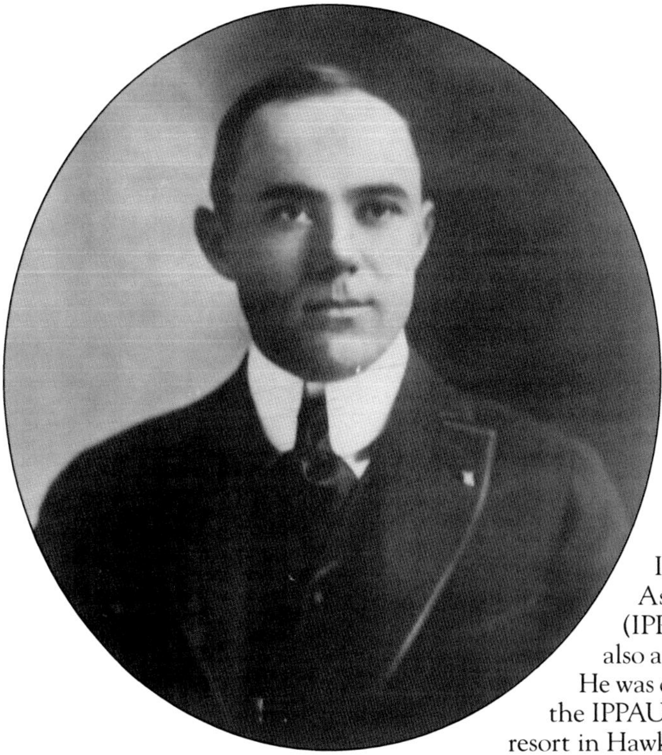

MAJOR BERRY. George L. Berry (1882–1948) was president of the International Printing Pressmen and Assistants' Union of North America (IPPAU) from 1907 to 1948. He was also a Democratic senator for Tennessee. He was directly responsible for establishing the IPPAU headquarters at the Hale Springs resort in Hawkins County.

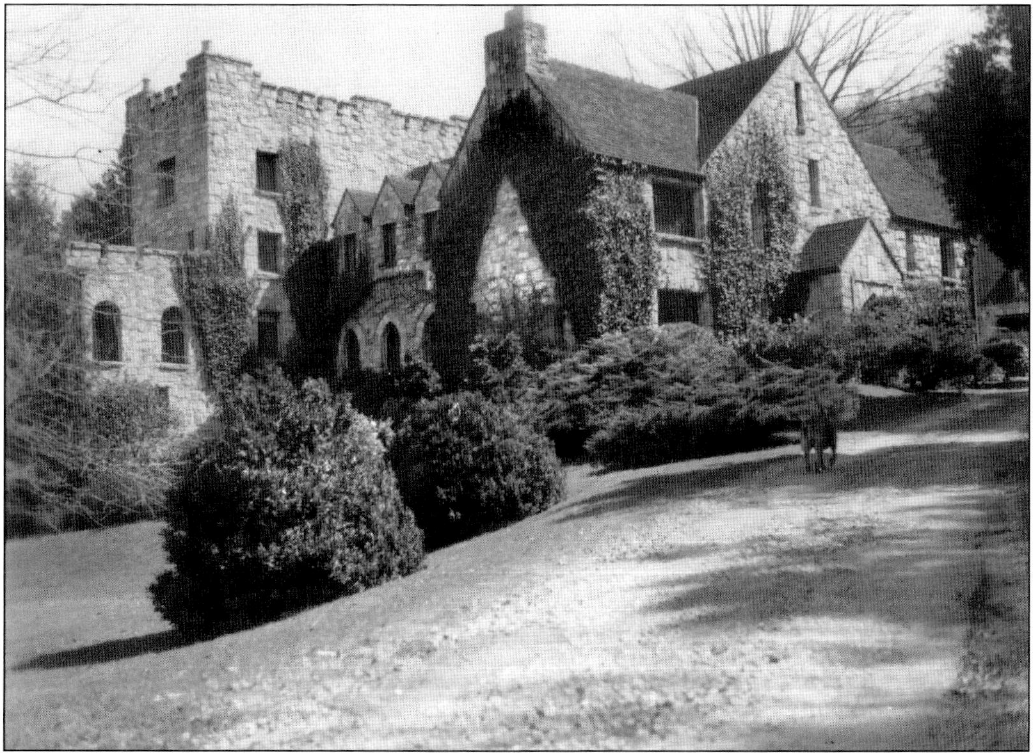

BERRY CASTLE. The presidential mansion at Pressmen's Home was built in 1928. George Berry found the plans for the gothic-style castle in Normandy, France. The four-story mansion boasted 36 rooms, an 8-car garage, and 10 bathrooms. For many years, it was one of the most beautiful and elegant homes in Tennessee.

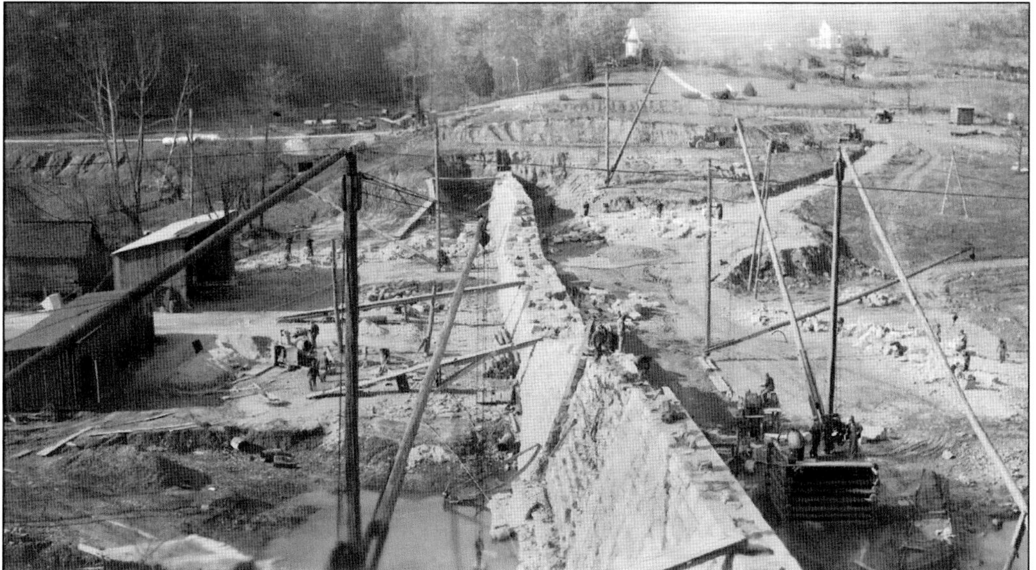

BUILDING DAM. The constant flooding at Pressmen's Home made building a dam across little Poor Valley Creek a necessity. A large man-made lake was a result. This photograph was taken February 24, 1936, after an overnight snowfall of 5 inches.

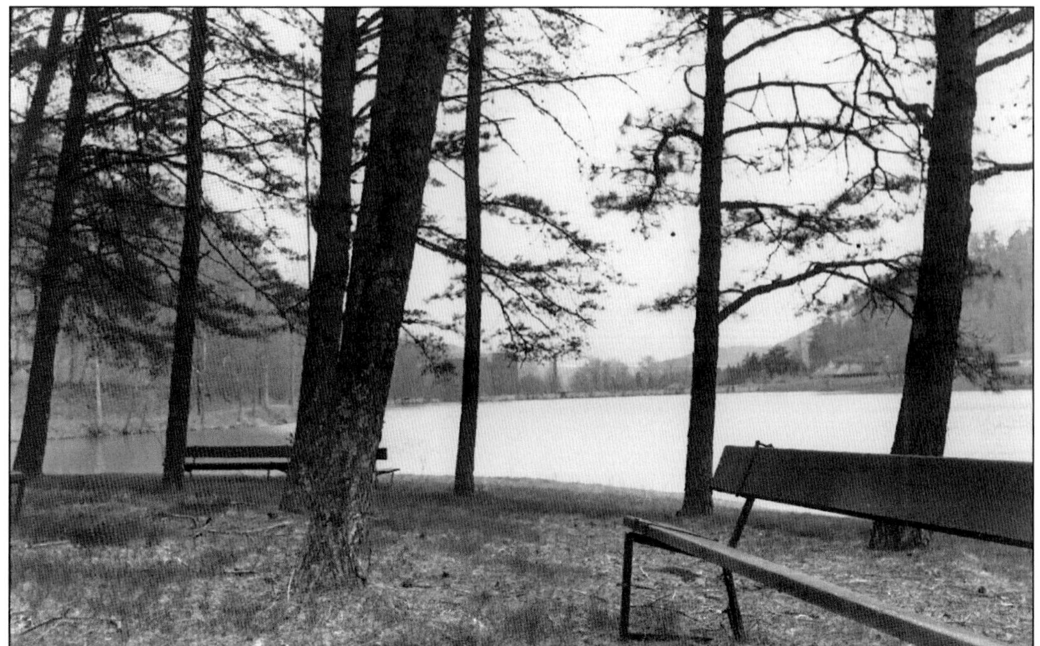

Scenic Lake. Here is a view of Pressmen's Home Lake with majestic Pine Mountain in the background. Patrons could enjoy the lake by canoeing, fishing, and horse riding on the miles of trails that surrounded the perimeter. There were also rental cottages along its banks. (Courtesy of Jim Caswell.)

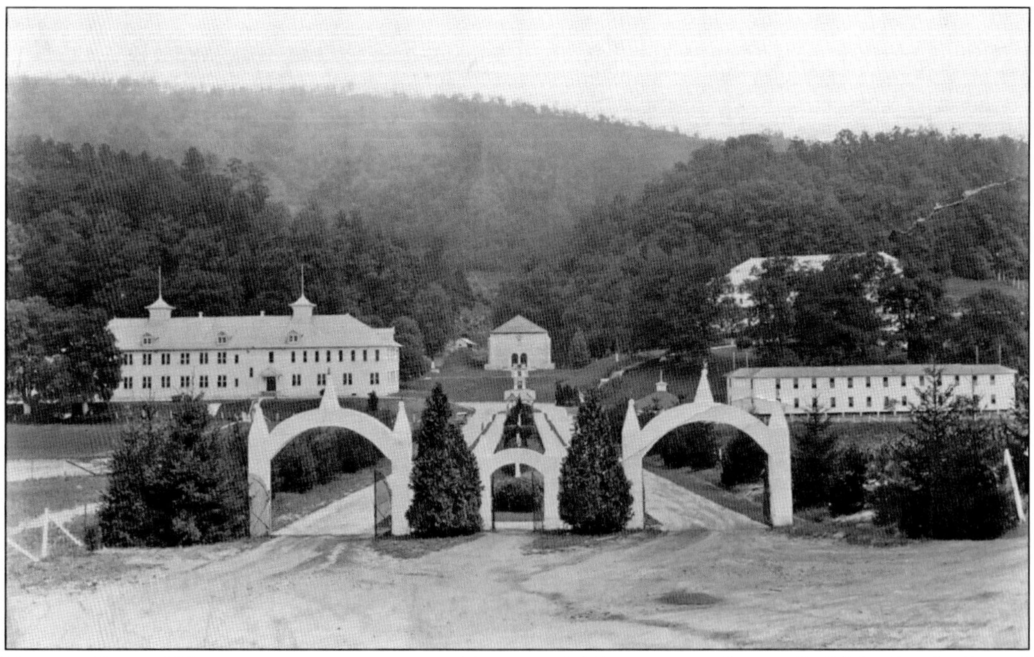

Pearly Gates. The stone entrance gates to Pressmen's Home were often called "the Pearly Gates" by old-timers. The Technical Trade School and Berry ball field are on the left. The Memorial Chapel and the mineral springs are center. The old hotel is upper right, and the indoor swimming pool is lower right. This photograph was taken in May 1926.

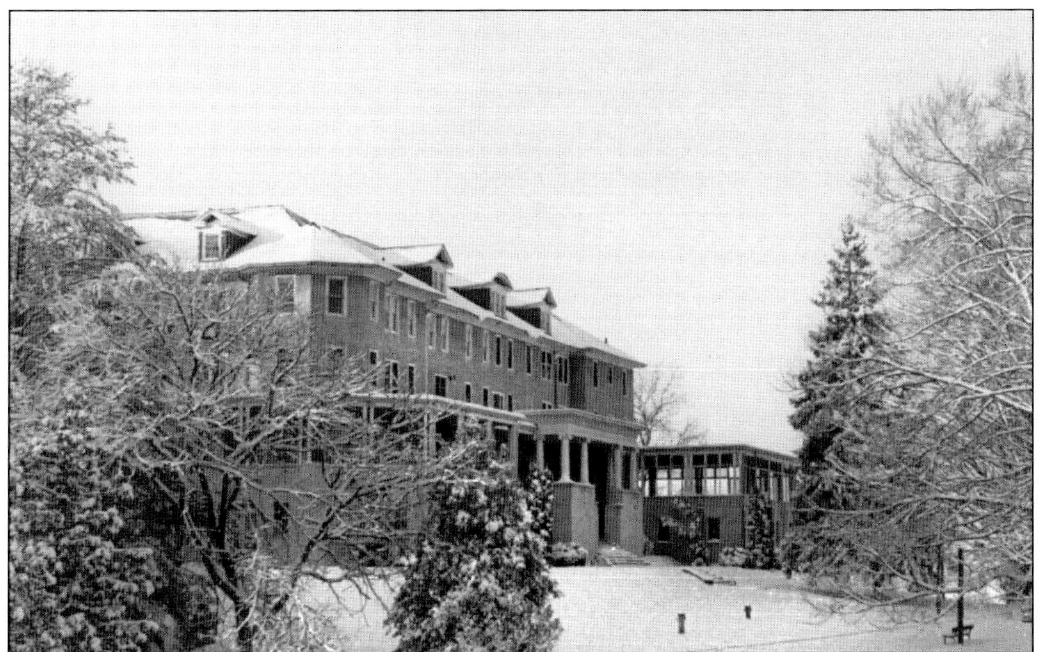

HOME BUILDING. The Hale Springs Hotel building was completed in 1911. The 300-room building was used as the American Legion Complex and Hotel until the Pressauna Tavern was built in 1926. The Hale building was then converted into a home for retired pressmen. Later the structure was used as an apartment building for workers and residents.

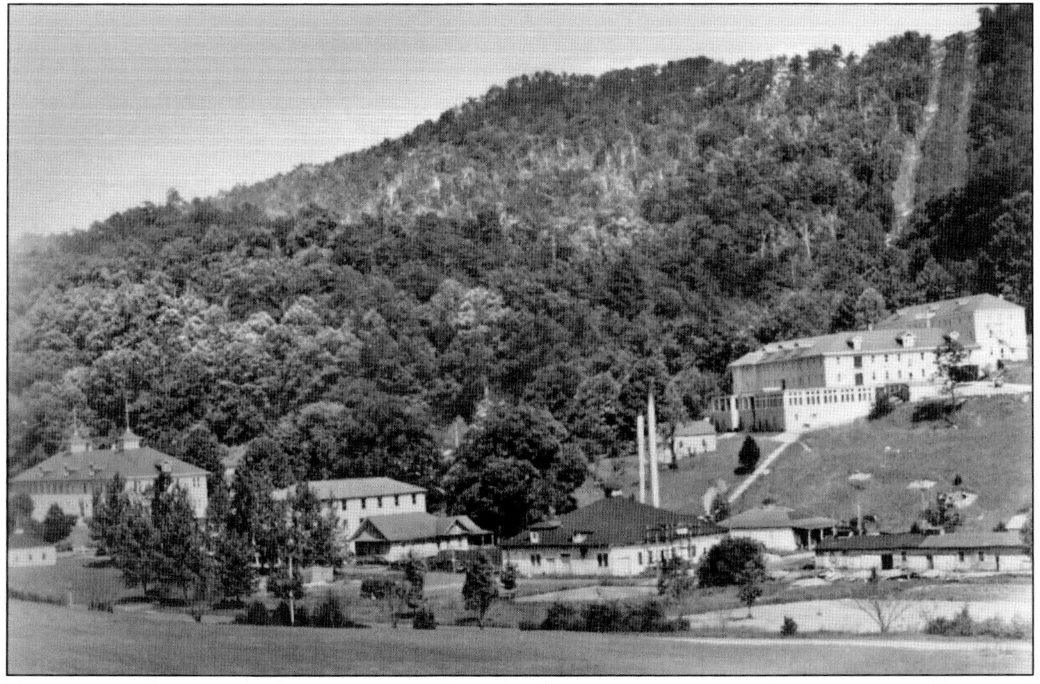

PANORAMIC. Pressmen's Home was a totally self-sufficient community. Members grew 300 acres of vegetable gardens and raised cattle, hogs, pigs, and chickens there. The IPPAU had its own water reservoir and power plant. There was also a telephone company and post office.

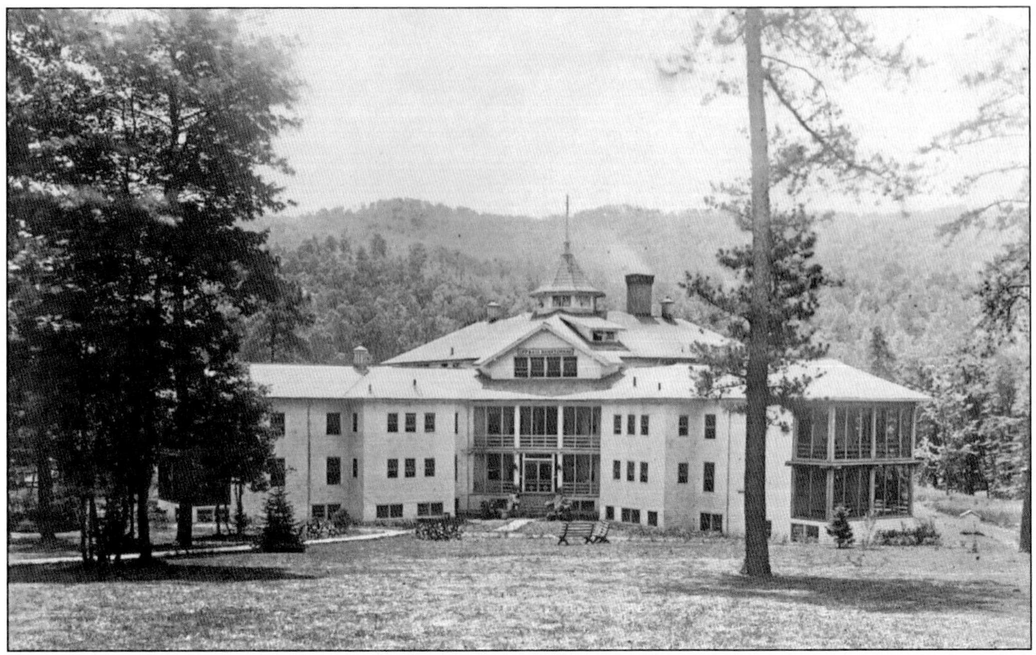

Sanatorium. The Tuberculosis Sanatorium at Pressmen's Home was built in 1911. The hospital was a four-story, four-wing white building in the shape of an equal-armed cross complete with an elevator. It was eventually equipped to handle 150 patients, whose beds were designed to slip onto sun porches for fresh air.

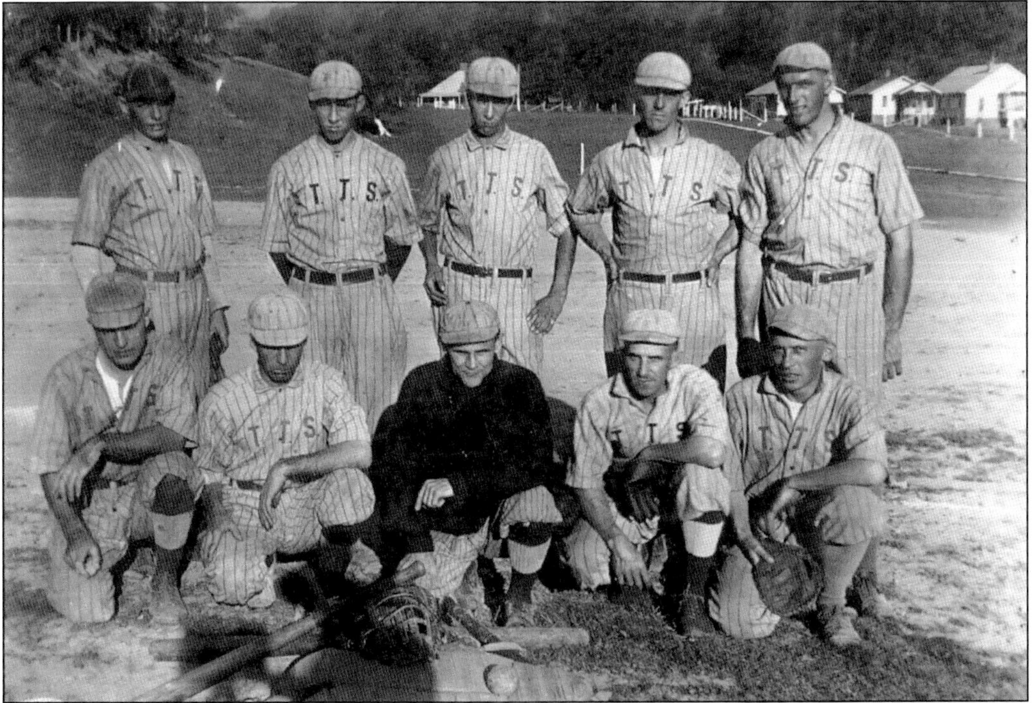

Ball Players. With every season, a new team of ballplayers turned out to bring the Pressmen's Home ball team into the winners' circle. This is the team for the 1924 season.

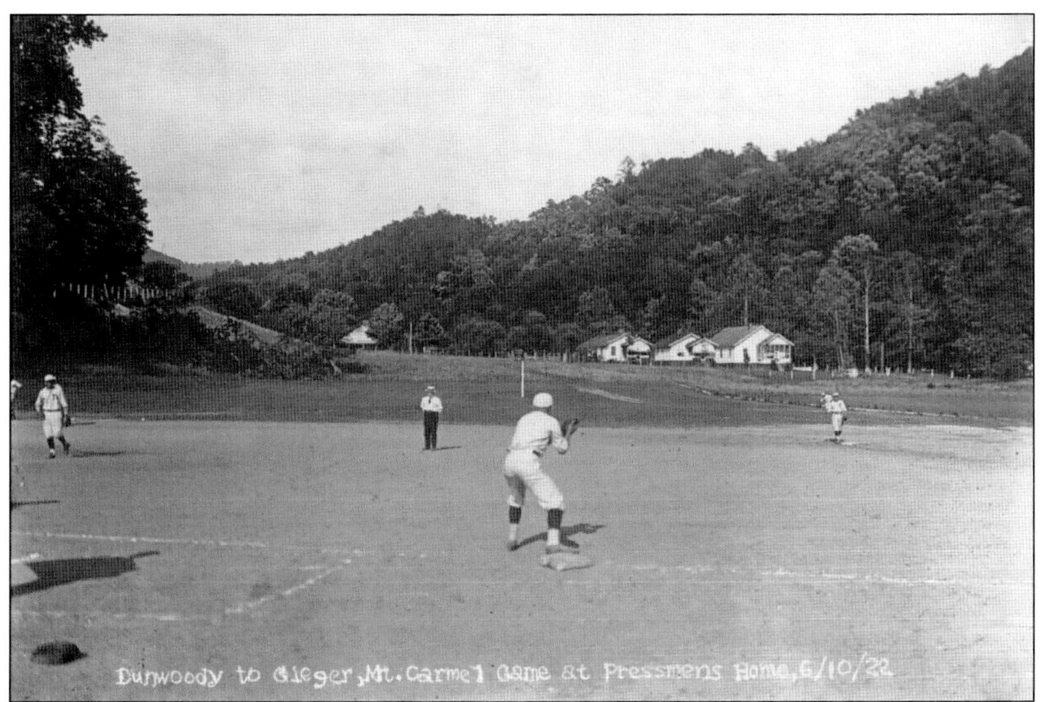

BERRY BALL FIELD. Baseball was a very important pastime at Pressmen's Home. The tradition began in 1910 and continued until 1967. At one time, the union boasted one of the best teams in the southeast, bar none. There was a men's and women's division, and both teams were award winning.

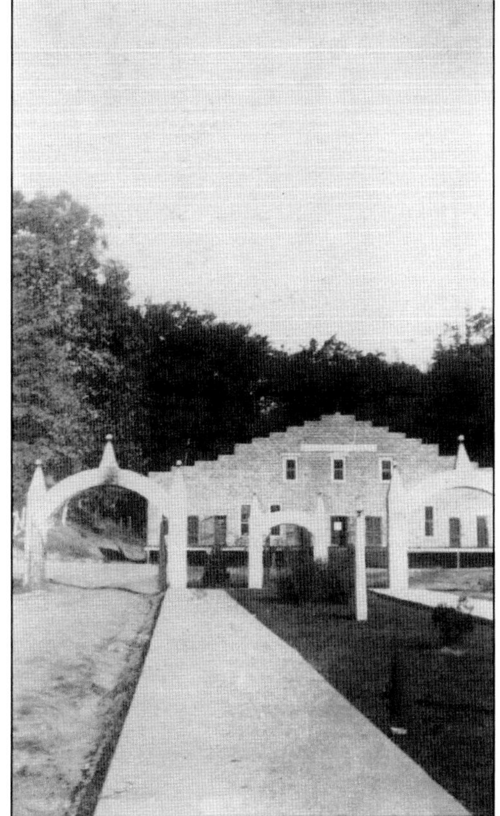

OLD MERCANTILE. The old Clinchfield Mercantile Company was opened in 1910, so the residents of Pressmen's Home could have access to groceries and farming supplies. The building also contained a post office and a barbershop. The mercantile was torn down in 1924 to make way for the Pressauna Tavern.

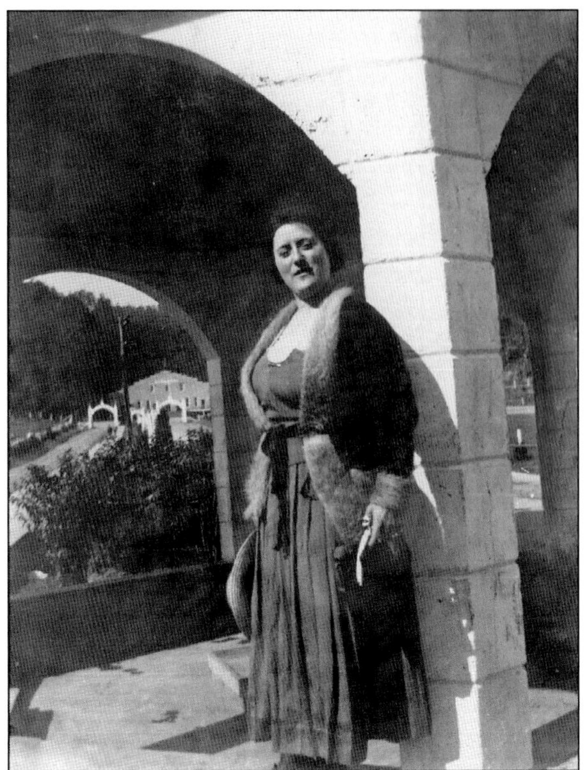

MARIE BERRY. As the wife of IPPAU president George L. Berry, Marie brought the grace and style of her aristocratic childhood in Santa Barbara, California, to rural Appalachia. Berry was responsible for bringing the Catholic Church to Hawkins County. She also founded Stone Mountain School for the children of Pressmen's Home and surrounding areas.

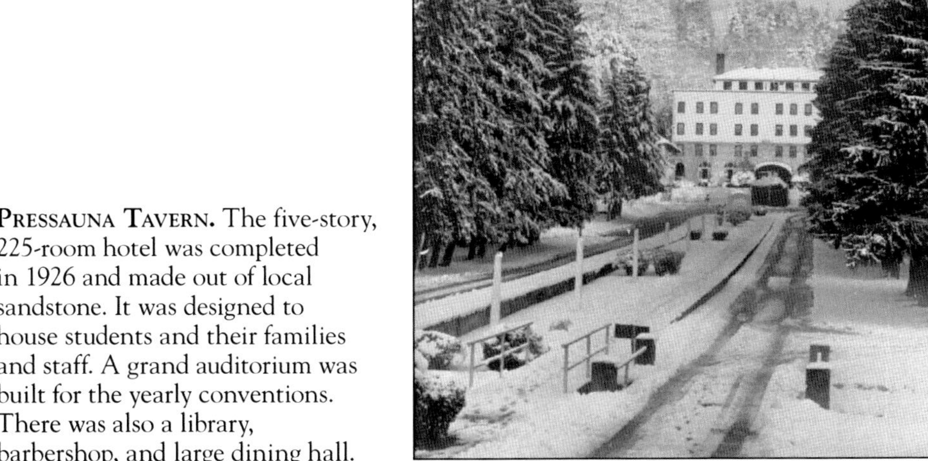

PRESSAUNA TAVERN. The five-story, 225-room hotel was completed in 1926 and made out of local sandstone. It was designed to house students and their families and staff. A grand auditorium was built for the yearly conventions. There was also a library, barbershop, and large dining hall.

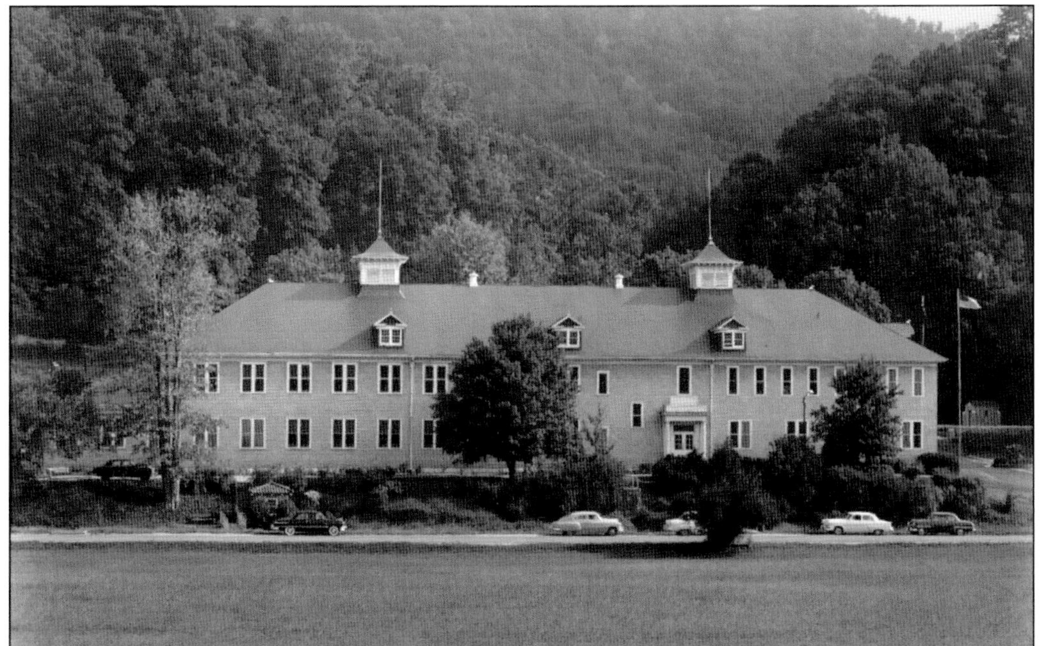

Old Trade School. The first IPPAU Trade School was completed in 1912. The building served as a school until a new one was constructed in 1947. The three-story structure housed the executive offices of the president and secretary-treasurer in addition to the accounting, records, and engineering departments.

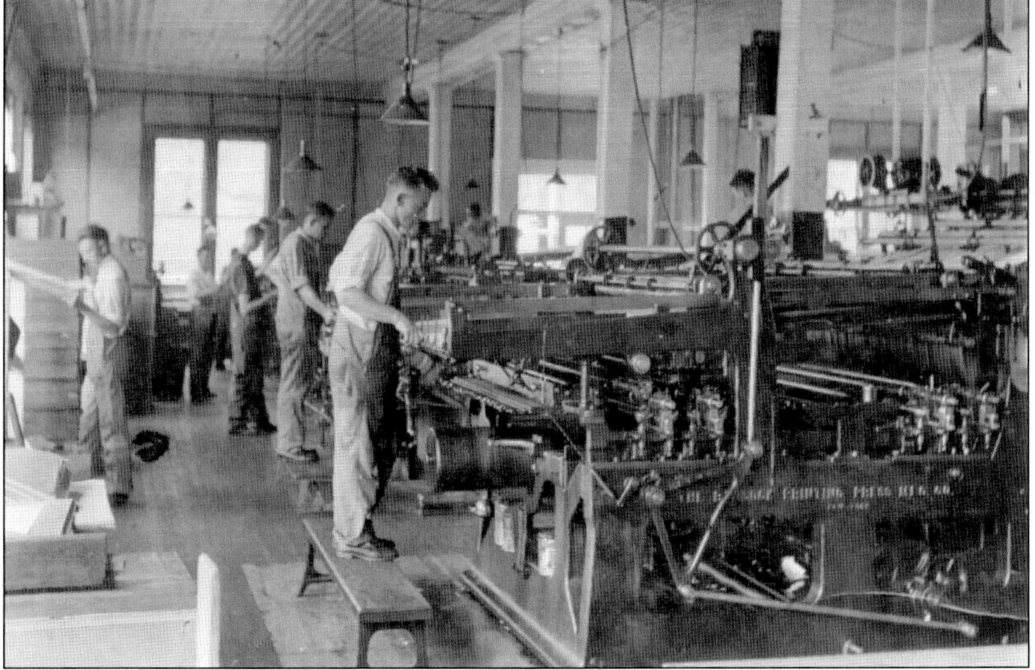

Pressmen Trainees. Here are apprentice trainees working the presses in 1923. Student pressmen came to Pressmen's Home from all over the country. On the third floor of the trade school, there were 40 dormitory rooms where students could board during their semester at the school.

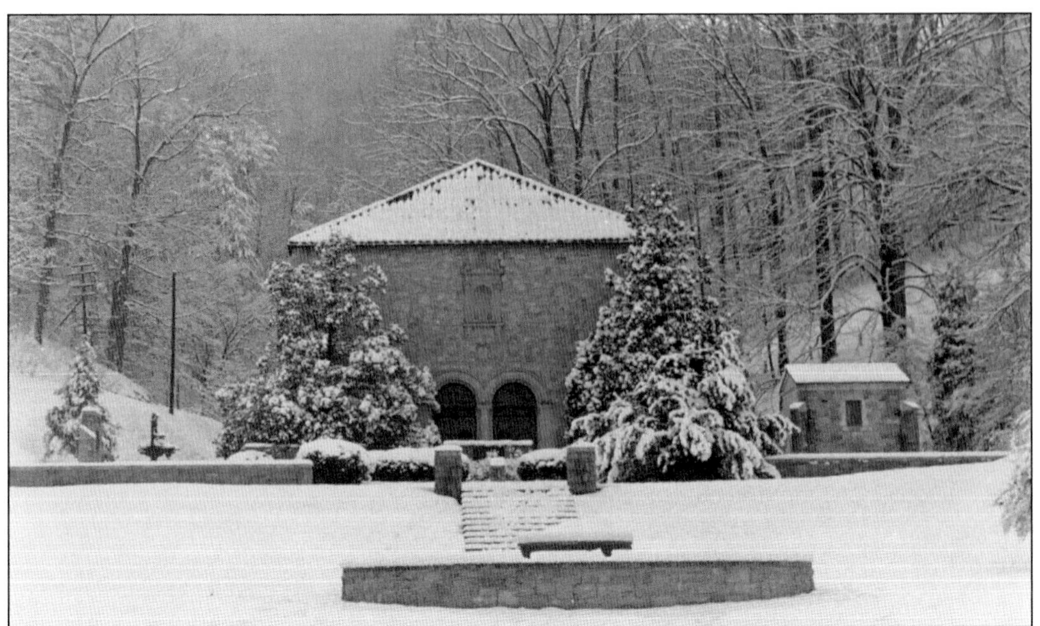

Memorial Chapel. This sandstone Italianate church was built in 1924 for the members of the International Pressmen and Assistants' Union of North America who died in World War I. Designed by renowned architect John Sheridan, the chapel was non-denominational. The legendary Sgt. Alvin York attended the dedication service. The carillon bells in the chapel rang five times a day. (Courtesy of Jim Caswell.)

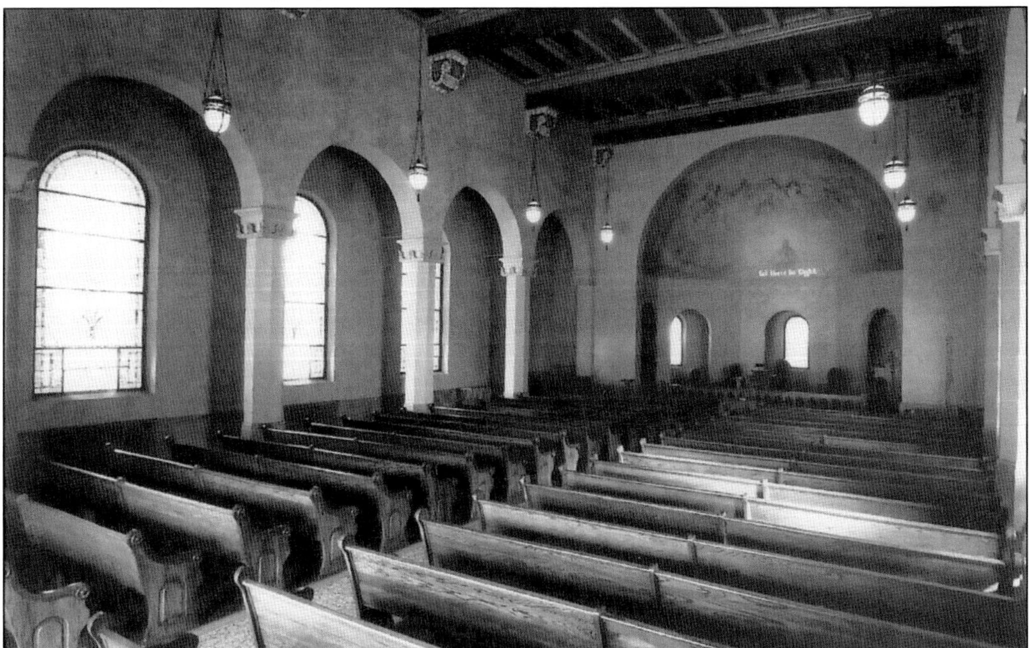

Chapel Interior. The interior of the chapel had a seating capacity of over 500 people. The ceiling had a fresco painting of Jesus Christ and angels painted by G. Harmon Simmons. The stained-glass windows were designed by Louis Comfort Tiffany. In 1948, a special crypt was built at the chapel to house the body of George L. Berry. (Courtesy of Betty Brooks.)

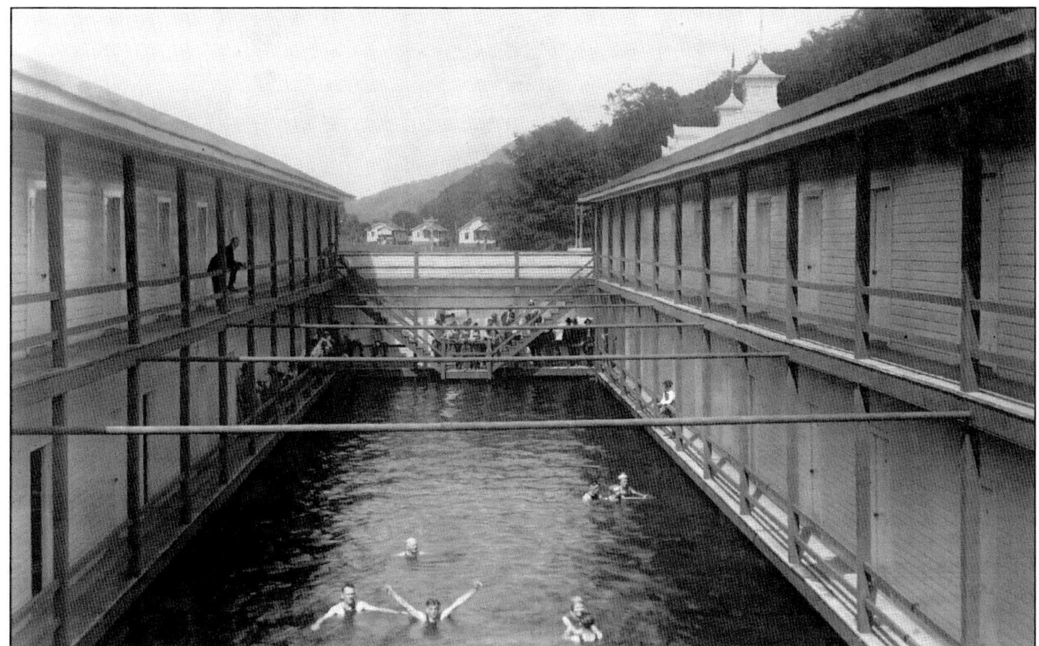

NATATORIUM. The 400-gallon year-round pool was dug in 1916 and later surrounded by a three-story building. The roof was retractable, allowing students to use the facilities year round. Bathhouses were built on all three floors around the pool. The building itself was demolished in 1960, but there continued to be a pool for many years.

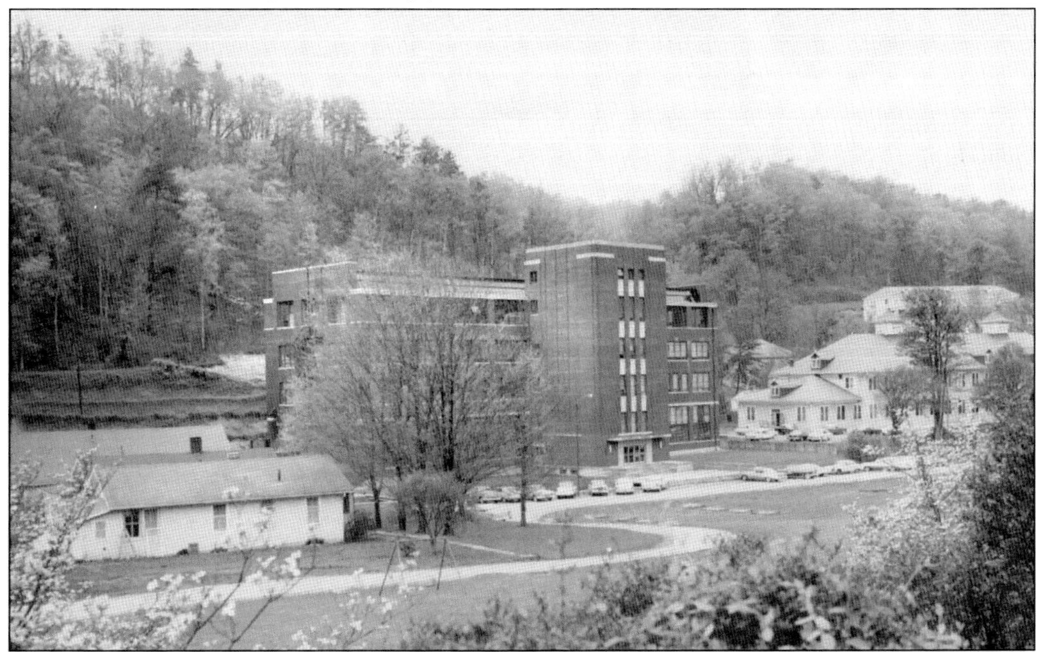

NEW TRADE SCHOOL. The new school building was constructed in 1948 at a cost of $1 million. The brick building was five stories high with the typesetting department on the first floor, school directors' offices on the second floor, the presses on the third floor, and a 1,000-person auditorium on the fourth floor.

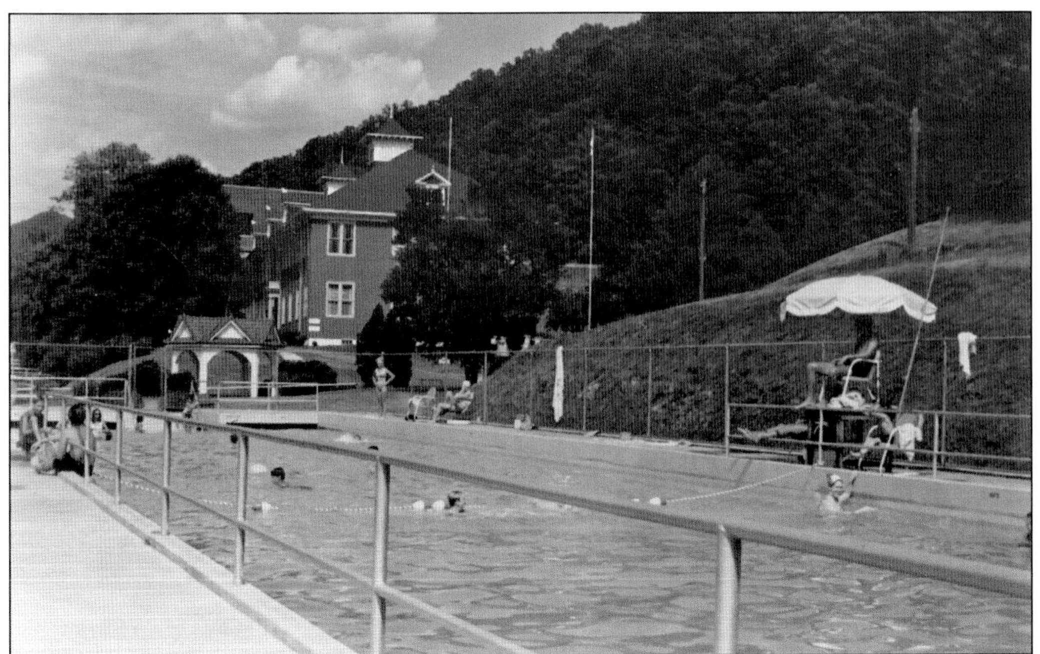

CAMELOT. In 1969, commissioners agreed to sell Pressmen's Home to land developers. The buyers were interested in building a secluded resort called Camelot. There was also a golf and country club with an 18-hole golf course. The luxurious resort offered swimming, horseback riding, and other recreational facilities.

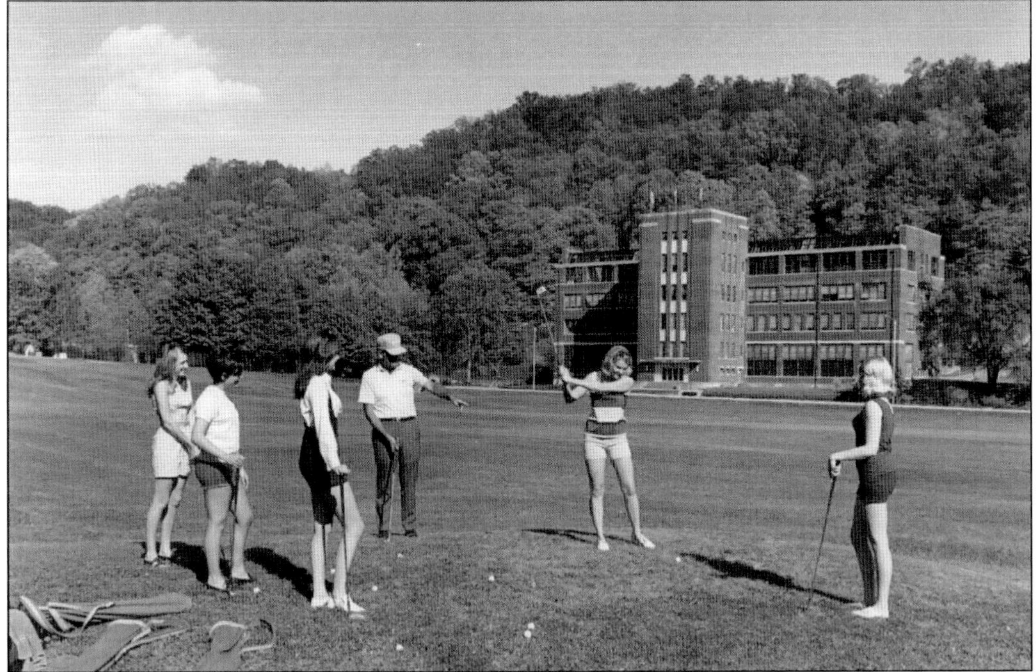

CAMELOT GOLF CLUB. After Pressmen's Home left for Washington, D.C., in 1967, a large golf course took the place of the pasture fields, and the cattle barns were turned into a country club. In this photograph, golfers put on a show for the photographer in front of the former Trade School.

Six

Towns and Communities

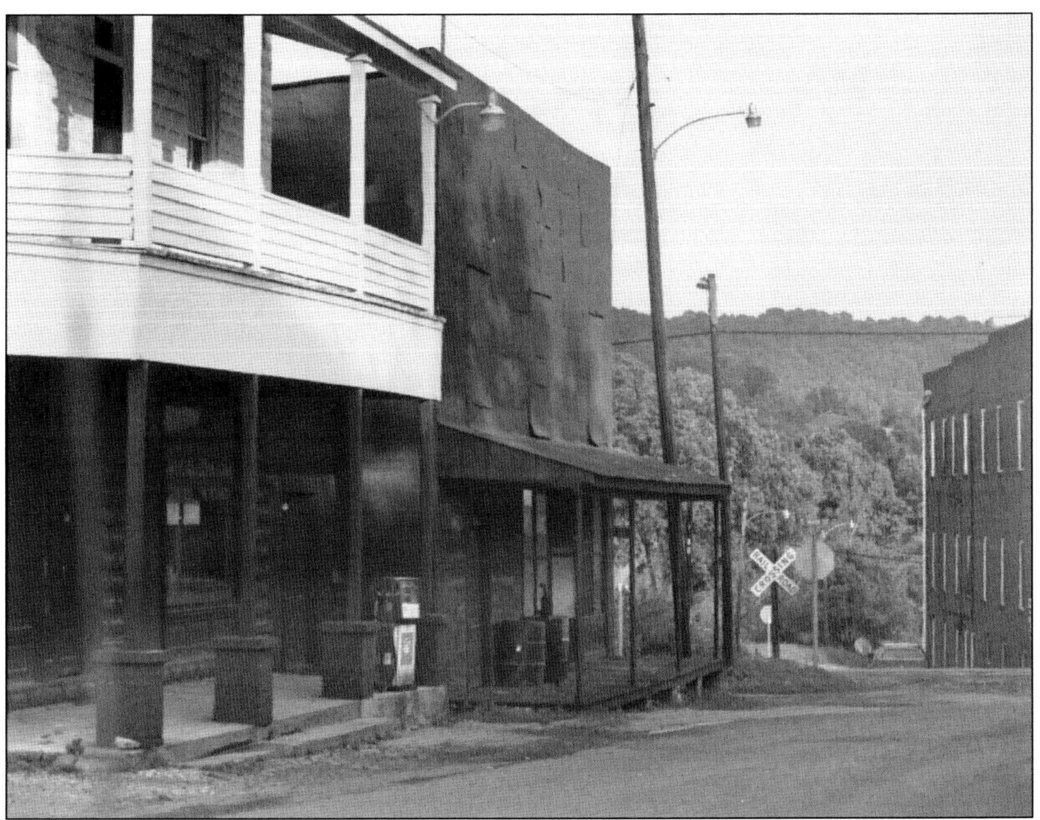

Bulls Gap. This little town was named for John Bull, who operated a stage line from Washington County down through Greene County. He maintained a station at present-day Bulls Gap. When the railroad came through in 1857, it was given the name "Rogersville Junction," but it eventually reverted back to Bulls Gap.

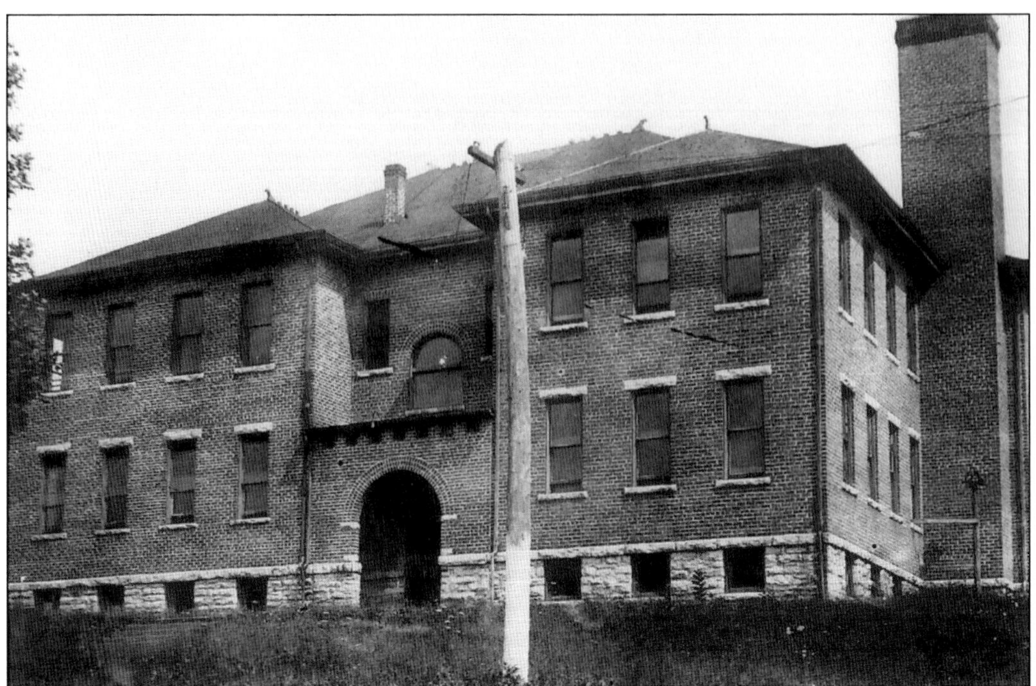

Bulls Gap High School. The old Bulls Gap High School, pictured about 1928, was built in 1916 succeeding an older frame building that is now a part of Wilson Funeral Home. The brick building was used until the 1960s when a new high school was constructed.

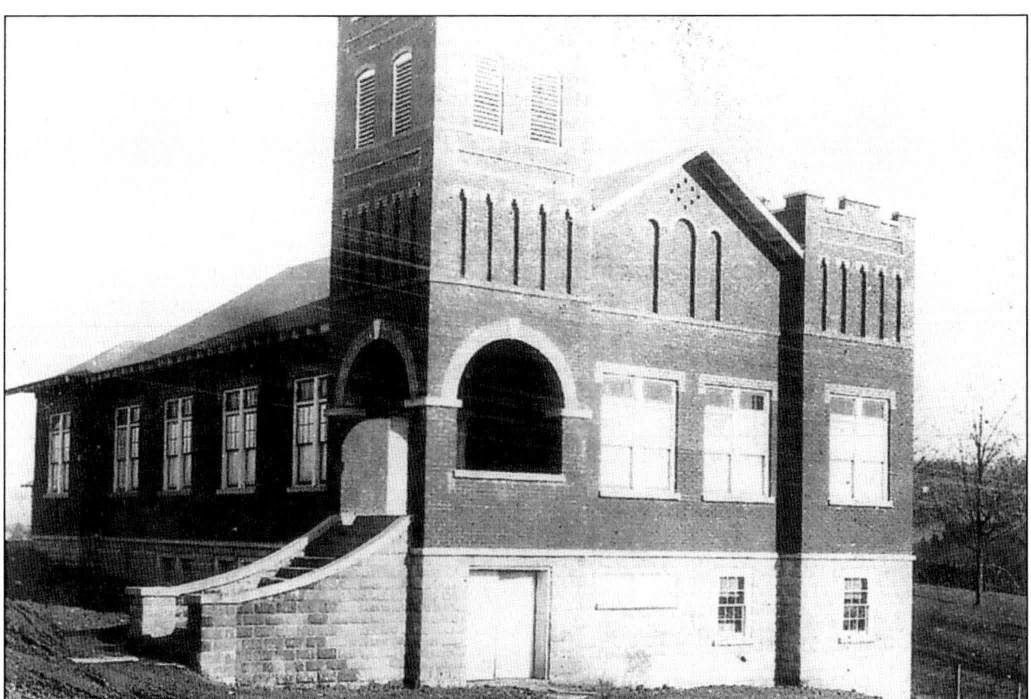

Bulls Gap Baptist Church. This brick structure was built in 1922 and served as the home of the Baptist Church in Bulls Gap for many years.

COUNTRY CHURCH. This is a 1905 postcard photograph of a beautiful Bulls Gap church now long since gone.

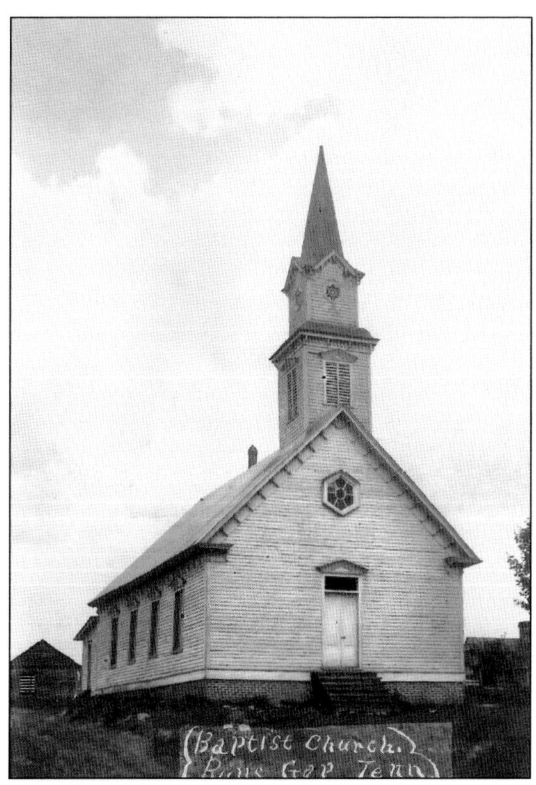

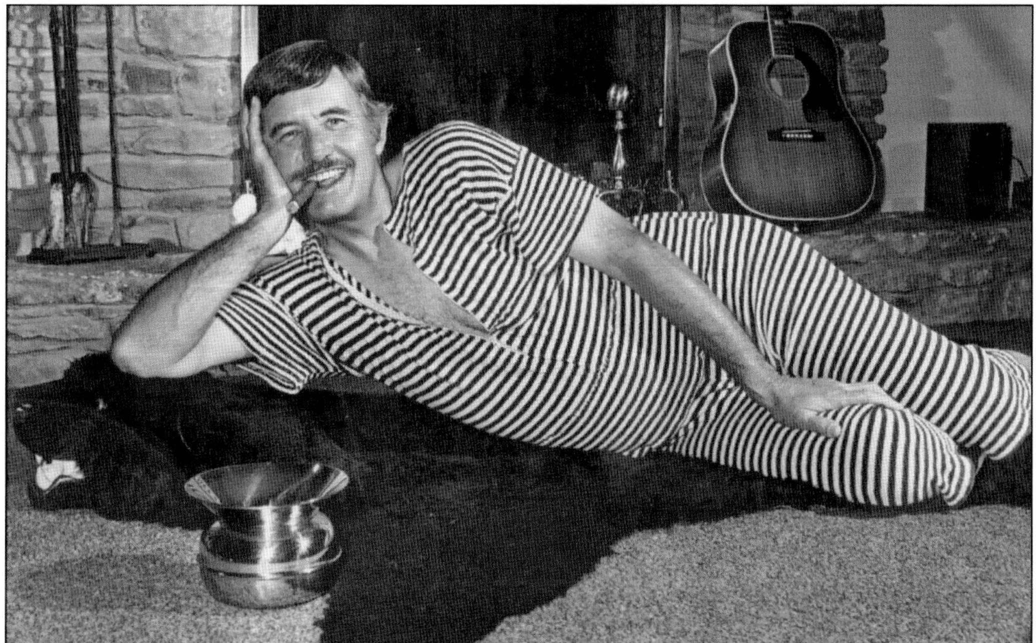

ARCHIE CAMPBELL. Perhaps the most famous son of Bulls Gap was Grand Ole Opry legend Archie Campbell, star of radio and television. His old homestead has been set up as a museum in the center of town. The crowd puts on an annual Archie Campbell festival each Labor Day weekend, which draws visitors from far and wide.

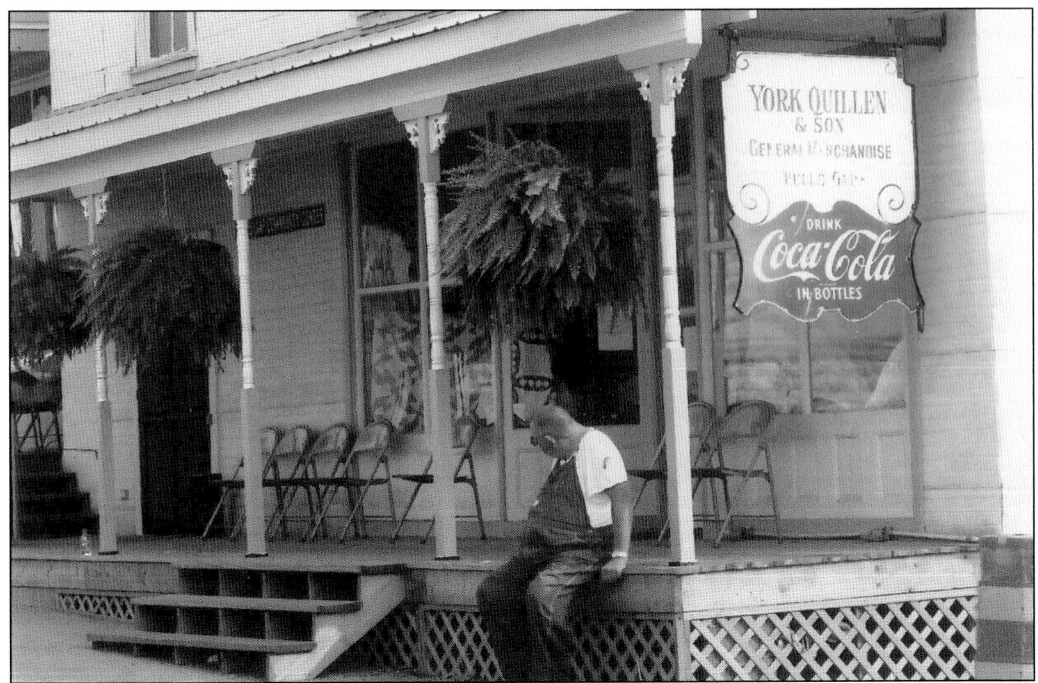

York Quillen Store. The old Quillen store was opened in the late 1800s. York Quillen is fondly remembered for his motto, "I've got it if I can find it." The building now serves as the Bulls Gap City Hall.

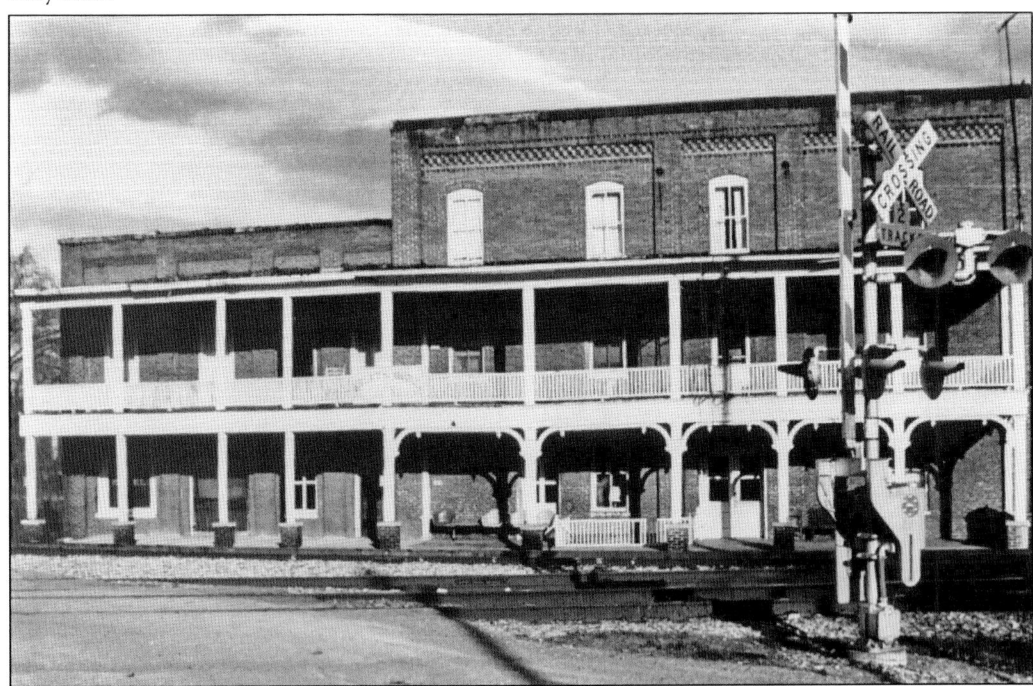

Gilley Hotel. The Smith Gilley Hotel on the railroad tracks in Bulls Gap was once a famous stopping place for fine accommodations on the East Tennessee, Virginia, and Georgia Railroad line built in 1884 following a fire that destroyed the original Smith Hotel.

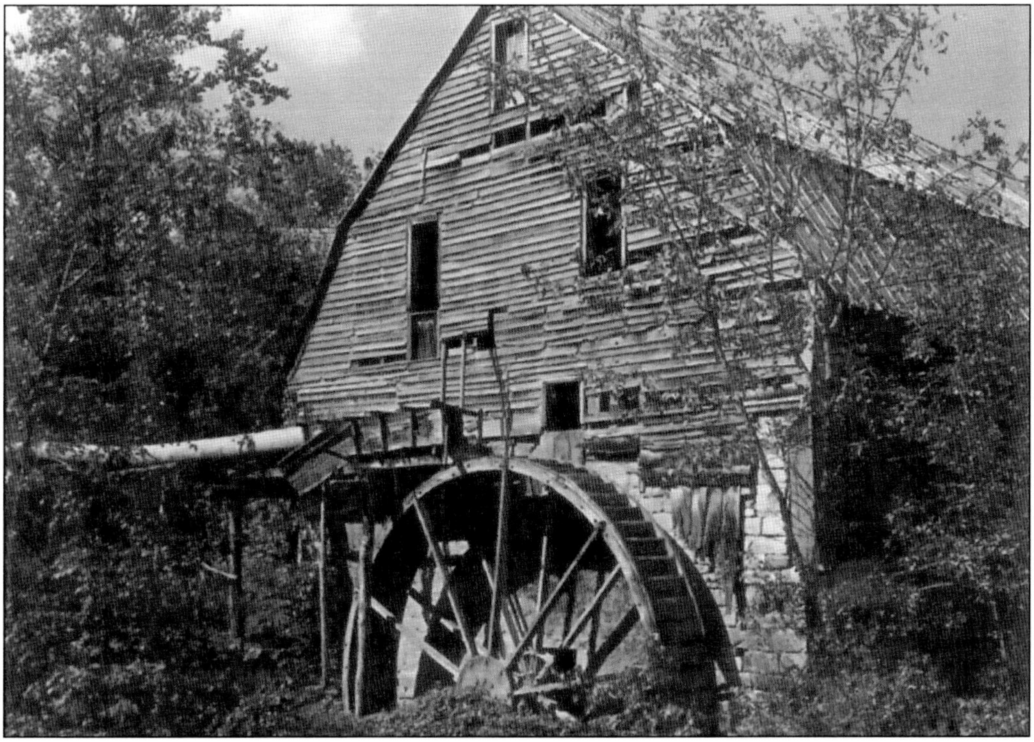

PATTERSON MILL. Robert Patterson built this mill on Patterson's Mill Creek, formerly known as Fall Creek. It also served as a fort during the frequent Chickamauga raids of 1775. The landmark stood for many years and was in the process of being placed on the National Register of Historic Places when it burned to the ground in 1975.

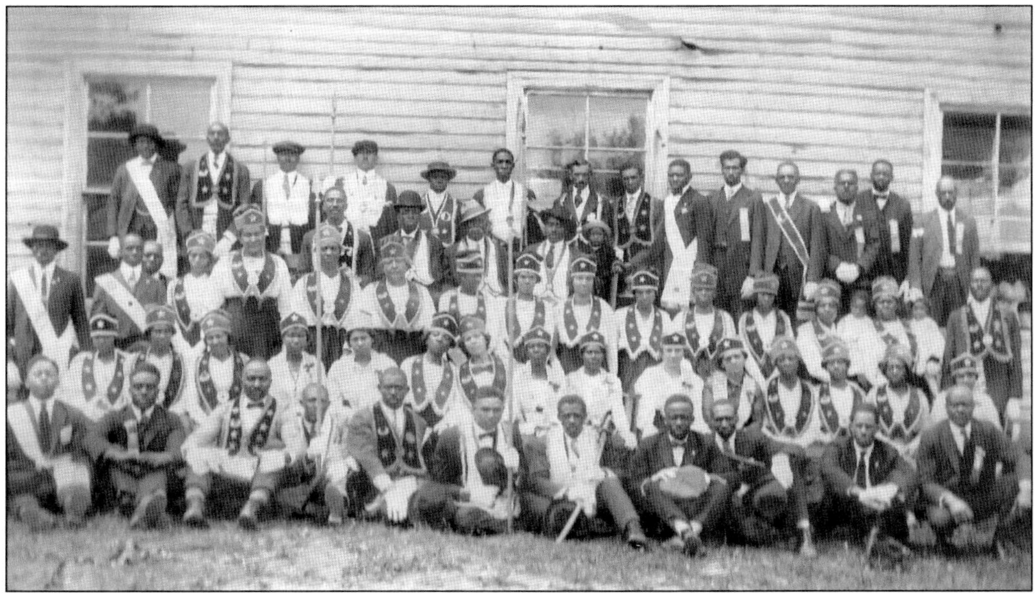

NEW CANTON LODGE. Here are the loyal order of African American Masons and the ladies of the Eastern Star. This photograph was taken around 1900 at the lodge in the new Canton community near Church Hill. (Photograph by Stella Gudger.)

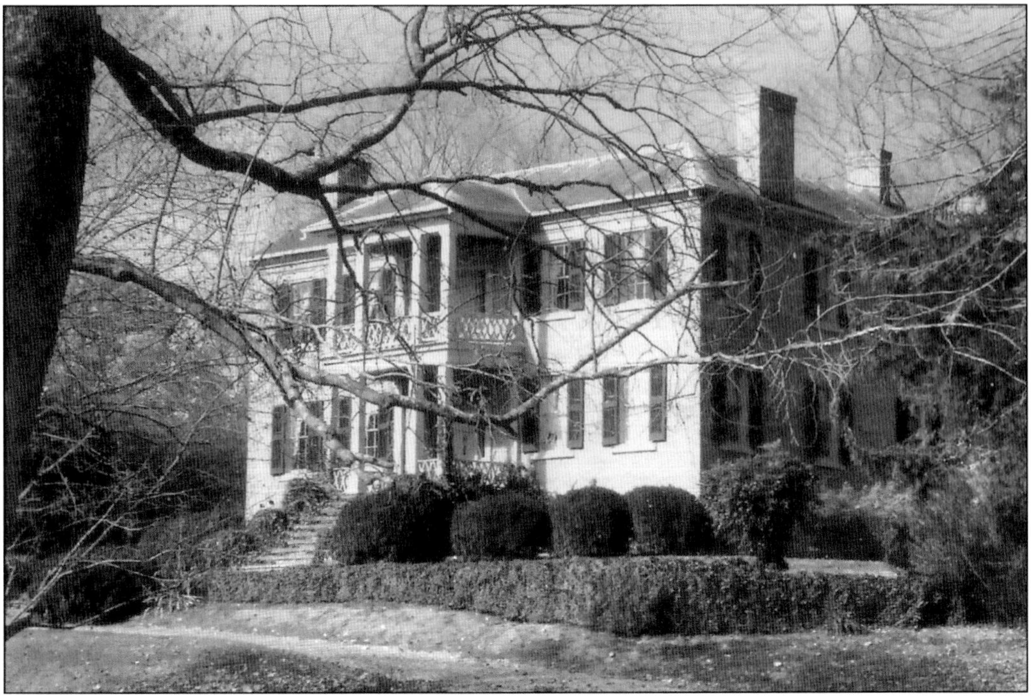

HORD HOUSE. The historic Hord house at New Canton was built around 1840 by Eldridge Hord. It was continuously occupied by four generations of the Hord family until the early 1990s when it was acquired by Carl Netherland Brown and his wife, Janet. Today the mansion has new owners who have restored it to its past splendor. (Photograph by Randy Ball.)

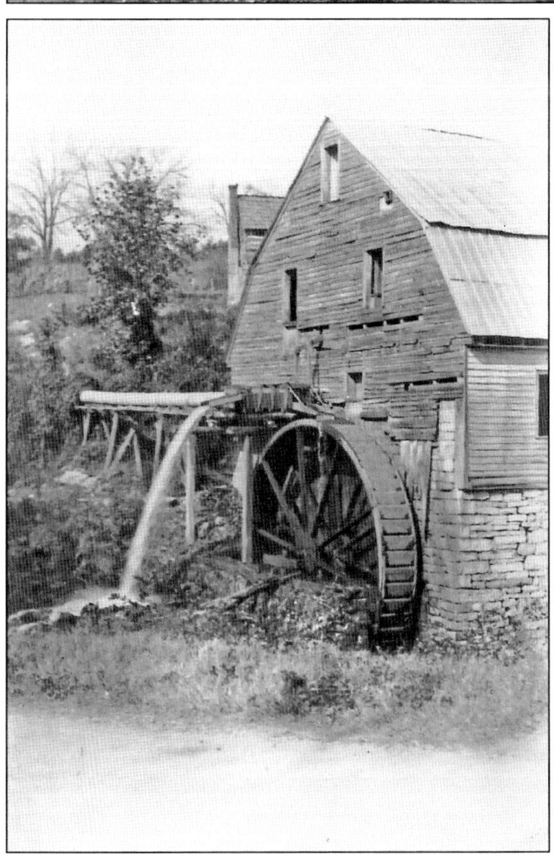

HORD MILL. The old Eldridge Hord mill at New Canton was also built around 1840. For many years, the mill served the community as a store and a mill for grinding corn and wheat. Today the structure is one of the last of the old gristmills still standing in East Tennessee.

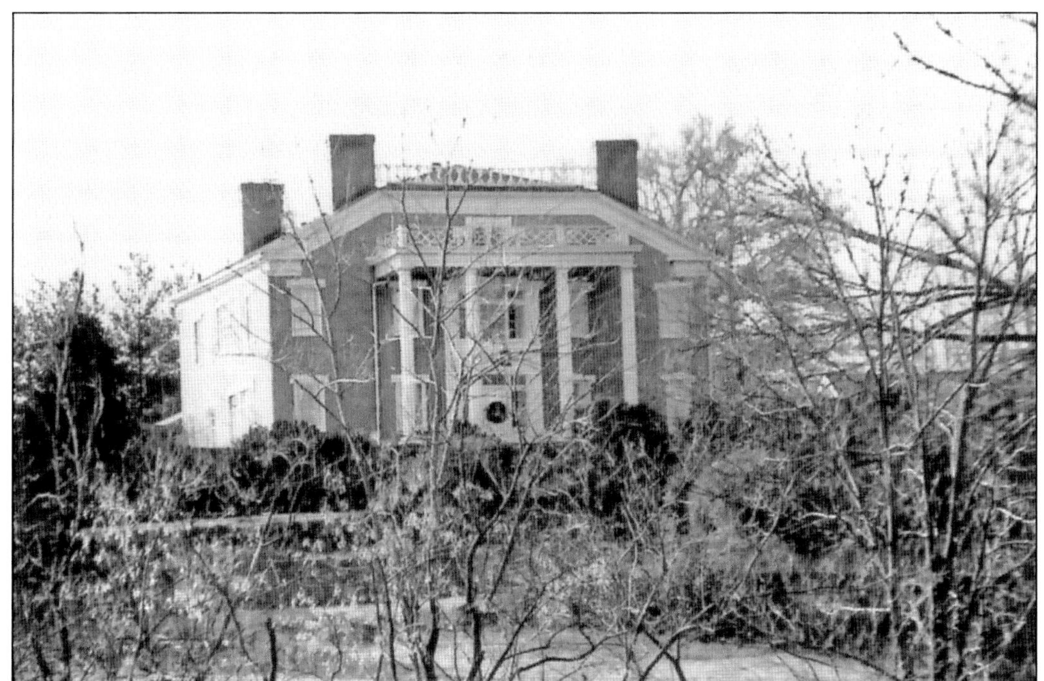

Rotherwood Mansion. This palatial home was built by Frederick Ross in 1818. The name was taken from Sir Walter Scott's *Ivanhoe*. It was here that Ross established a very successful iron furnace and a nail factory and later a woolen mill and a silk mill. (Photograph by Randy Ball.)

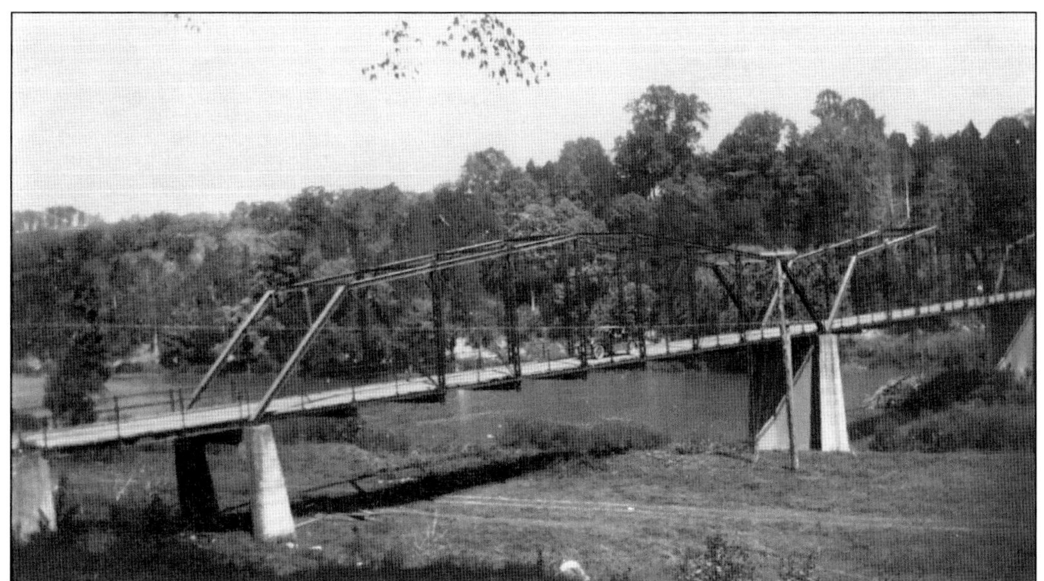

Rotherwood Bridge. Since 1818, there has been a bridge across the north fork of the Holston River. The first one was built by Frederick Ross. This photograph was taken in 1926. (Courtesy of Barbara Beets Combs.)

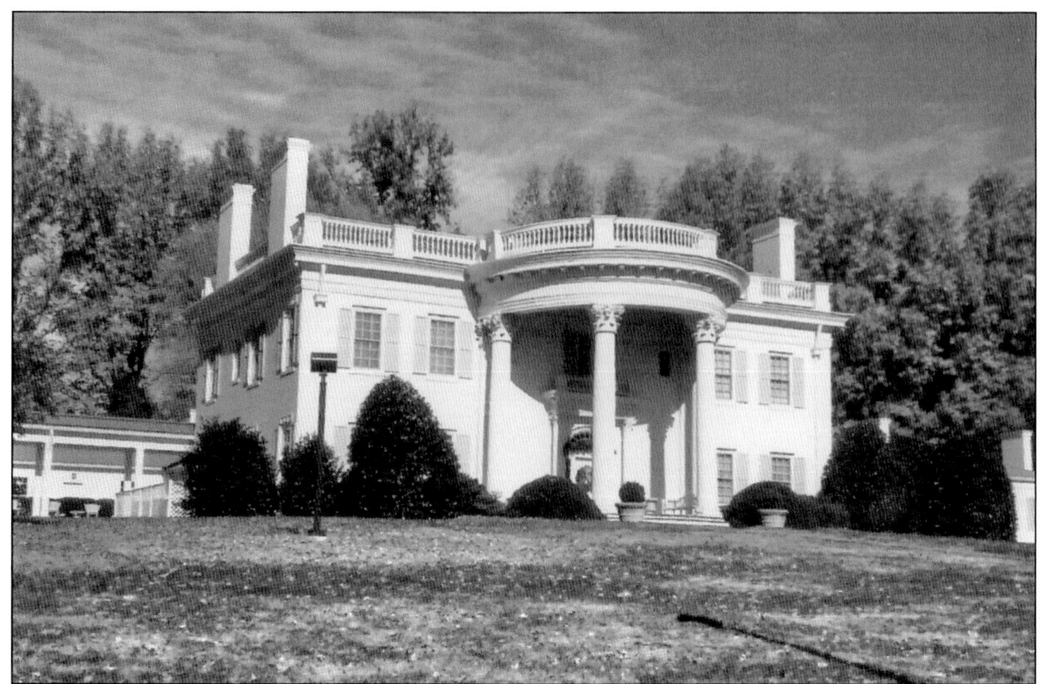

ALLANDALE MANSION. This beautiful old home was built by the Brooks family in 1949. They called it Allandale, though it was later dubbed, "the Kingsport White House." The house was built on property formerly owned by the Ross family. (Photograph by Randy Ball.)

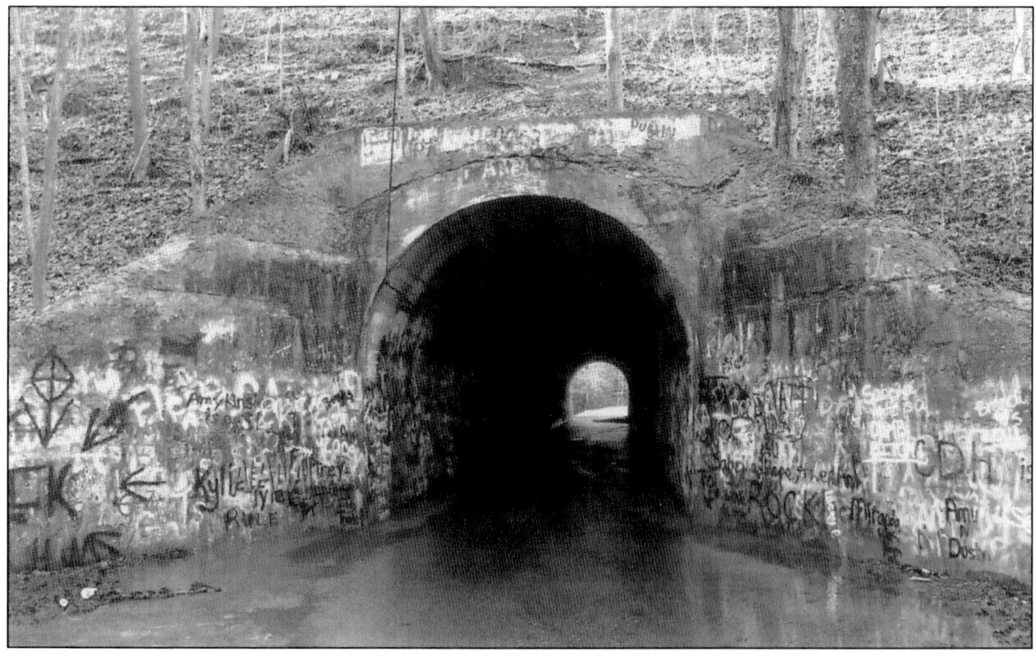

SENSABAUGH TUNNEL. Located on Big Elm Road in the Solitude section of North Hawkins County is the infamous Sensabaugh Tunnel. Railroad workers were killed near the tunnel in the early part of the 20th century. Since that time, many superstitious locals consider it one of the most haunted places in Hawkins County. (Photograph by Randy Ball.)

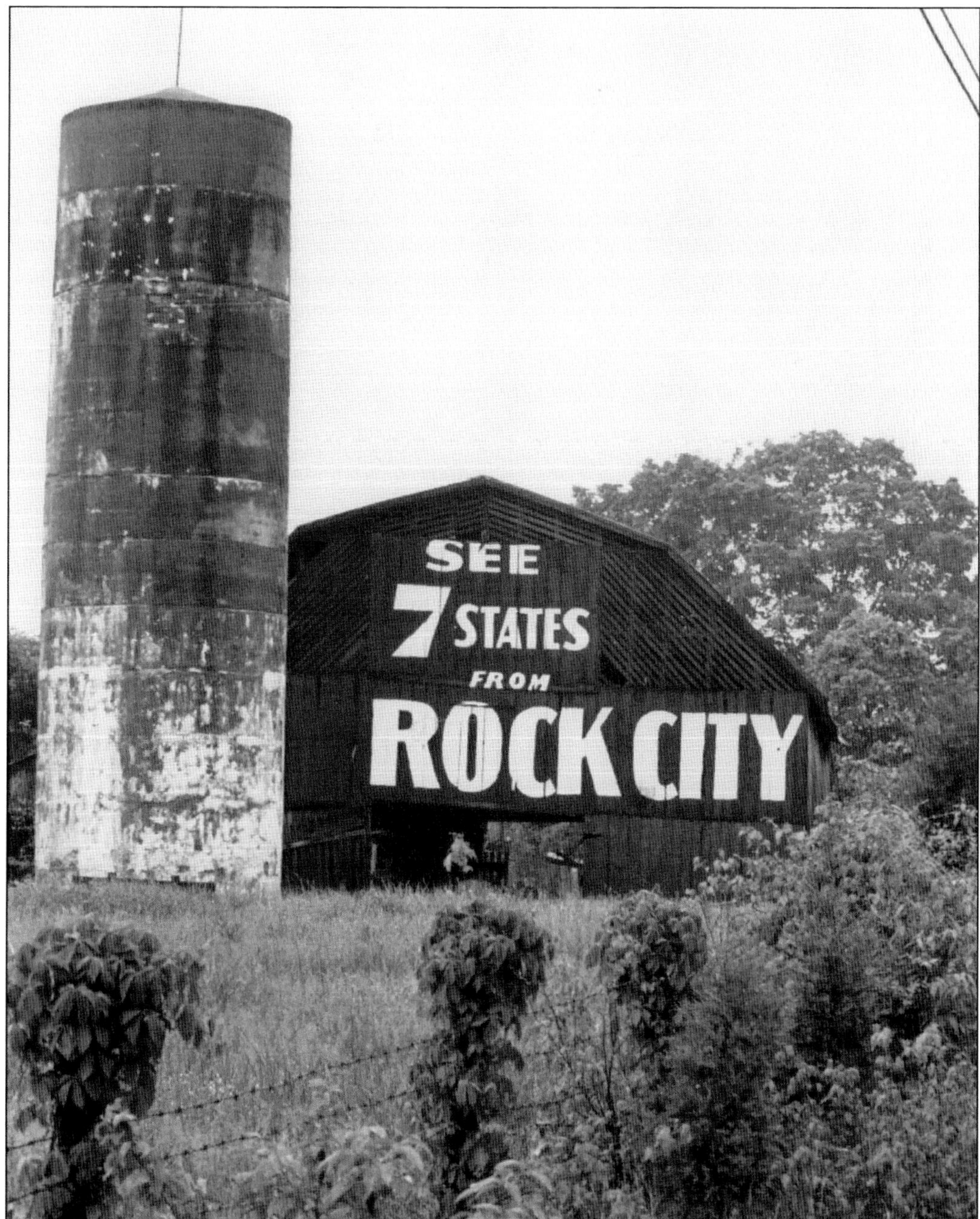

See Rock City. Soon after Rock City opened on May 21, 1932, owner Garnet Carter enlisted the help of a young barn painter named Clark Byers, who was hired to travel the nation's highways and offer to paint farmers' barns in exchange for letting him paint three simple words: "See Rock City." This barn is located in the Burtons Corner community near Rogersville. (Photograph by Randy Ball.)

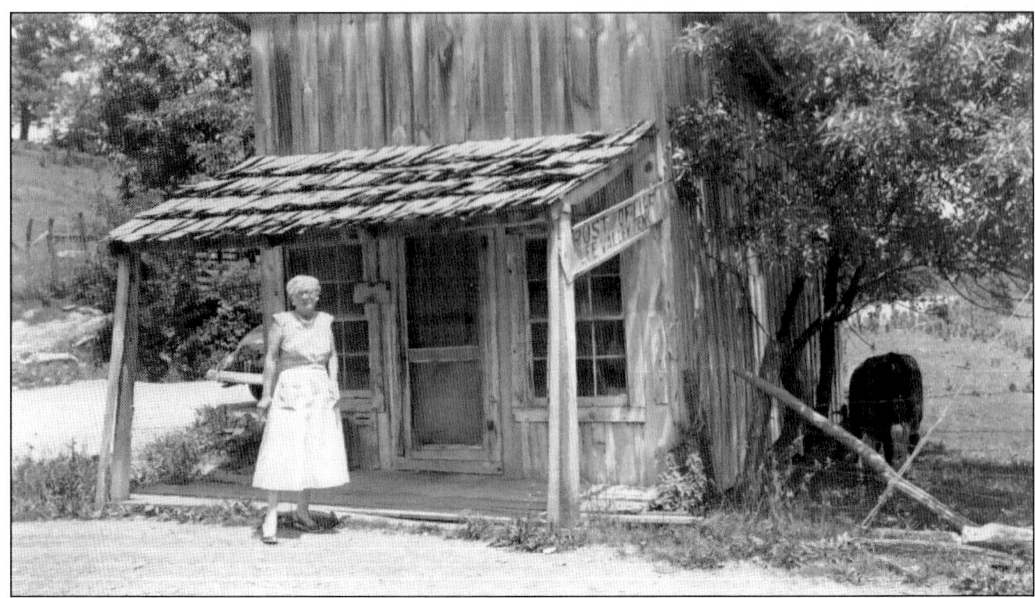

POST OFFICE. For many years, each community in Hawkins County had its own individual post office. This one was in Lee Valley near Clinch Mountain. An unidentified postmistress stands out front.

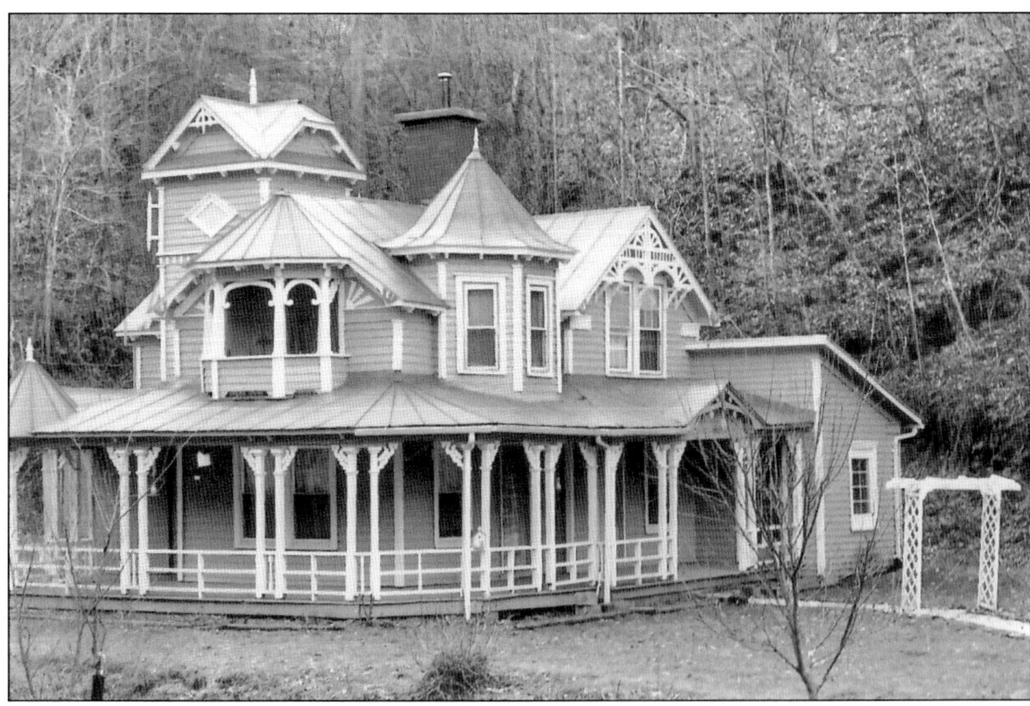

MILLER HOME. Dr. Albert Miller's home at Edison was built in the early 1900s and is supposedly the first prefab home built in Hawkins County. It came in on the train to Rogersville and was hauled over Clinch Mountain in wagons where it was erected. It is supposed to have been purchased from Sears and Roebuck. (Photograph by Randy Ball.)

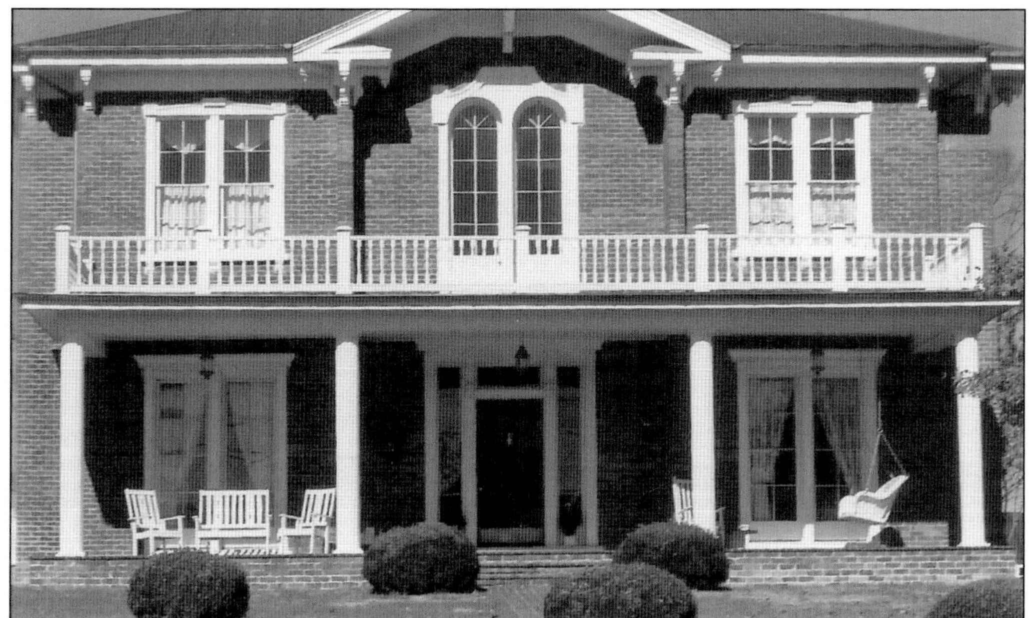

CHESNUTT HOUSE. The historic Chesnutt Roark house on Highway 113 between Rogersville and St. Clair was built about 1842 by Rodham Chesnutt. For many years, the mansion was the home of Samuel P. and Effie Chesnutt Roark. The house has remained in the same family since its construction and has recently been restored to its original antebellum splendor. (Photograph by Randy Ball.)

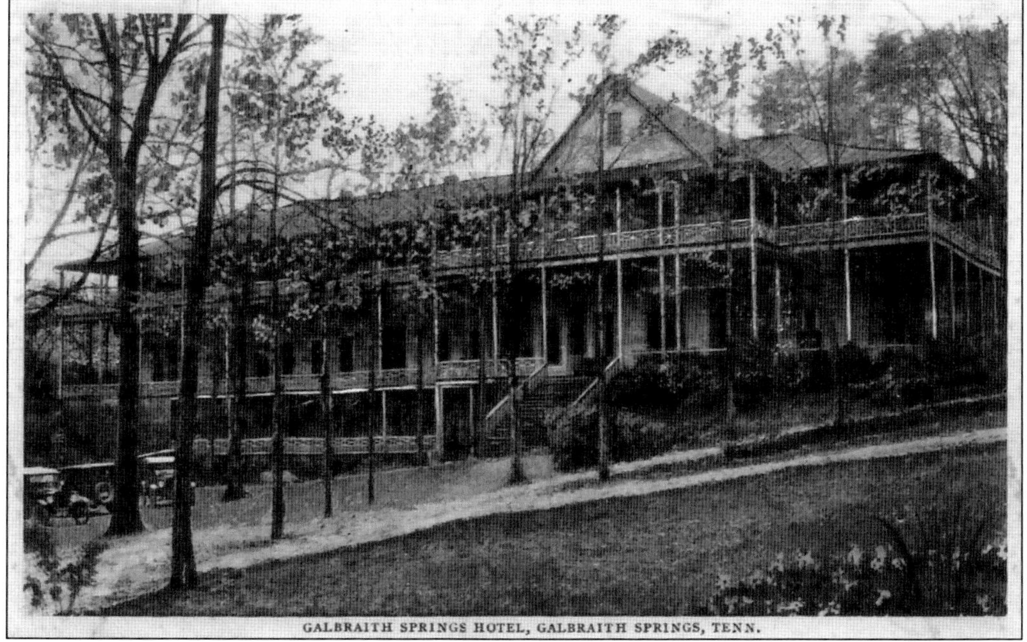

GALBRAITH SPRINGS HOTEL, GALBRAITH SPRINGS, TENN.

GALBRAITH SPRINGS. This famous resort spa was opened in the 1850s in the Mooresburg community. It was founded by the Galbraith family. The resort featured a three-story rambling hotel, a large dance pavilion, a bowling alley, and swimming facilities. The health spa offered meals, lodging, recreation, and the opportunity to build a cottage nearby.

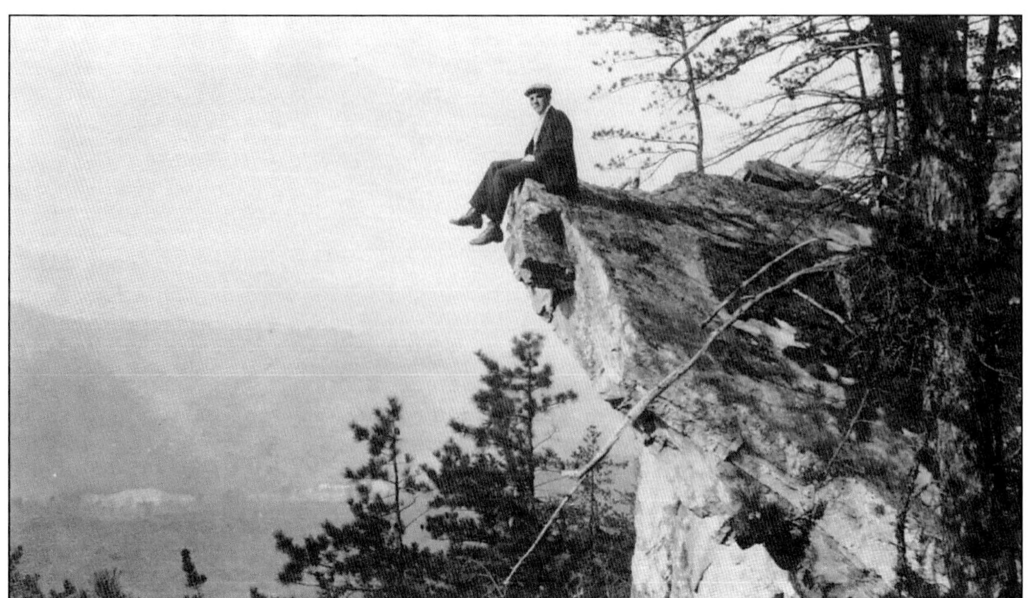

DEVIL'S NOSE MOUNTAIN. Located in the Striggersville community is one of Hawkins County's most majestic landmarks. The mountain's odd shape is thought to be the reason for its unusual name. Over the years, many people have climbed the Devil's Nose and gazed from its lofty heights.

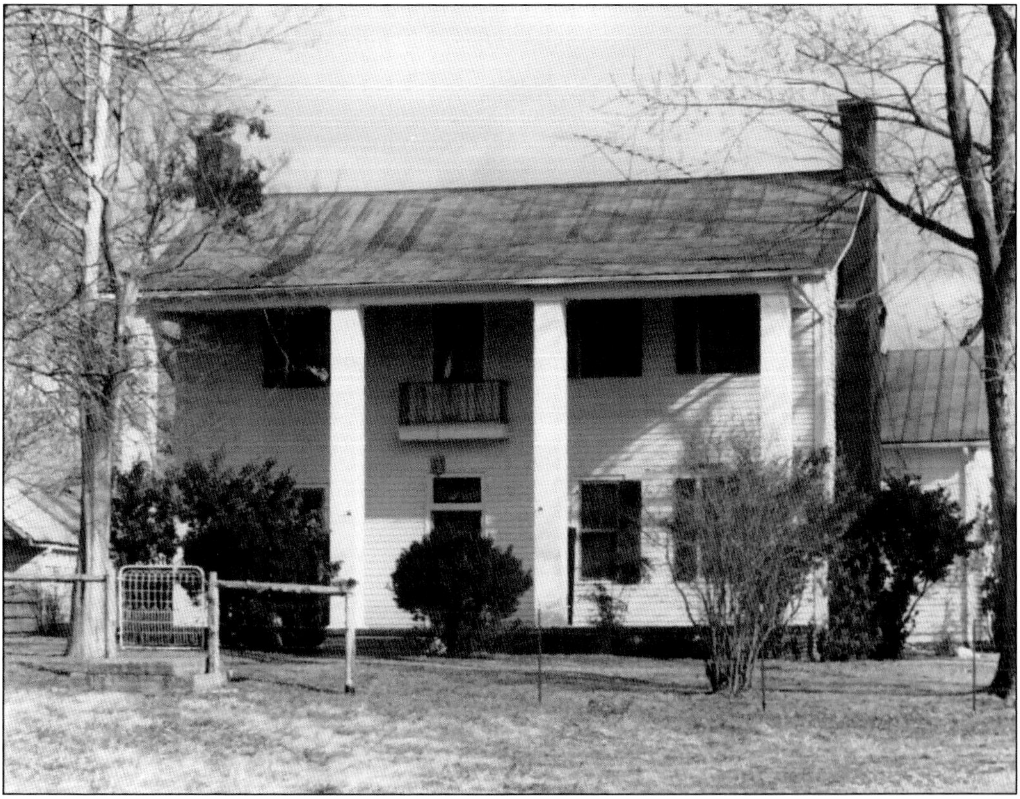

MILL BEND. The historic Burem house on Mill Bend Road was built in the 1860s. The Colonial-style home boasted 15 rooms. It was torn down in the 1990s. (Photograph by Randy Ball.)

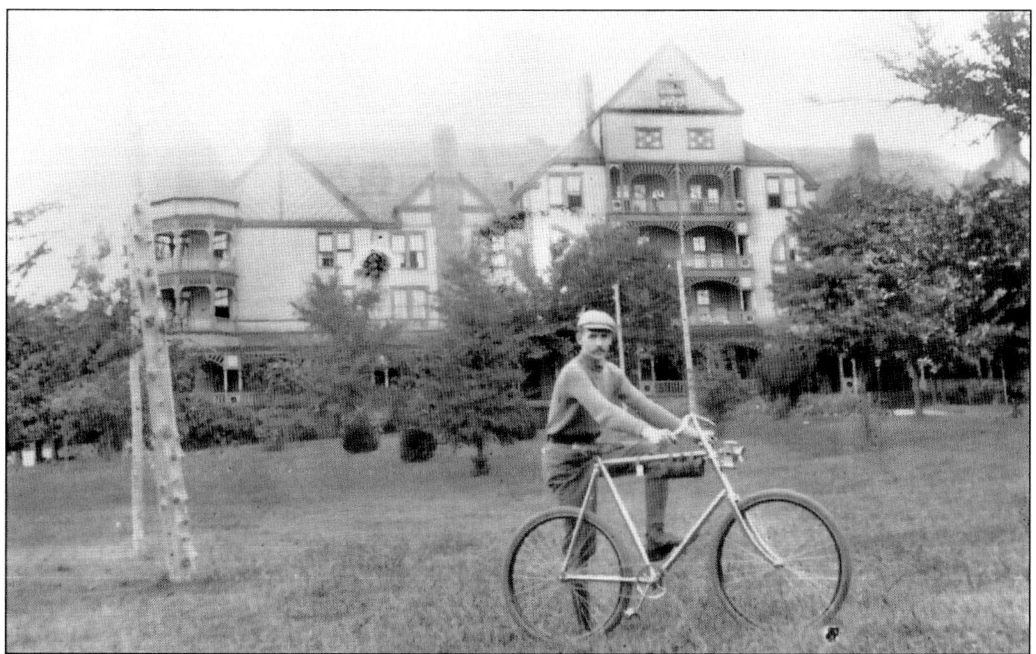

Tate Springs. The old Tate Springs resort was located near the north end of Hawkins County at Bean Station. The grand luxury resort boasted a five-story hotel with swimming pools and a golf course. Guests to the resort included the Vanderbilt, Melon, and Ford families. (Courtesy of Randy Ball.)

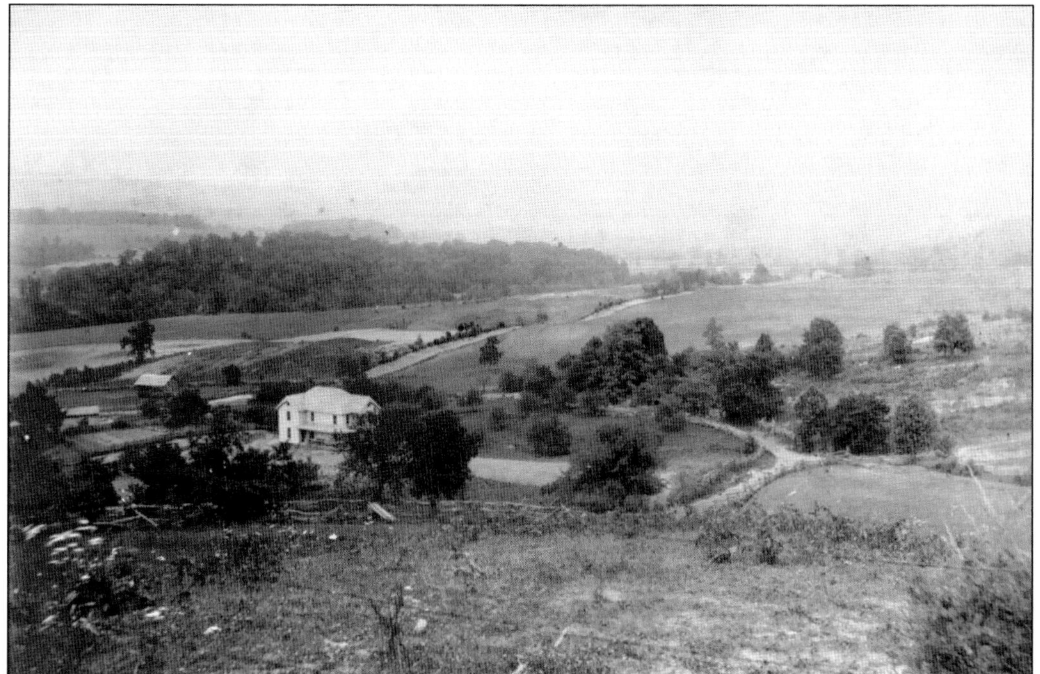

Choptack. The community of Choptack is located between the Rogersville town knobs and Stone Mountain. The unusual name given to the valley comes from the echo of a tree being chopped on a nearby ridge.

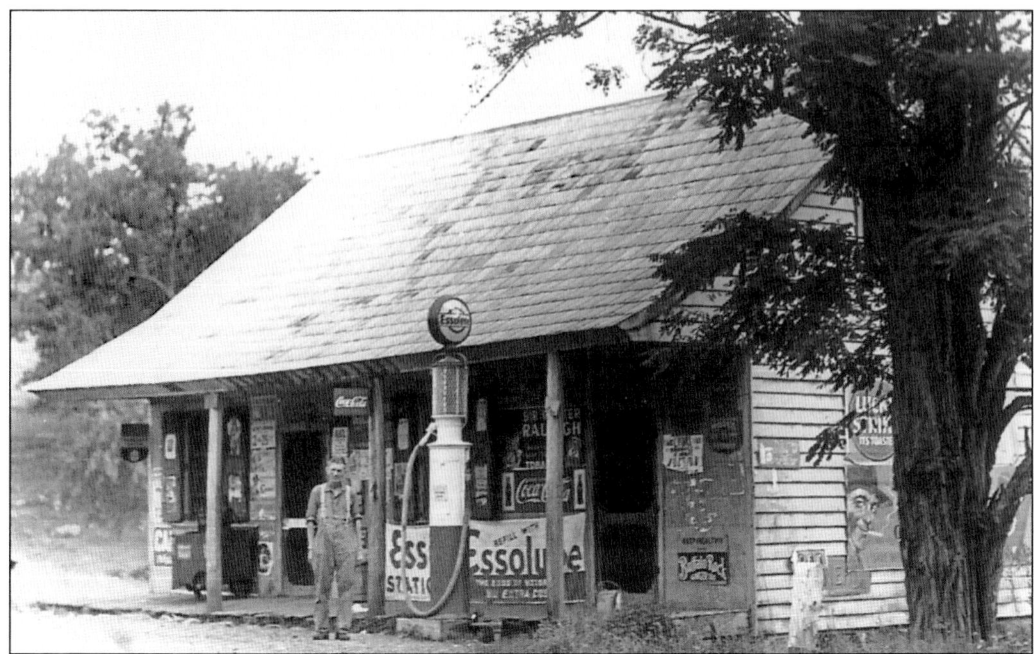

Yellow Store. The Yellow Store was built in 1795 by Jacob Miller. It served as a trading post for many years. It was about 3 miles from the town of Surgoinsville. This photograph was taken in 1936. W. J. Thurman, who ran the store for many years, is standing by the gas pump. The store was destroyed by a tornado in 1955. (Courtesy of Betty Brooks.)

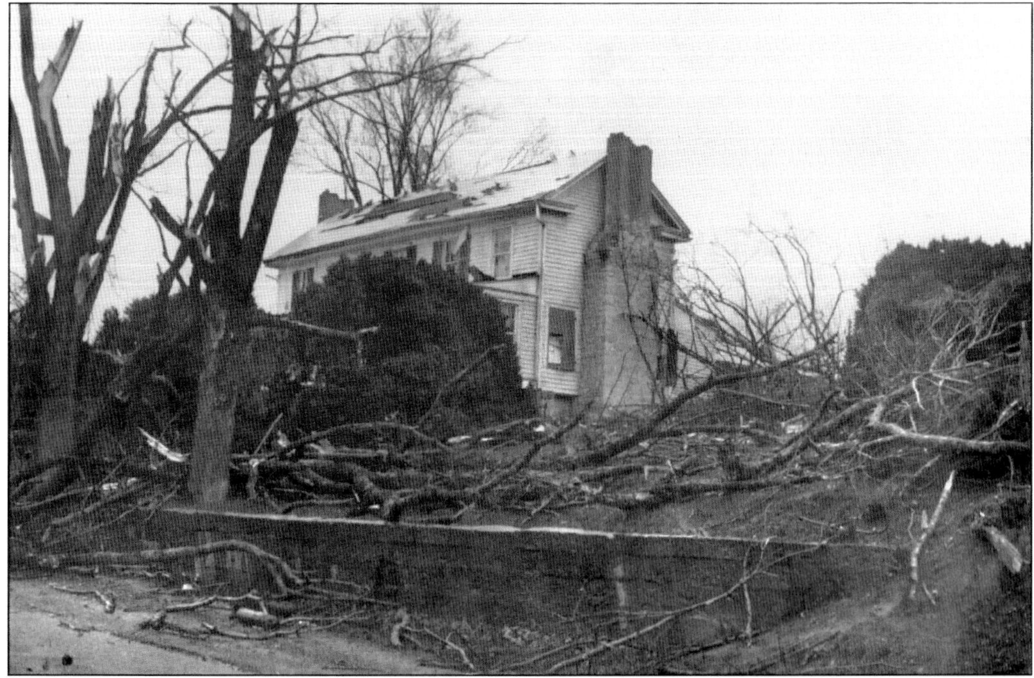

Smith House. Located on Highway 346, the Frank Smith house near Yellow Store in Surgoinsville narrowly escaped the 1955 tornado that destroyed many neighborhood houses and stores. Today it is owned by Thomas and Sally Childs Shelburne.

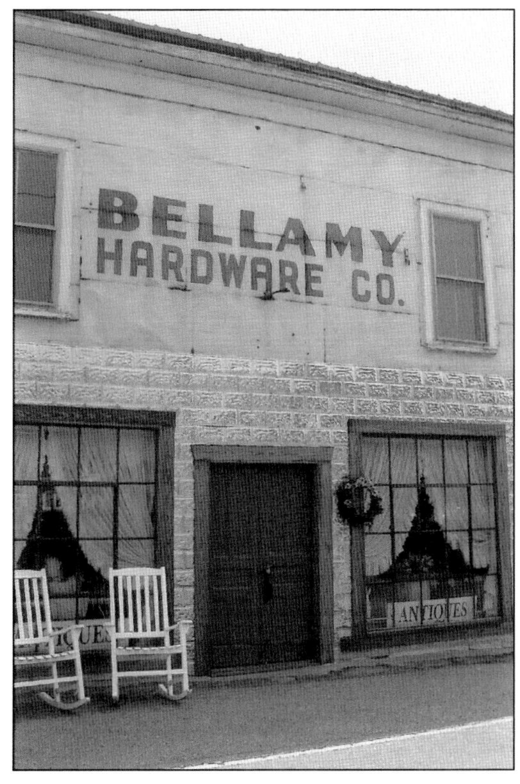

Bellamy Store. The Bellamy Store was built around the turn of the 20th century as a hardware and general store for the town of Surgoinsville. The train ran directly behind the store, and many times coffins were stored overnight in the upstairs storeroom. Today the store serves as a bluegrass theater. (Photograph by Randy Ball.)

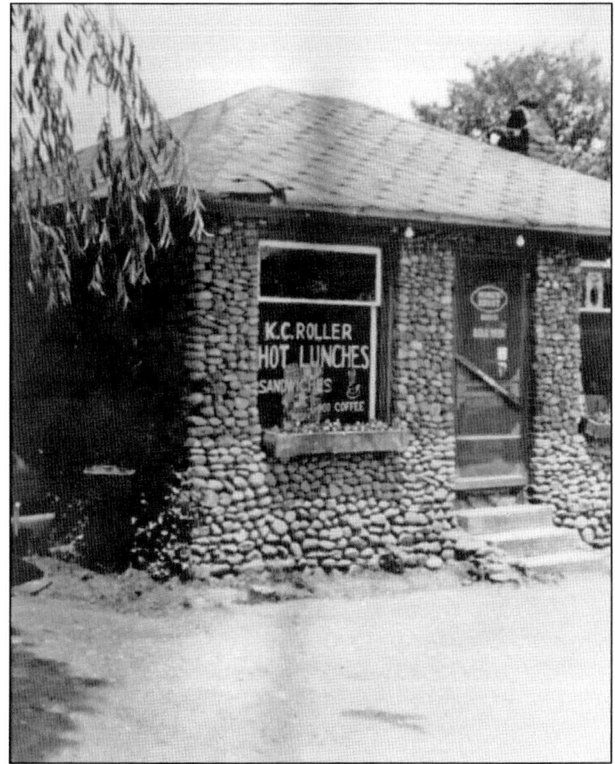

Rock House. Located on the Old Stage Road in Surgoinsville, the Rock House was one of Hawkins County's most recognizable landmarks. Pres. Franklin Delano Roosevelt and his secretary stopped there in the 1930s on their way to Washington from Warm Springs, Georgia. The Roller family operated the store for many years and later turned it over to Joyce Greer.

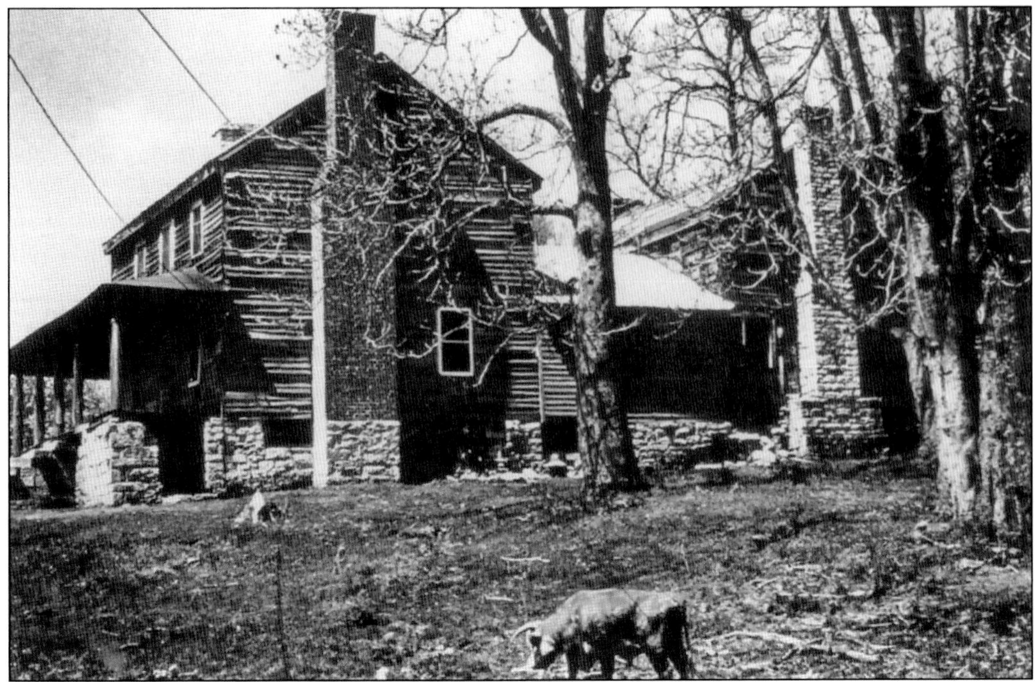

MAXWELL LYONS HOUSE. This large log cabin was traditionally thought to be the home of American Revolutionary War hero George Maxwell. The large log structure was built by William Lyons around 1800 and served as an inn and tavern. It also boasted a large gathering room for the purpose of dancing.

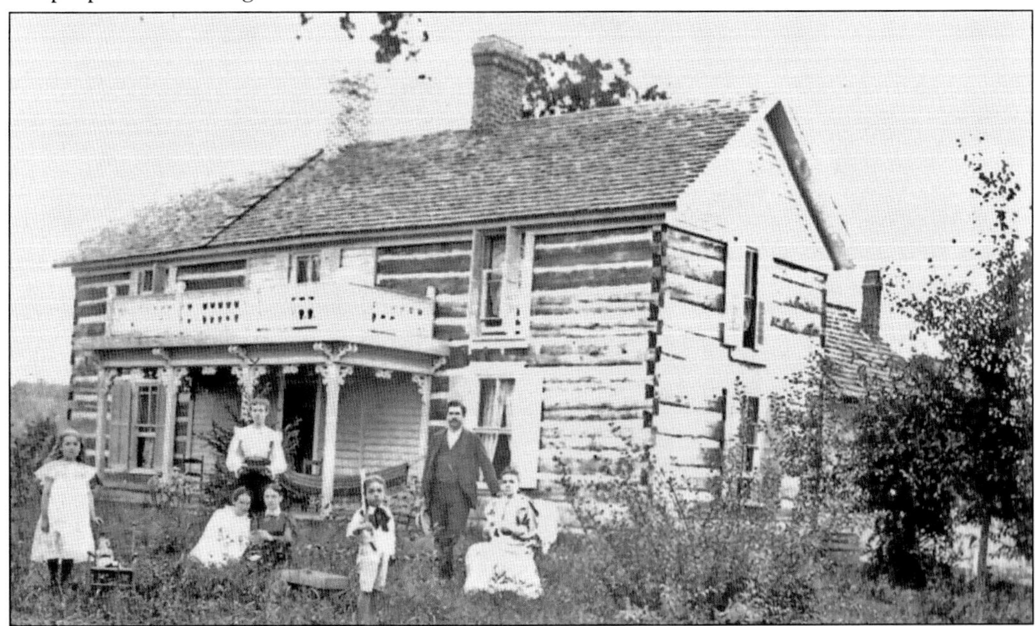

LYONS HOUSE. The log home of Dr. William C. Lyons is a double log pen built in Surgoinsville in 1891. Dr. Lyons was the son of Clinton Gallaher Lyons, a veteran of the Civil War. It was later the home of Dr. Lyons' son Dr. Conner Lyons, longtime physician and mayor in Surgoinsville. (Photograph by Randy Ball.)

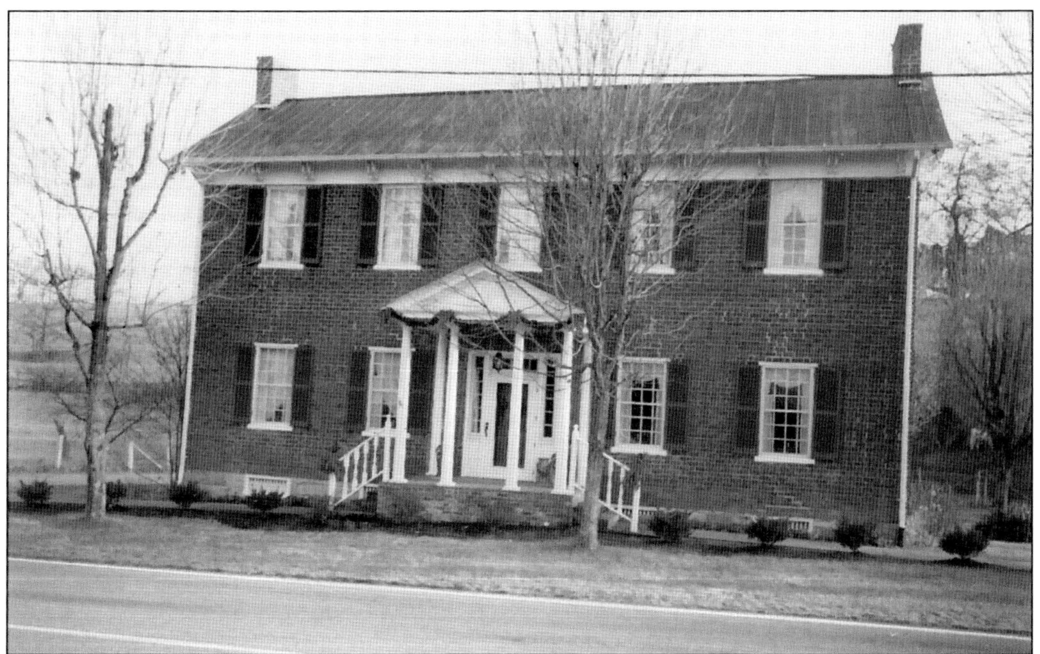

Fudge Farm. This Federal-style mansion was built in 1824 by German immigrant Conrad Fudge. The farm has remained in the Fudge family through five generations and still retains many of its original outbuildings and heirlooms. The home is listed on the National Register of Historic Places.

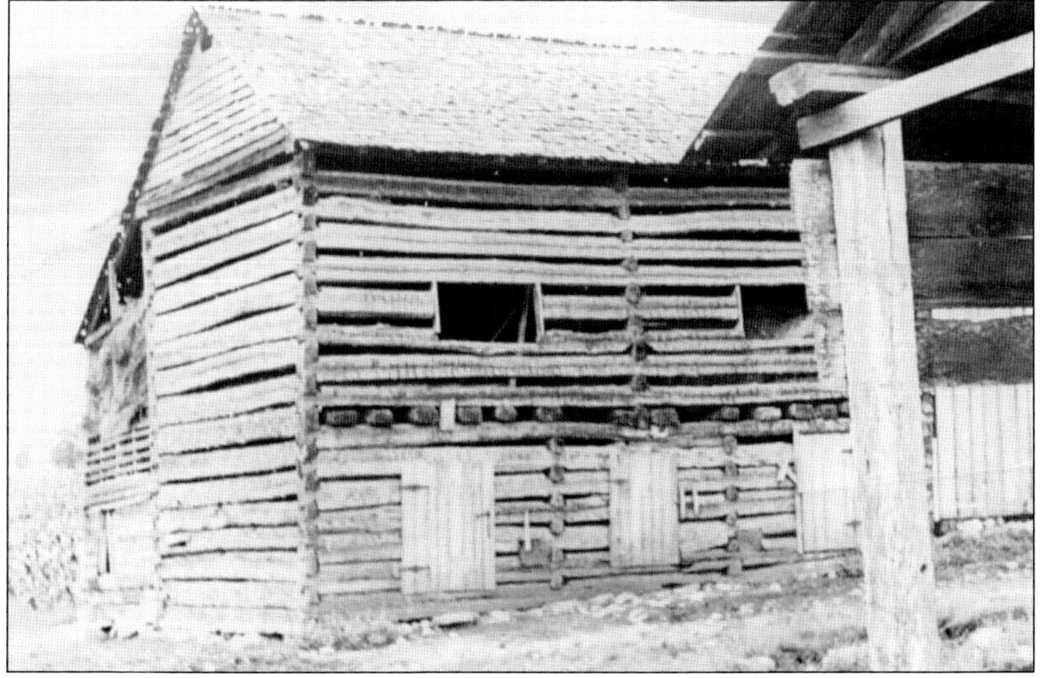

Double Pen Barn. The huge double pen barns at the Fudge Farm were constructed in 1824. A store was maintained here throughout the 1800s.The barn complex was also used for square dances for Surgoinsville residents during this time frame.

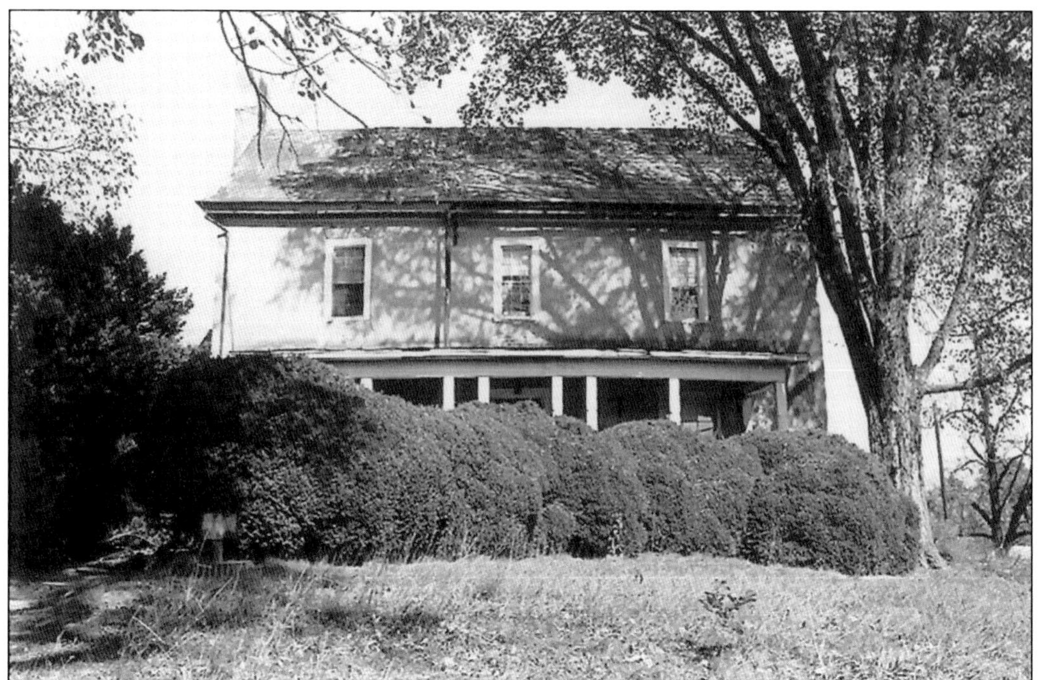

STONY POINT. Located on a rock ledge in the community of Stony Point is the Armstrong Mansion. Built in 1780, it is one of the oldest brick structures in Tennessee. Prince Louis Philippe, who later became king of France, visited there in 1797. The house is listed on the National Register of Historic Places.

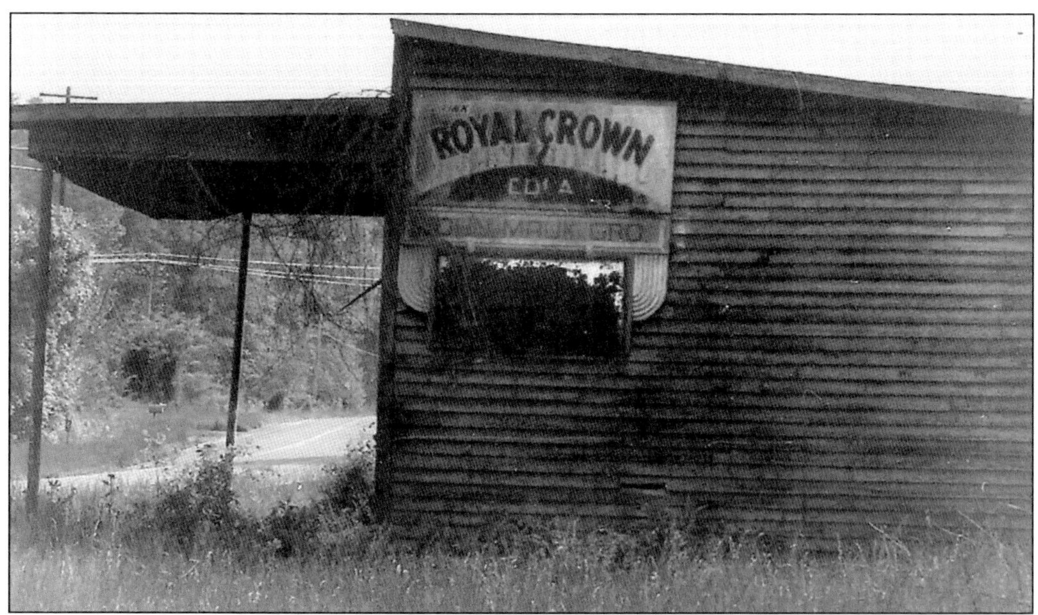

JOHN MAUK STORE. On the corner of Phipps Bend Road and Highway 346 are the remnants of John Mauk's store. It was once the hub of the Stony Point community. John Mauk ran the store for many years on the barter system. Many old-timers gathered at the store around the potbellied stove and discussed the events of the time. (Photograph by Randy Ball.)

New Providence. Founded in 1780 by William Armstrong III, New Providence Presbyterian Church was organized by famous pioneer preachers Rev. Samuel Doak and Rev. Charles Cummings. The cemetery there claims several American Revolutionary War veterans and 28 Confederate veterans. (Photograph by Randy Ball.)

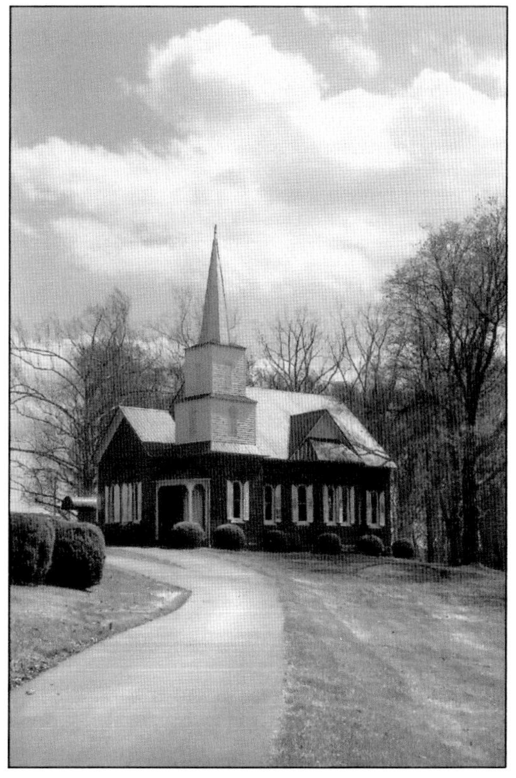

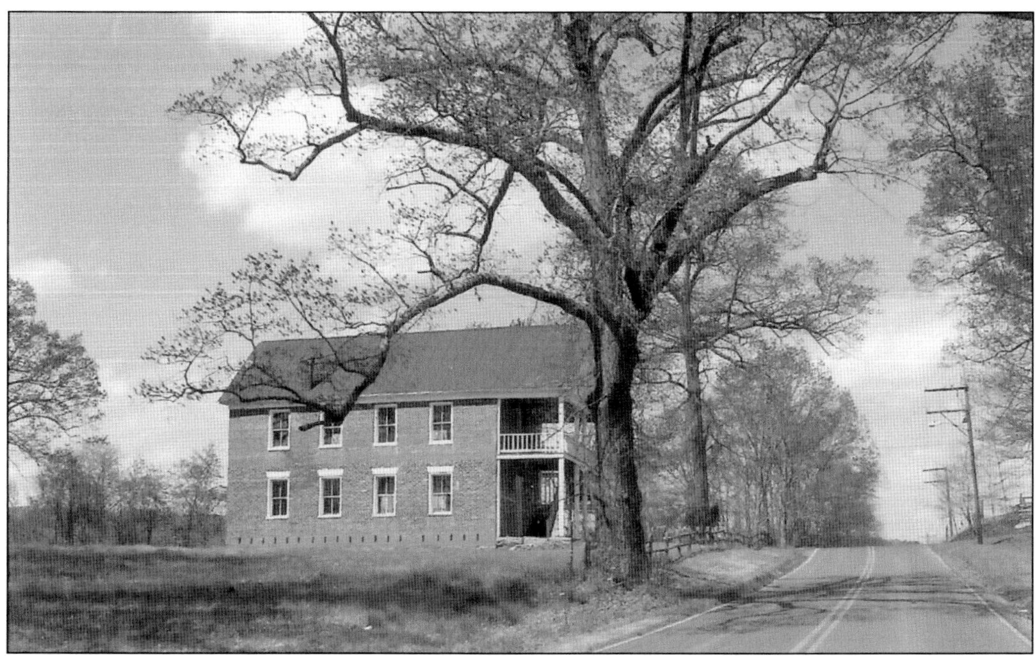

Maxwell Academy. This old school at Stony Point was established in 1856 and named after American Revolutionary War hero George Maxwell. The land was donated by William Armstrong. The present brick building was erected in 1901 to replace the original building that burned. The school closed in 1942. (Photograph by Randy Ball.)

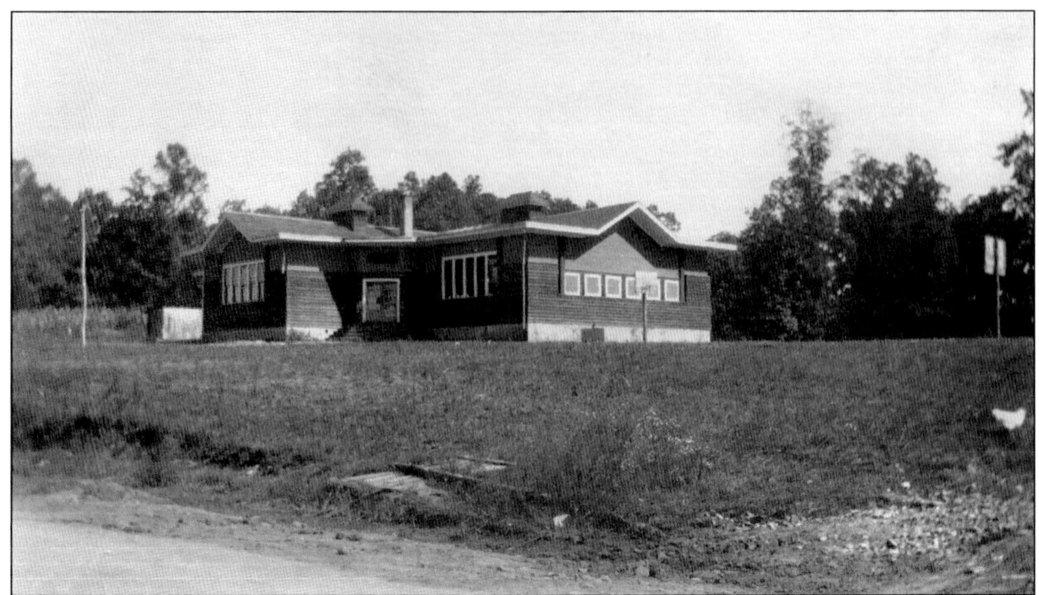

SURGOINSVILLE HIGH SCHOOL. The first high school building in Surgoinsville was erected in the 1920s. Today the old school stands empty and in a state of disrepair. (Courtesy of Barbara Combs.)

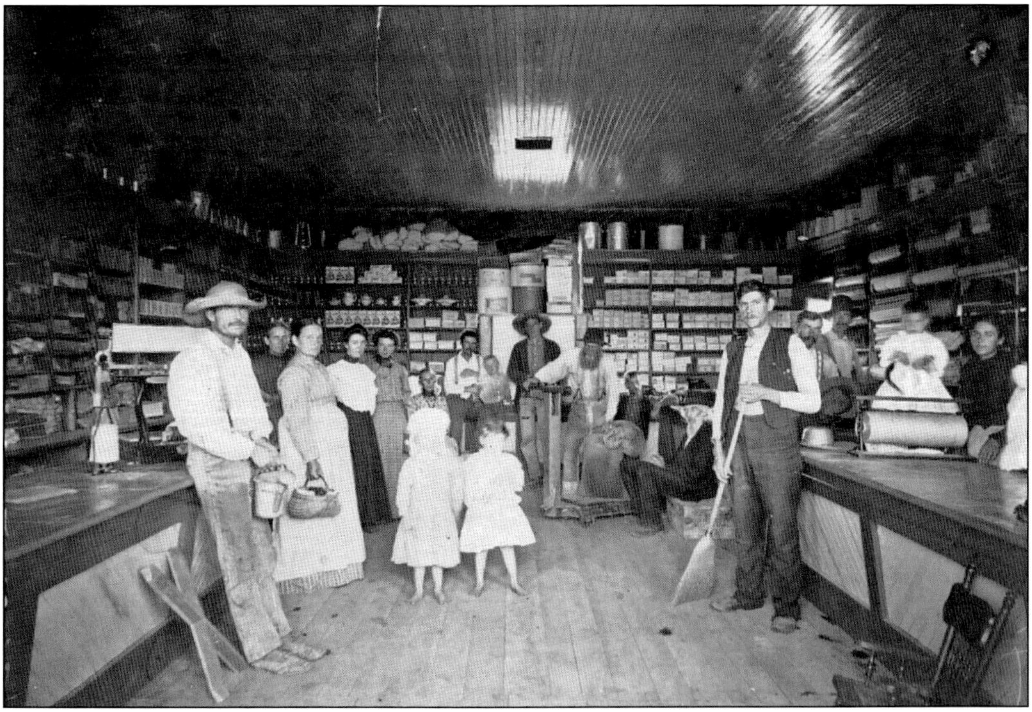

DAVIDSON'S STORE. Located on Carters Valley Road, this business was originally called Looney's Store. The store first opened in 1902 and operated for nearly 30 years until it became a causality of the Great Depression. Seventy years later, a descendant of the Looney family, William Davidson Sr., reopened the store in the 1990s.

Seven

Hawkins County This and That

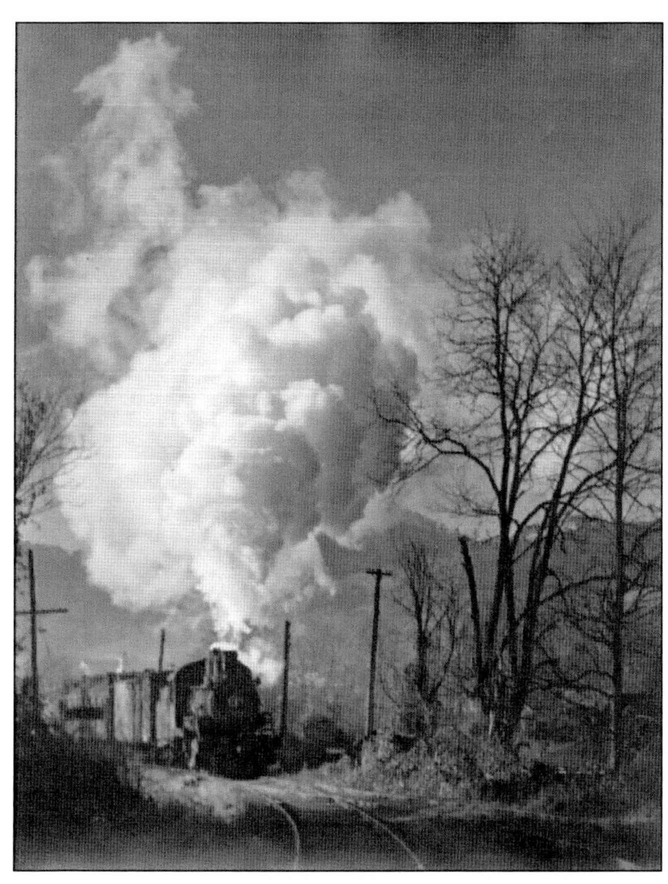

Old No. 03. The old steam engine train, once a familiar site in Appalachia, has now vanished from the landscape. This photograph was taken on a bitterly cold January morning in 1931. The little sleepy town of Rogersville is shown in the background.

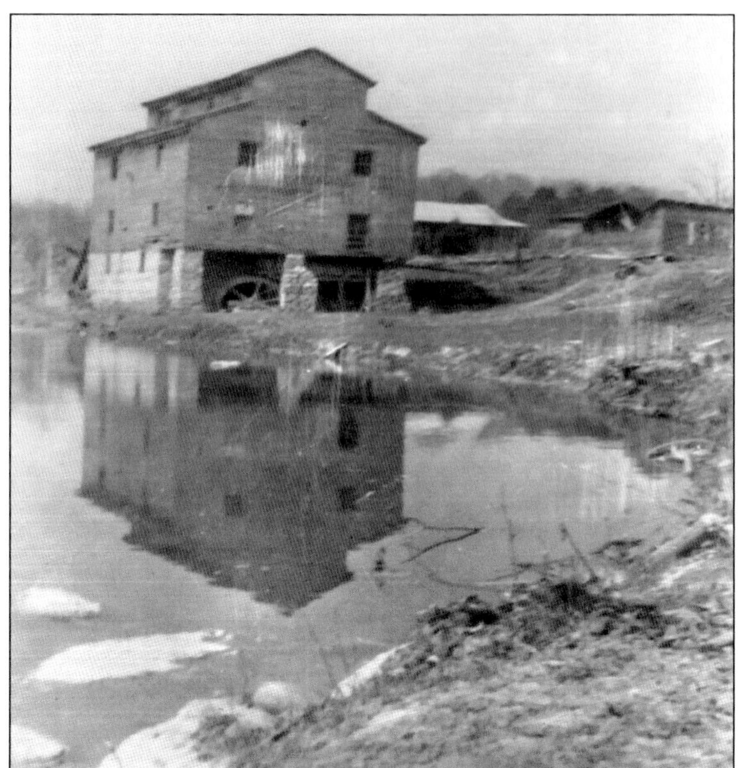

KIRKPATRICK MILL. Once located on the Holston River section of the Kirkpatrick farm, the old gristmill serviced the community for many years. It was built in the mid-1700s by John Kirkpatrick. The old mill was torn down to make way for Cherokee Lake.

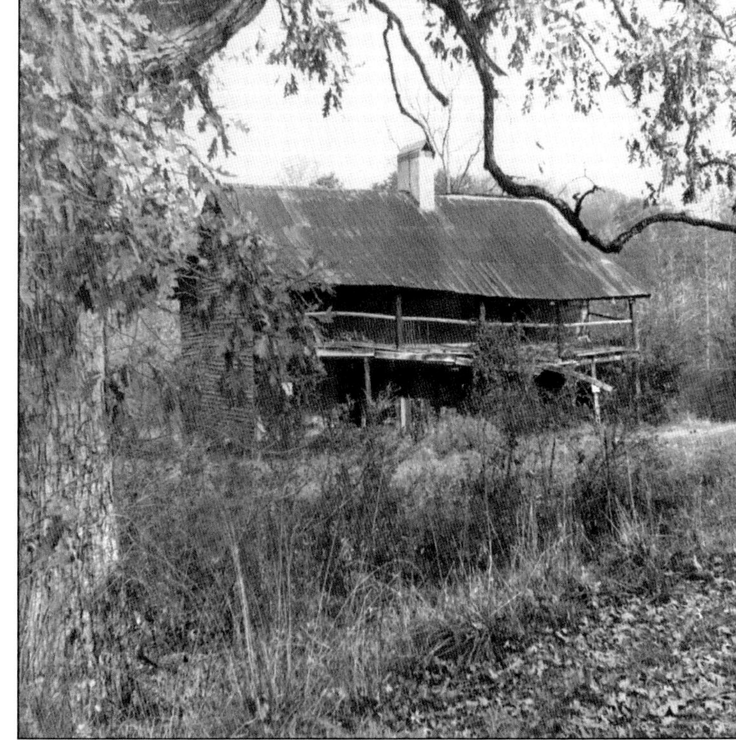

KIRKPATRICK HOMESTEAD. A part of the Kirkpatrick complex, this house was erected in the 1700s by early settler John Kirkpatrick. Next door a general store once stood, which was managed by the Farmers Alliance. (Photograph by Randy Ball.)

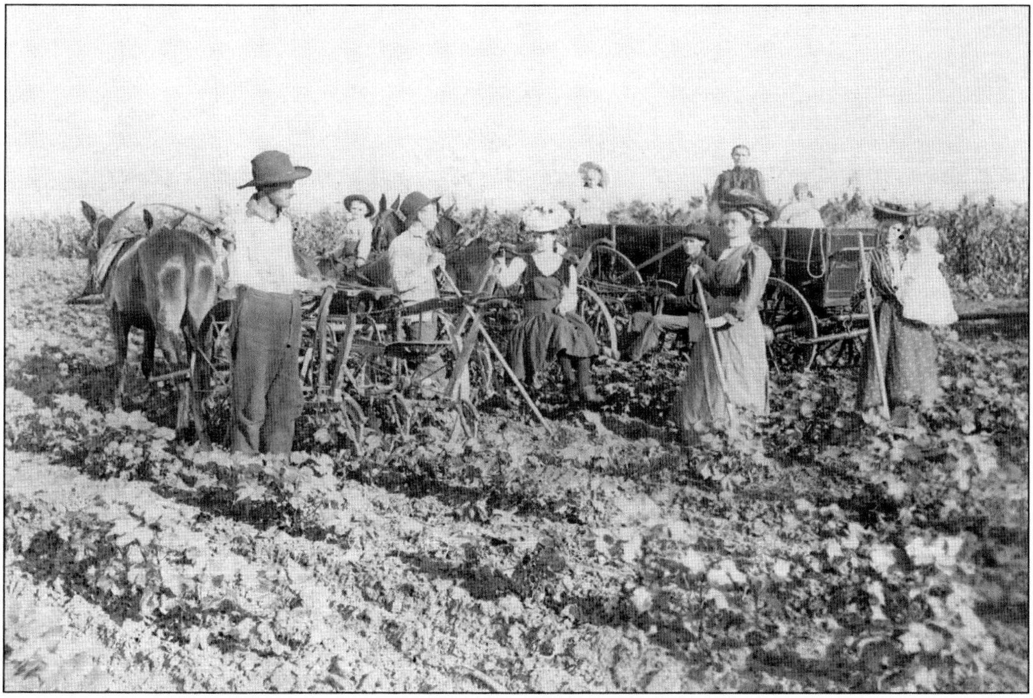

Old Times. William Henry Greene, Alma Jones Greene, Sally Buttry, Jane Cope, and others are shown working the Greene farm in Clinch Valley in 1899.

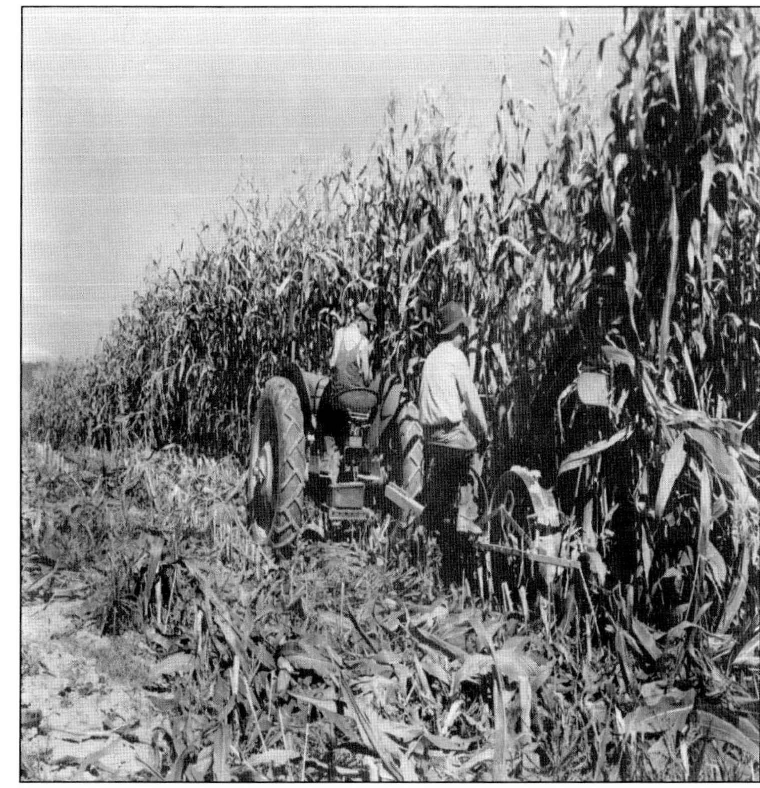

New Times. Thomas and Andrew Greene, grandsons of William Henry Greene, are shown working the same farm 50 years later but with a much easier means.

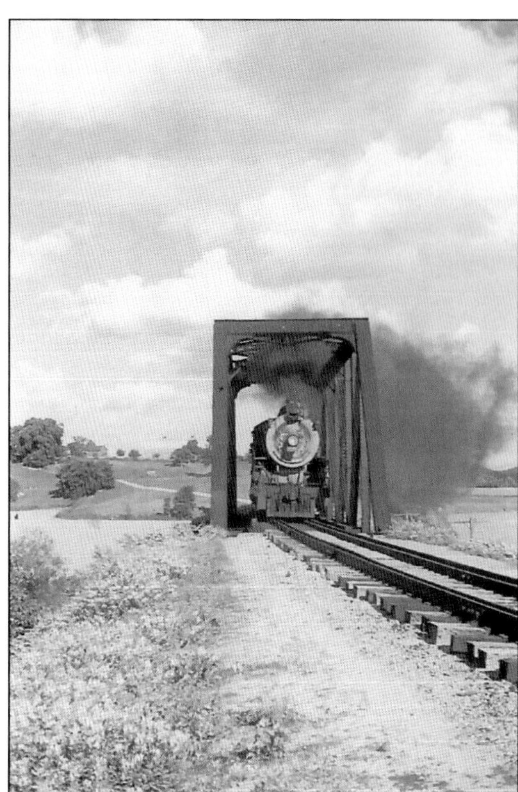

Train Crossing. This passenger train is shown leaving Bulls Gap in 1939. In the early days, train travel was one of the most convenient and comfortable ways to make a trip.

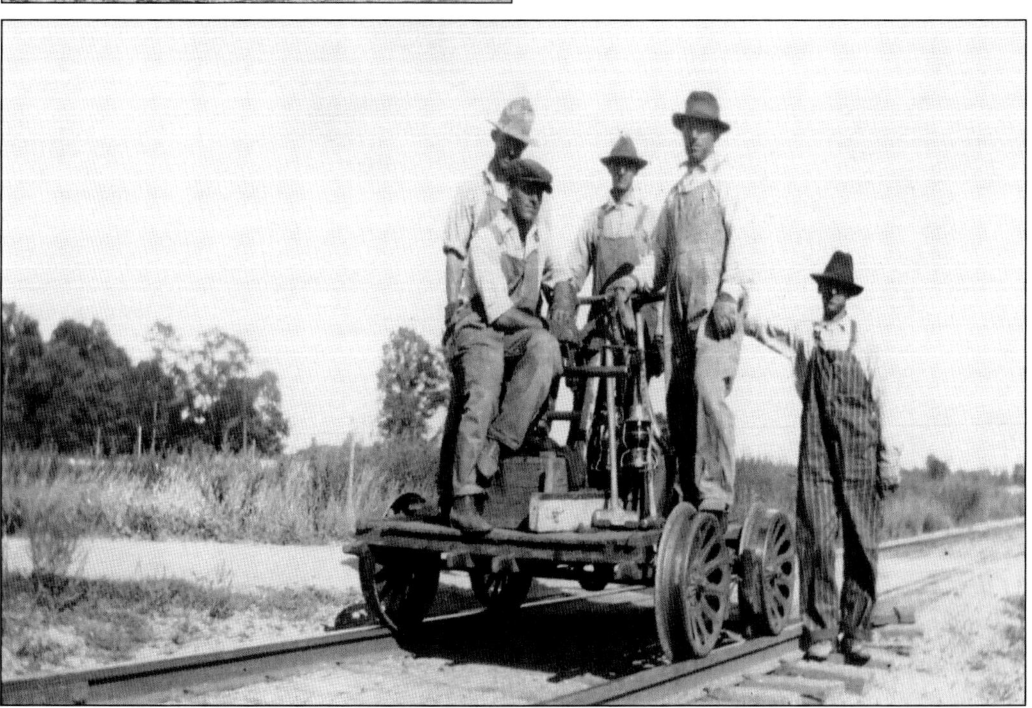

Handcar. Back in the early part of the 20th century, there was more than one way to ride the rails. An early railroad crew riding the rail through the Persia community can be seen in this image.

WELL DIGGING. The Ferrell family dug wells in Hawkins County for over 100 years. This photograph was taken in 1902.

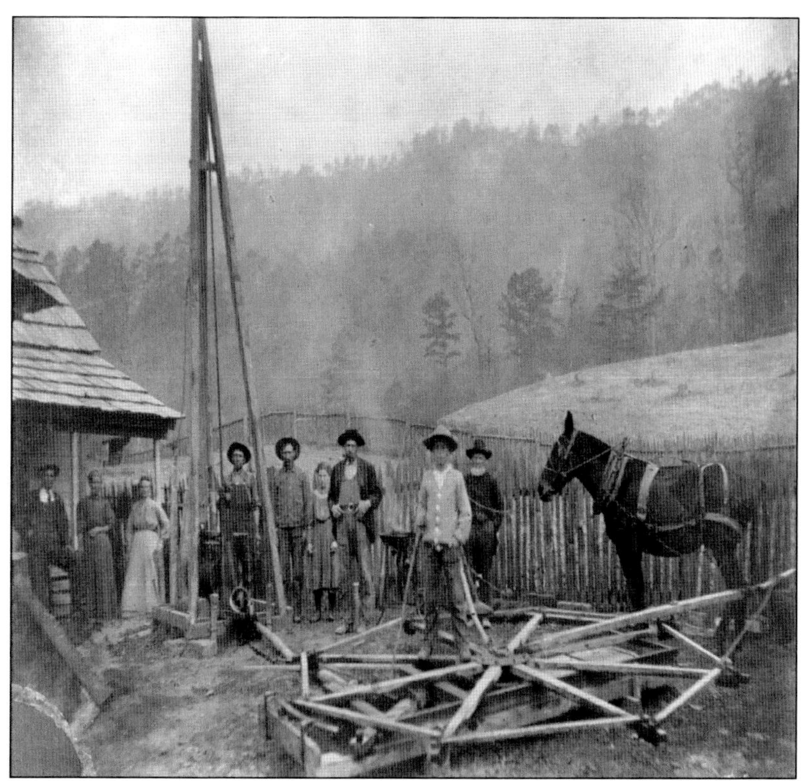

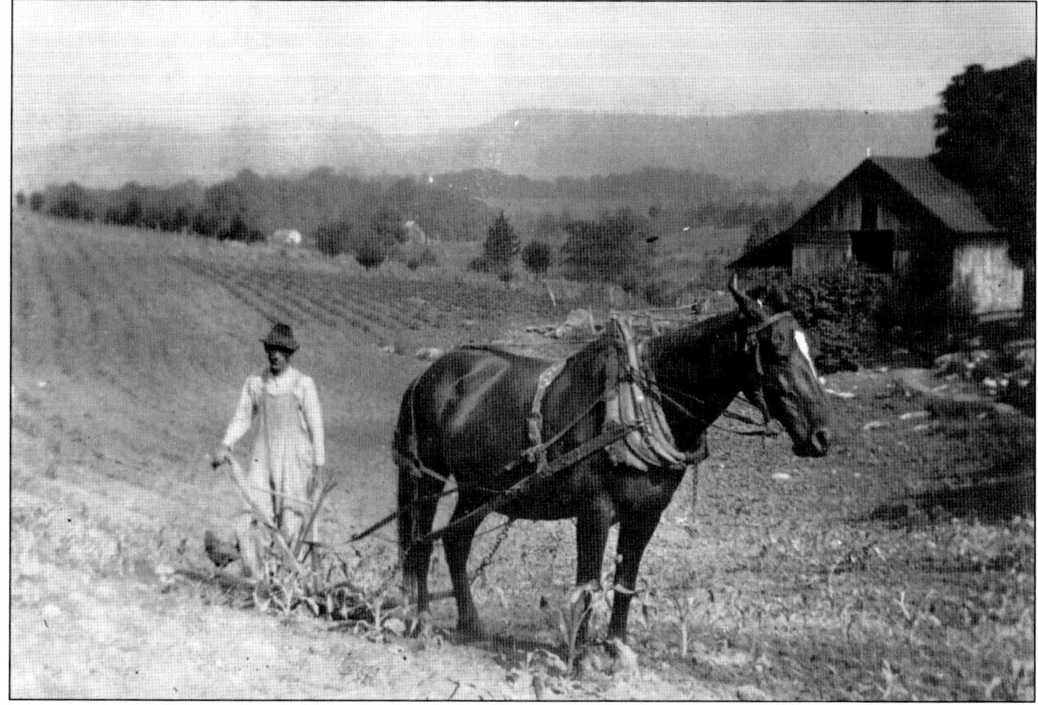

PLOWING. John Ferrell cane be seen plowing in the String Town community of Hawkins County. The bull tongue plow was very important to Appalachia farmers.

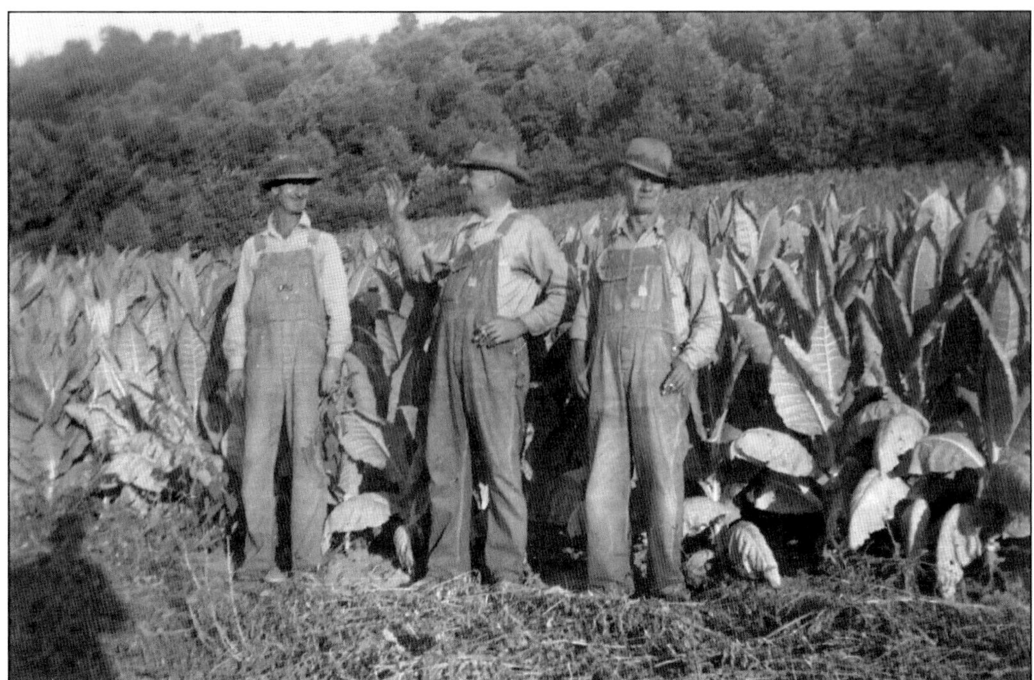

Tobacco. For many years, tobacco was the backbone of the Hawkins County economy. In this 1945 photograph, unidentified farmers are cutting tobacco in Striggersville under the Devil's Nose Mountain.

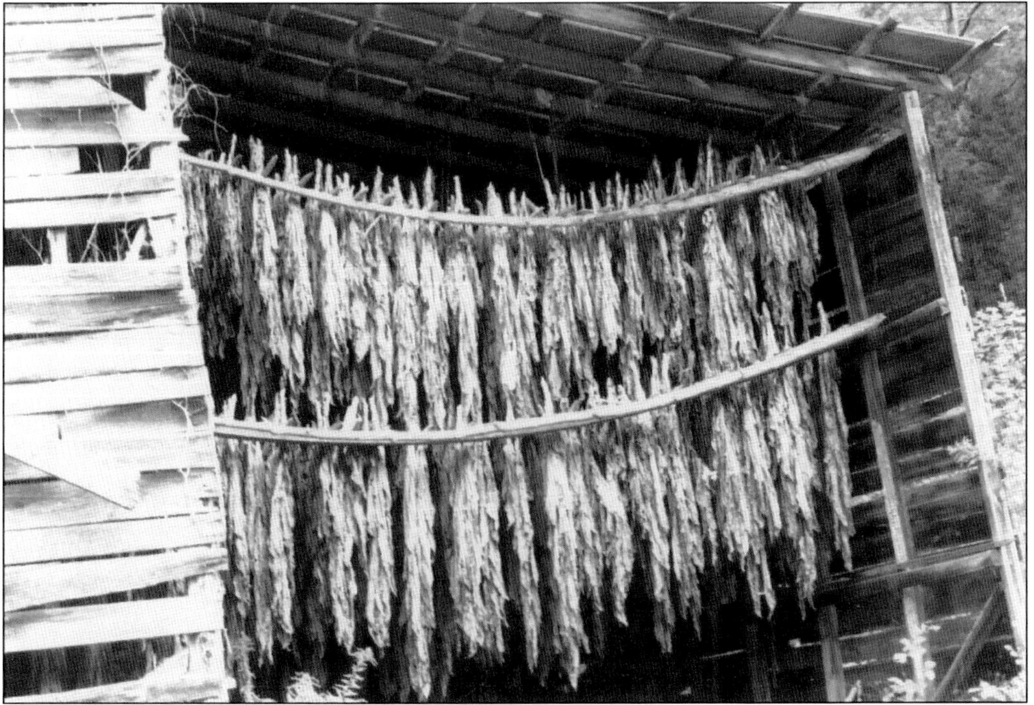

Curing. This image shows tobacco curing in a barn in the Hickory Cove community. (Photograph by Randy Ball.)

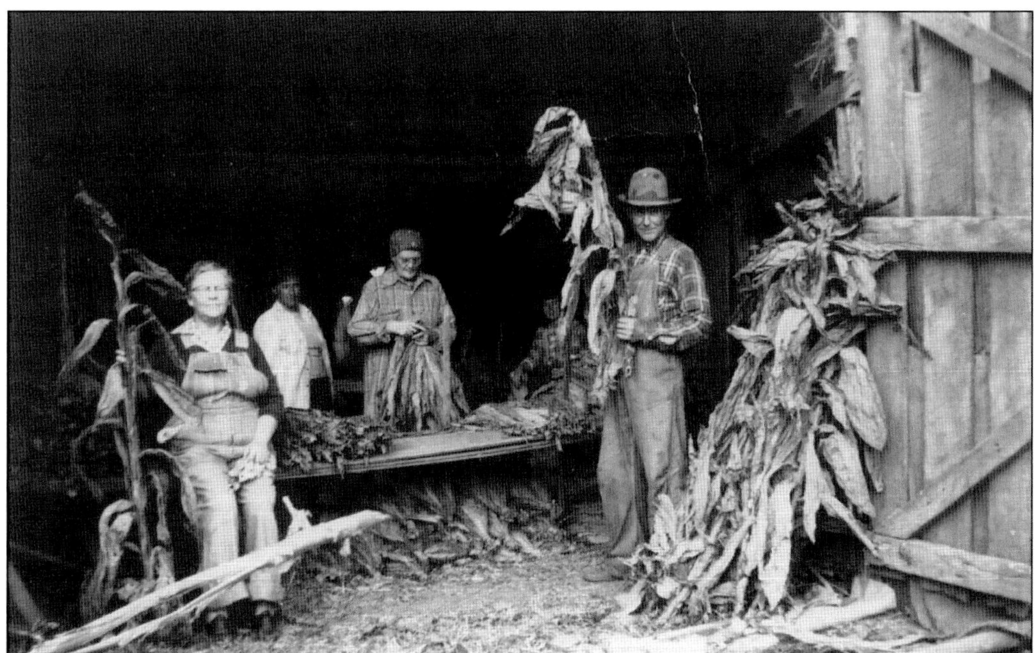

GRADING. After the tobacco had cured in the barn for about six weeks, the leaves were stripped from the stalks and graded. The leaves were then tied according to their quality. From left to right on a cold October day in 1953, Belle Ashe, unidentified, Matilda Trent, unidentified, and Arch Ashe are grading tobacco in Striggersville.

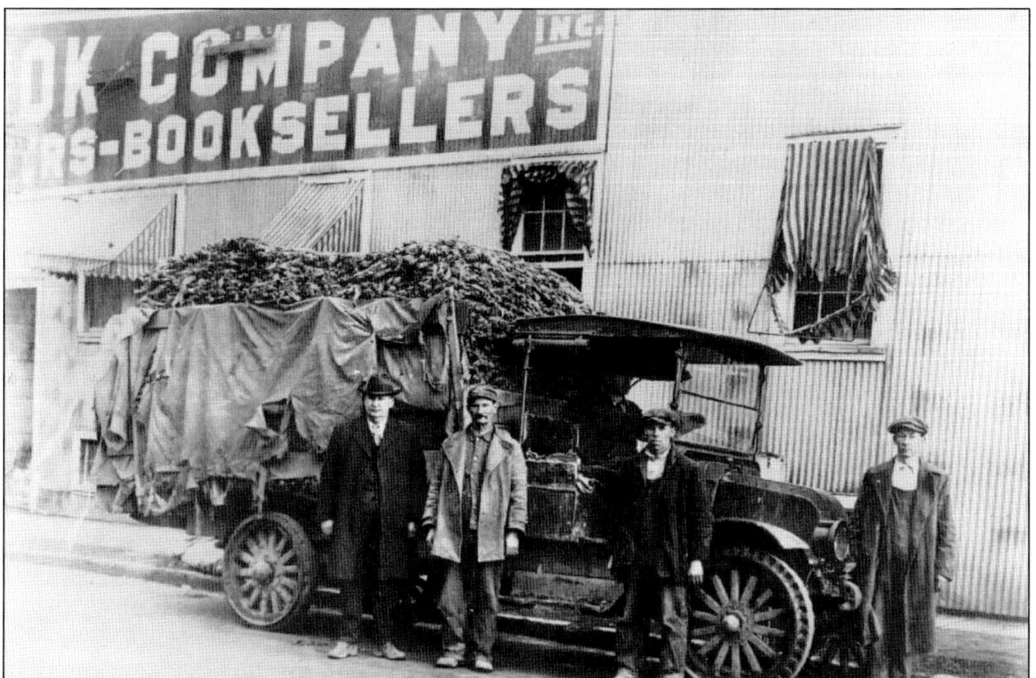

MARKET DAY. The first tobacco warehouses came to Rogersville in the 1930s; up until then, farmers had to travel a great distance to get their tobacco crop to market. This photograph shows farmers arriving at auction with a load of tobacco in 1924.

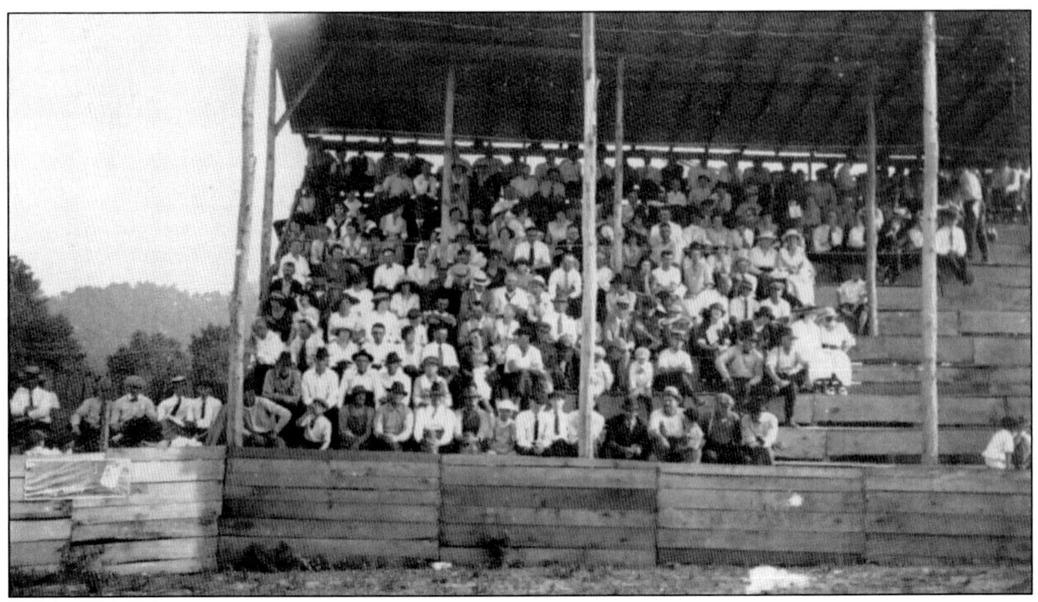

Fairgrounds. The annual Hawkins County Fair was held on Reno Street in Rogersville for many years. This photograph shows the grandstand on the fairgrounds known as Rogers Field. The property was used for several events including circuses and carnivals. The fairground was closed when a growers warehouse was built on the site in the 1940s.

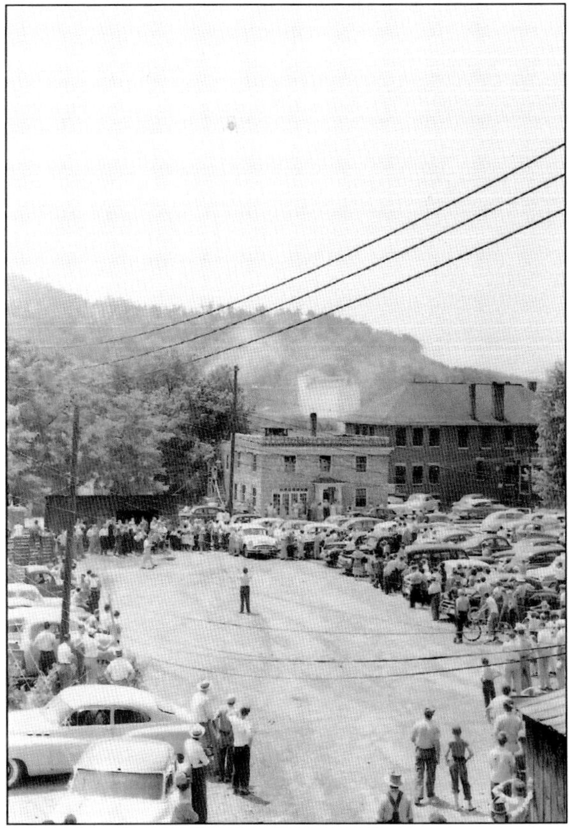

Visitors. A large crowd is shown on the back of Rogersville Street awaiting the arrival of Gov. Winfield Dunn's helicopter. The now razed Rogersville City Hall building and jailhouse are in the background.

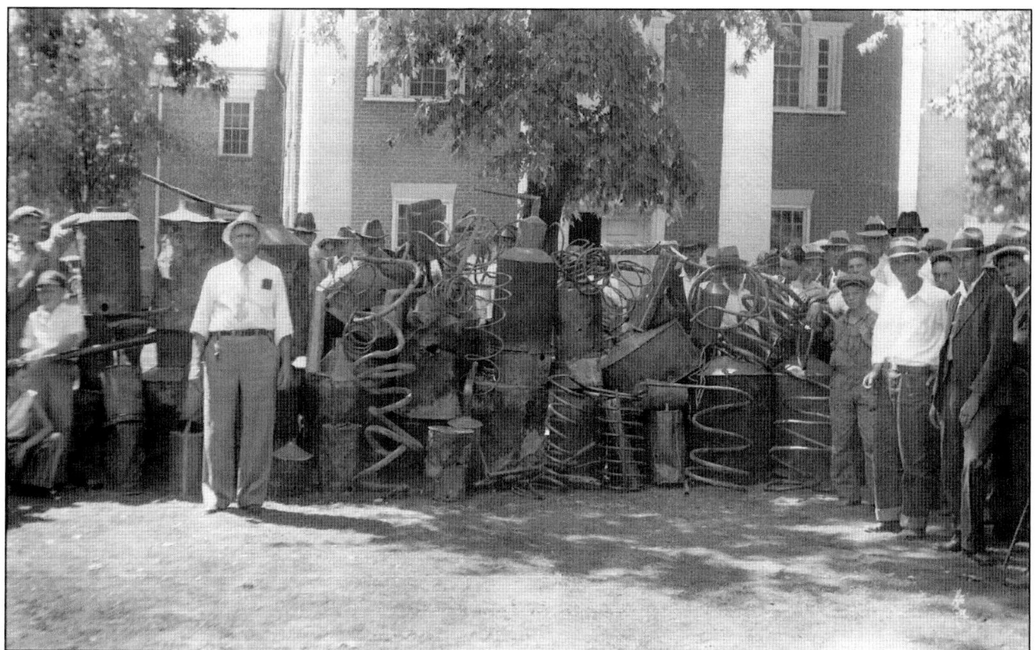

Moonshine. The Scotch-Irish settlers brought their expertise of whiskey making to the Appalachian Mountains and to the hills of Hawkins County. Shown here are several confiscated moonshine stills on display in front of the courthouse in 1936.

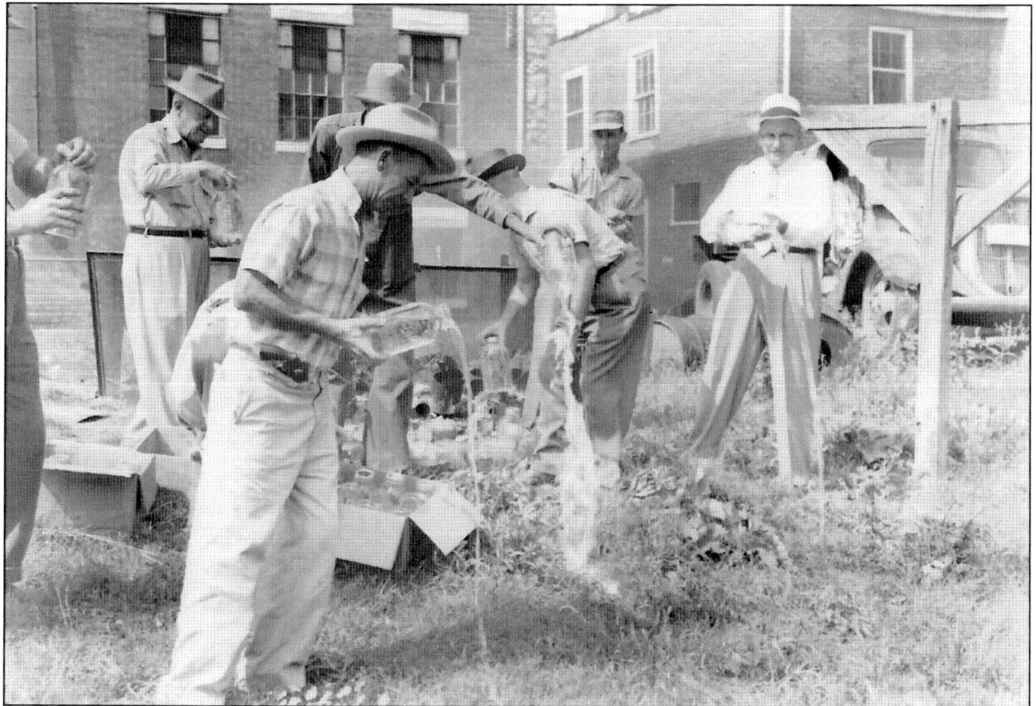

Official Pour Out. After a sufficient amount of moonshine and other confiscated liquor had been seized, the county would have an official pour out. Law officers and local church representatives were usually in charge of the pour outs.

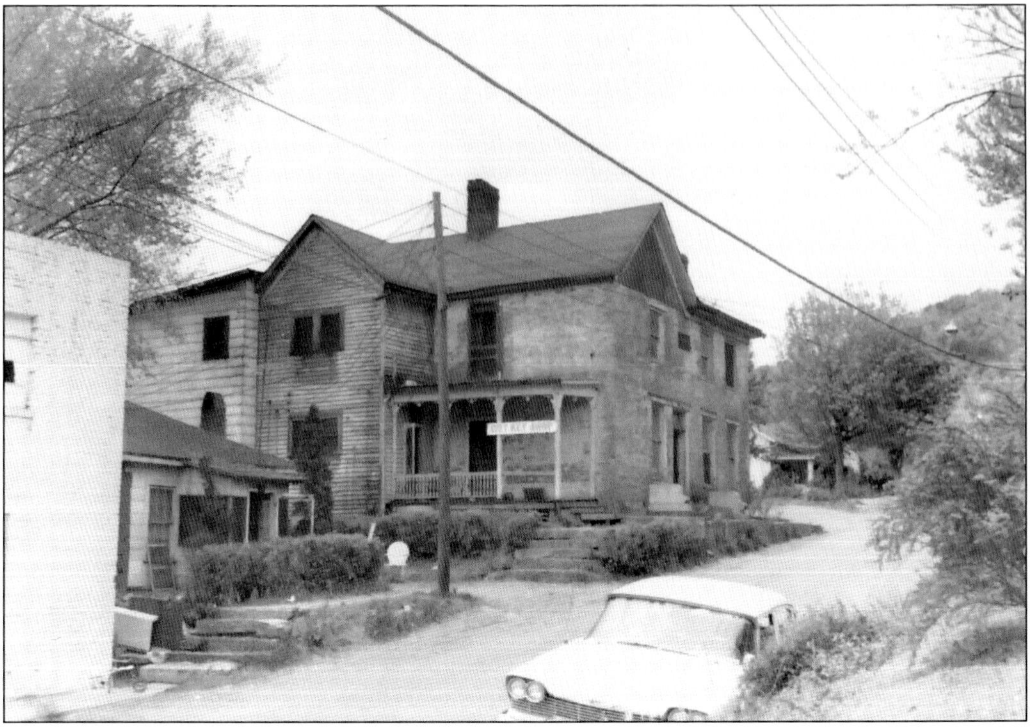

City Key Shop. The log part of this building was built in 1800 and was known as the Samuel Powell law office. A locksmith by the name of "Key Bill" Sandidge ran the shop for many years until his death in the 1970s.

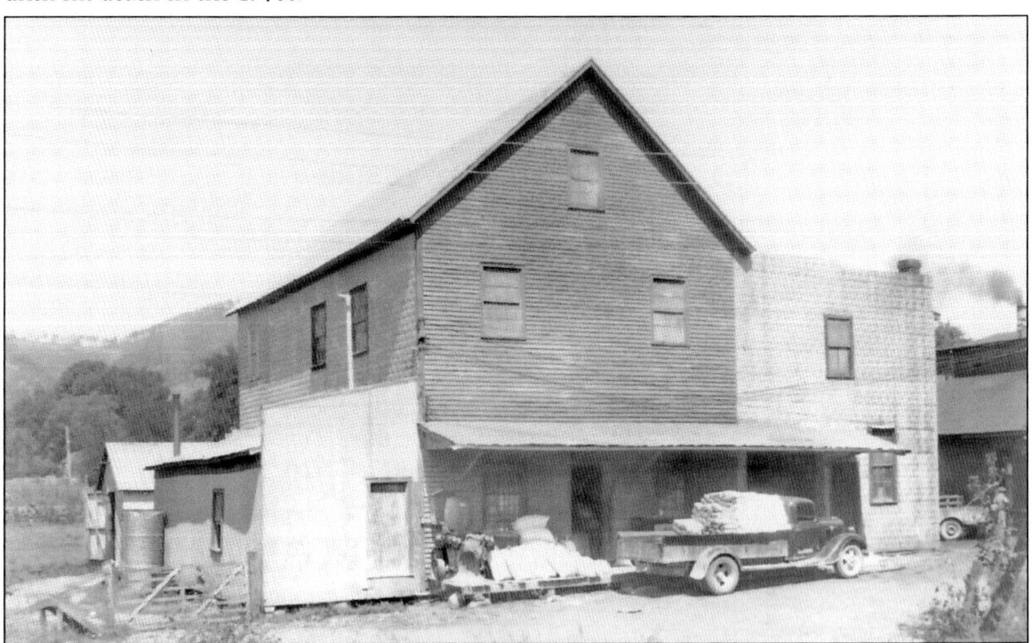

Horton Feed and Seed. This building first served as the Rogersville Electric Company and later as the Horton Feed and Seed mill. The structure was torn down in the 1990s to make a parking lot for Crockett Spring Park.

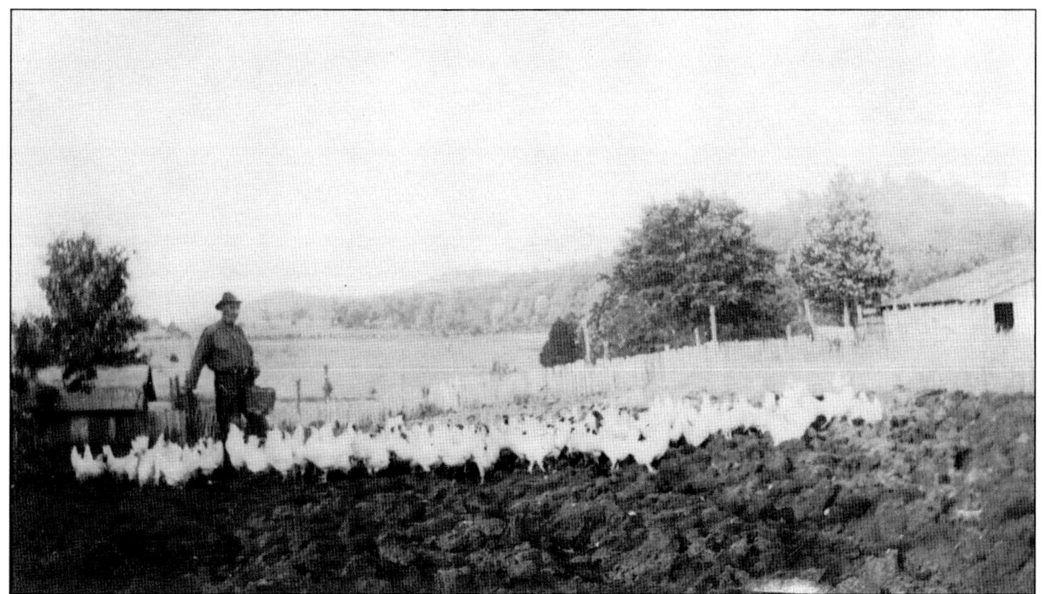

Dad Looney's Chickens. This image shows Dad Looney of Carter's Valley with his flock of award-winning chickens in 1939. Looney ran a store and a farm in the community for many years.

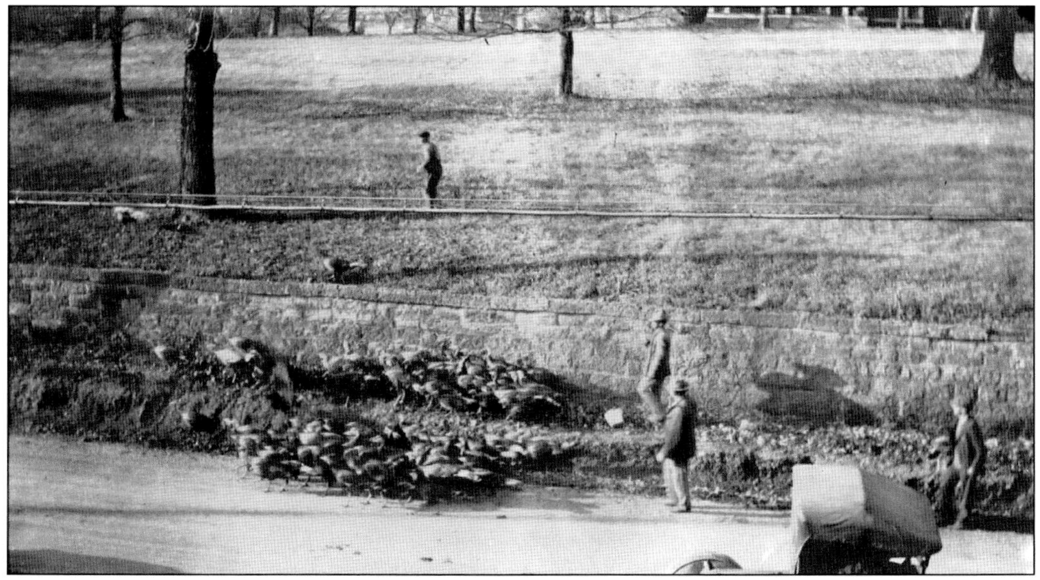

Turkey Drive. This is the 1924 Turkey Drive through Main Street in downtown Rogersville. These farmers from the Beech Creek community are driving their flock to the William Davis Harmon poultry house.

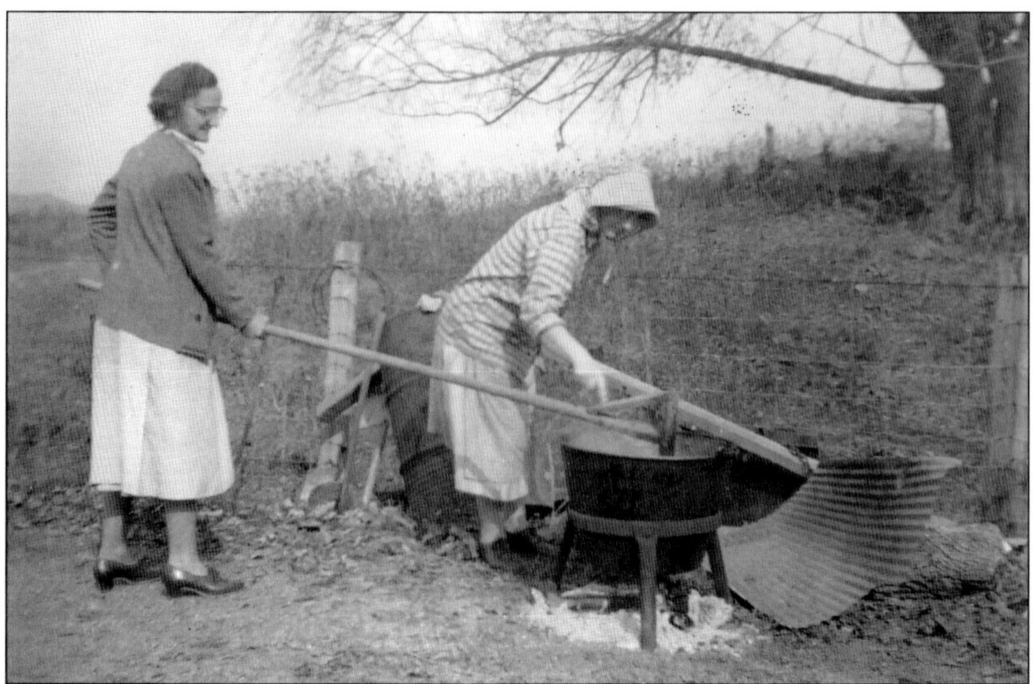

APPLE BUTTER. Matilda Trent (left) and Mamie Sizemore are making apple butter in the Striggersville community. The ladies made it in a brass kettle over an open fire as their ancestors did long ago.

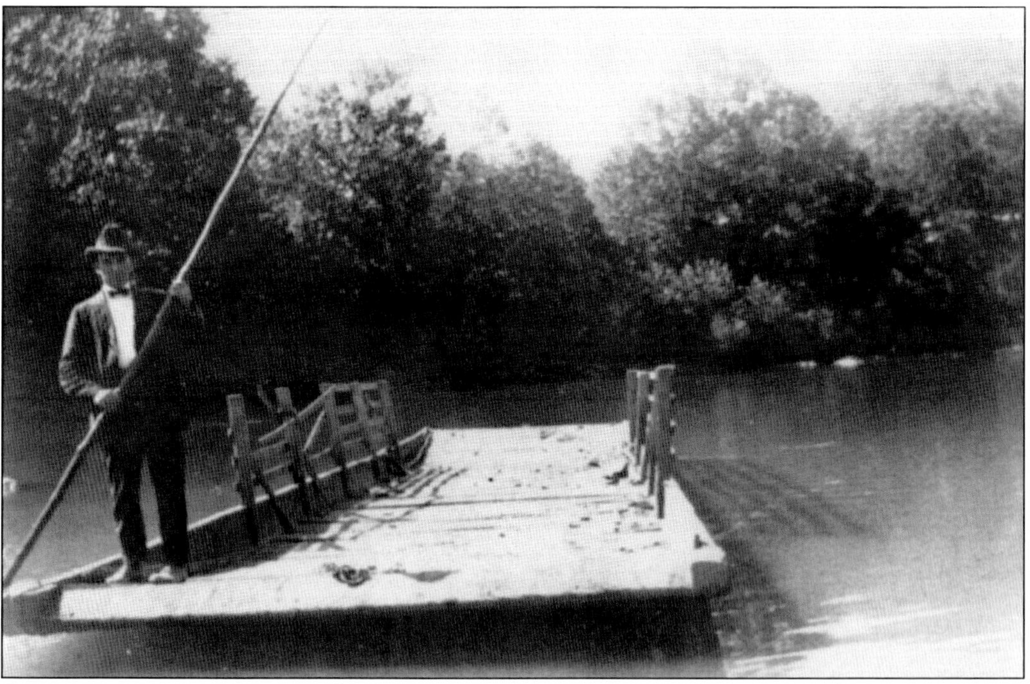

CHRISTIANS BEND'S FERRY. Will Thomas is shown crossing on the ferry at Christians Bend in 1924. The expense of building a bridge across the Holston River caused a great need for ferries in Hawkins County, especially for farmers who had to get crops to market.

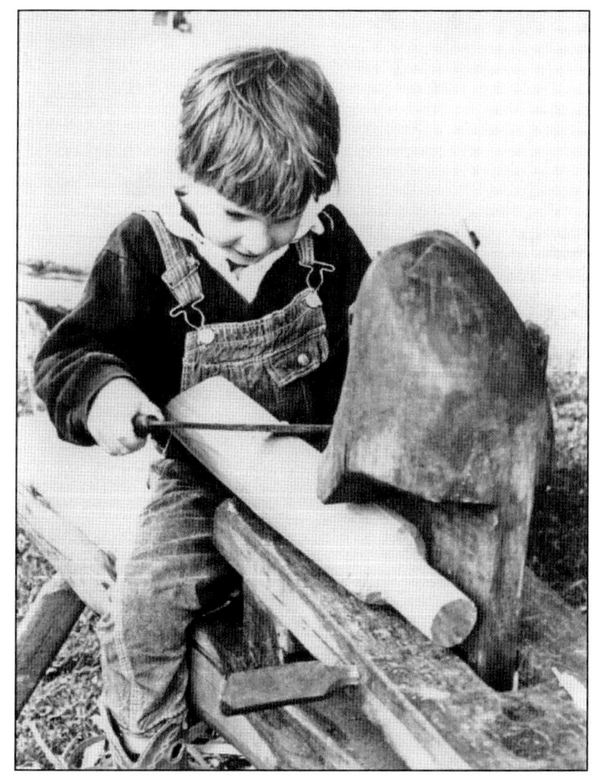

Wood Lathing. One of the most important traditions of the Appalachian Mountains was to teach the children a trade. Wood lathing was very important for making furniture and shaping shingles. (Photograph by Randy Ball.)

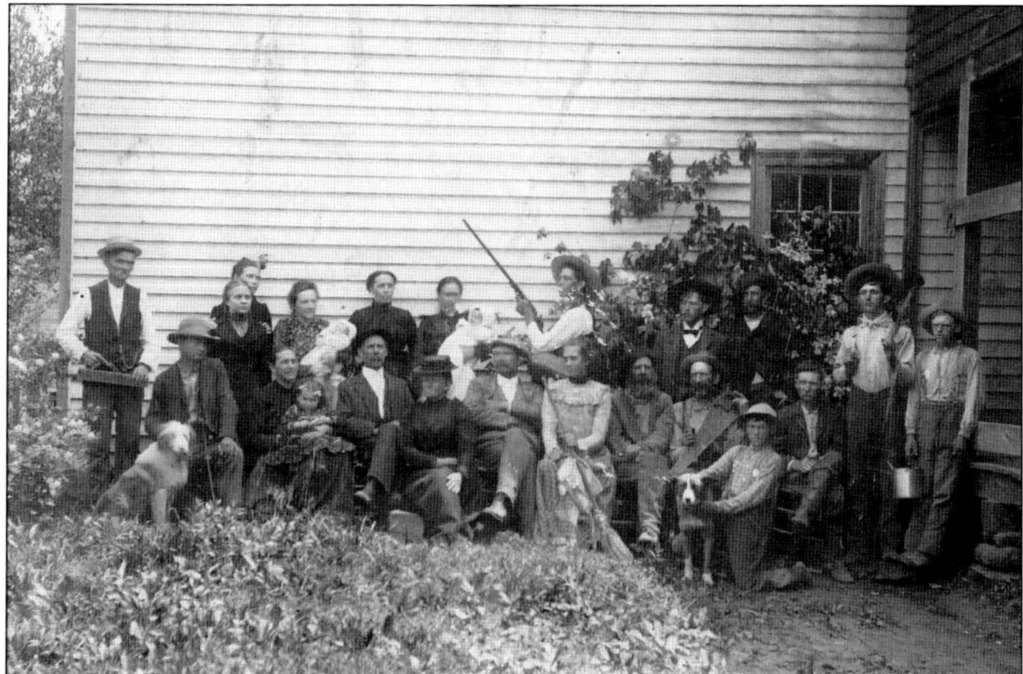

Looney's Store Gathering. Here is a community gathering at the side of the Looney store in 1903. A closer look reveals that each person in this photograph is holding up an object illustrating his or her particular profession. (Courtesy of Bill Davidson.)

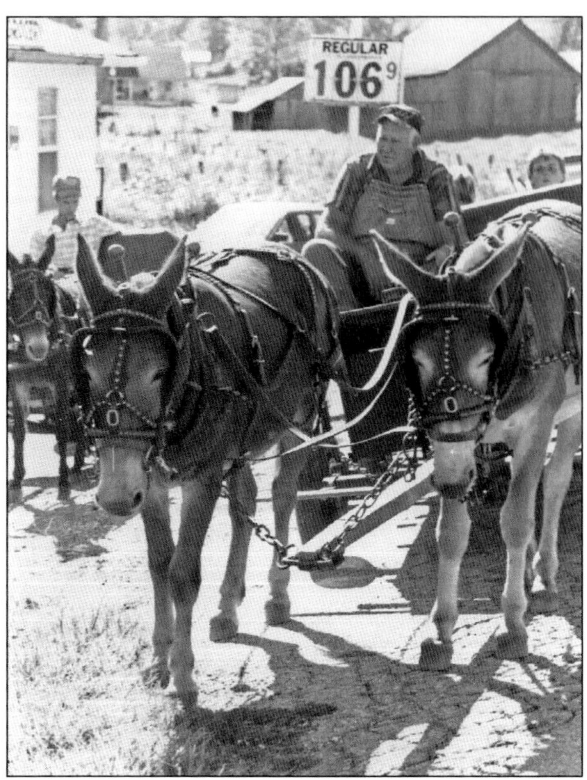

A Good Mule. In the mountains of southern Appalachia, few things were as important to a farmer as a good team of mules. (Photograph by Randy Ball.)

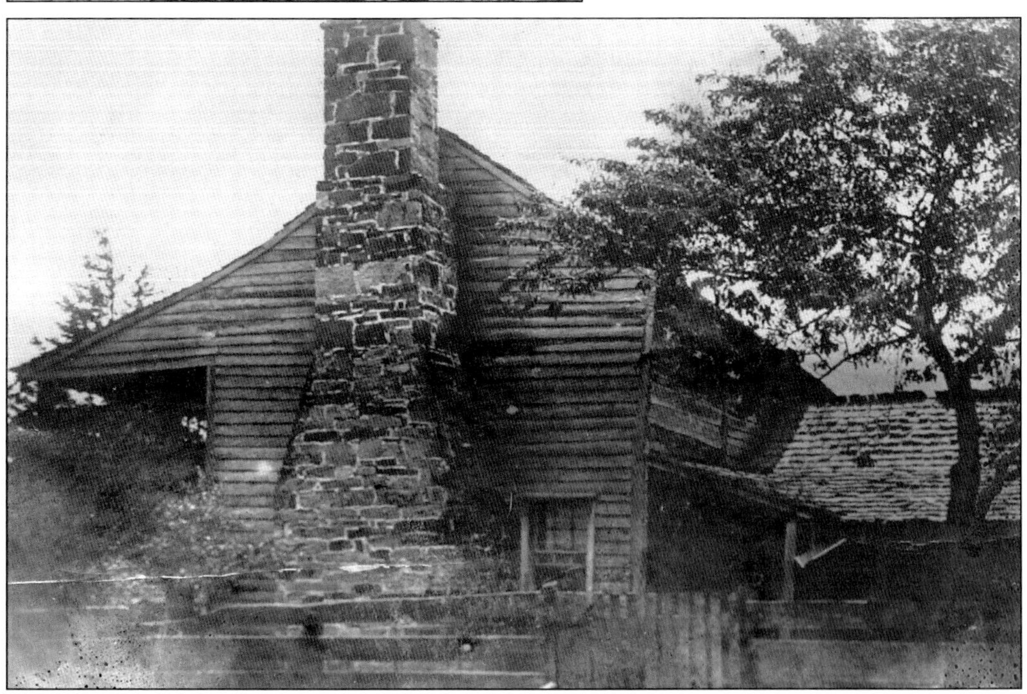

Michael Looney Homestead. The old Fisher's Creek homestead of long hunter and settler Michael Looney was built in 1789. The Looneys were one of the first families in the new frontier of Tennessee. (Courtesy of Bill Davidson.)

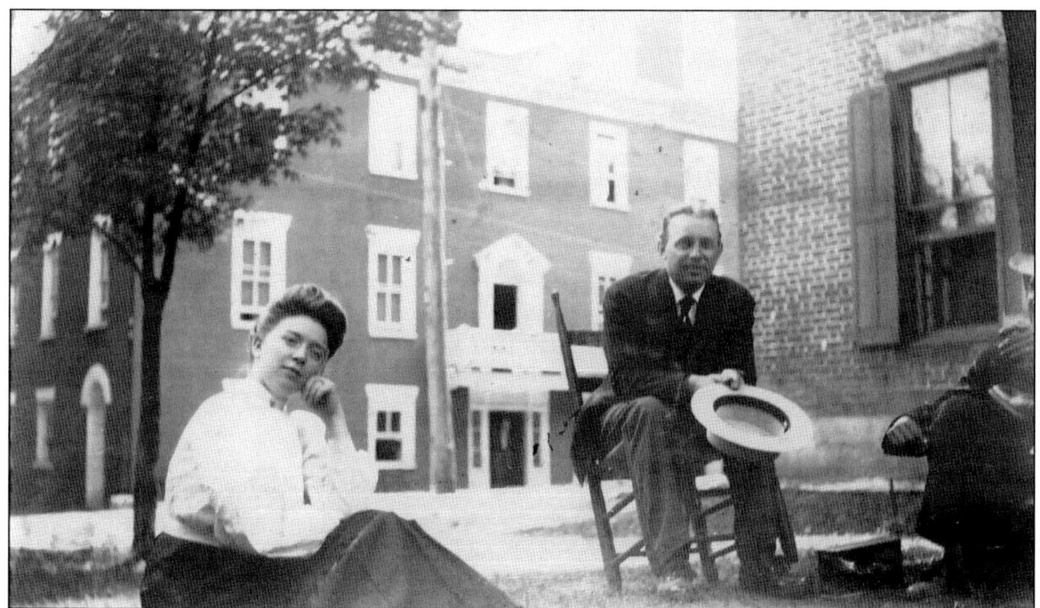

Saturday Afternoon. Kay and Hugh Kyle are shown passing a Saturday afternoon in the side yard of the Kyle house on Main Street in Rogersville. The 1824 Hale Springs Inn is in the background.

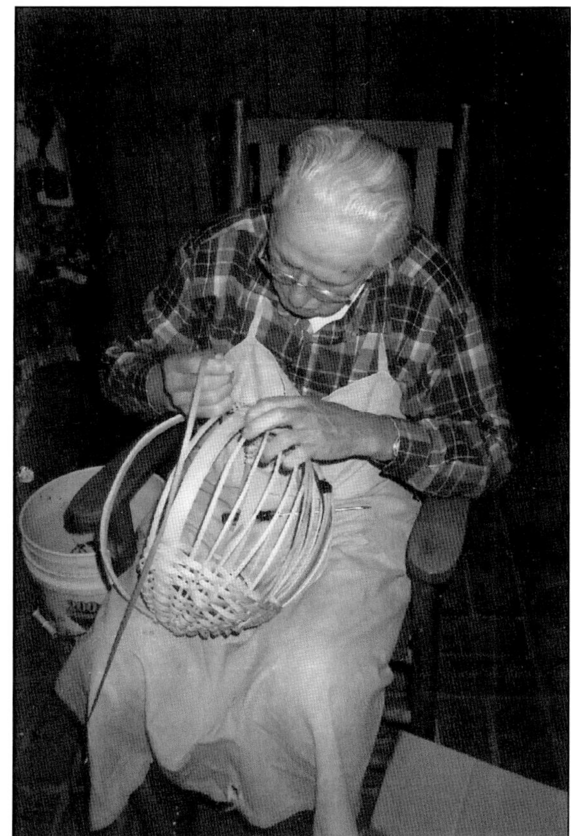

Basket Maker. The late Ezekiel Davis of the Sulphur Springs Valley community was a Renaissance man of Appalachian crafts. He was taught at an early age to make baskets by his mother, Minnie. His father, Jim, taught him how to make oak buckets and log cabins. (Courtesy of Eileen Absher.)

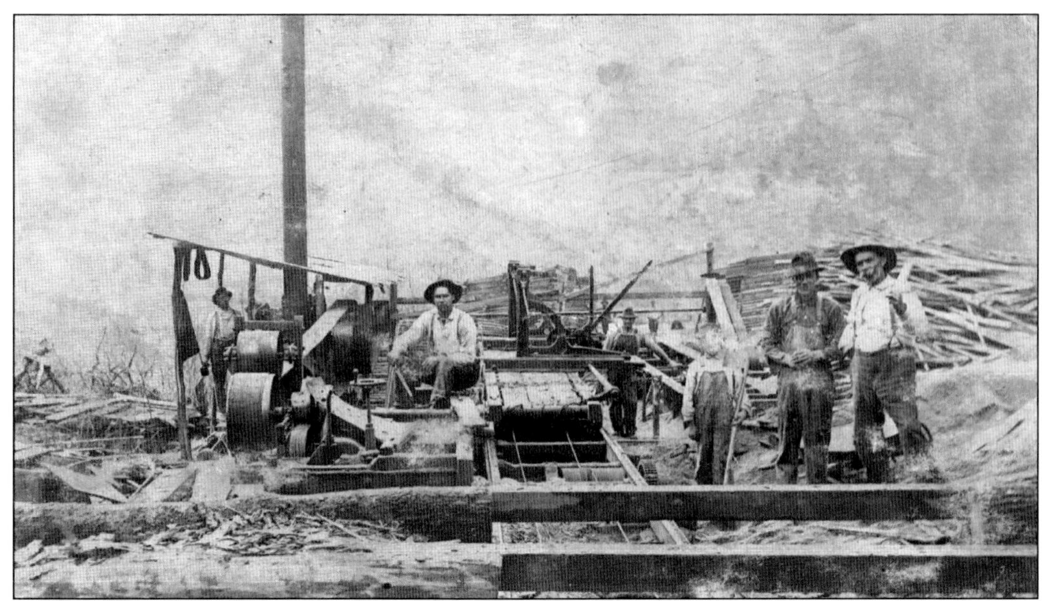

SAWMILL. Here is the Emmitt Davidson Sawmill in Carters Valley in 1903. The Davidsons and the Looneys ran the mill for nearly 50 years. (Courtesy of Bill Davidson.)

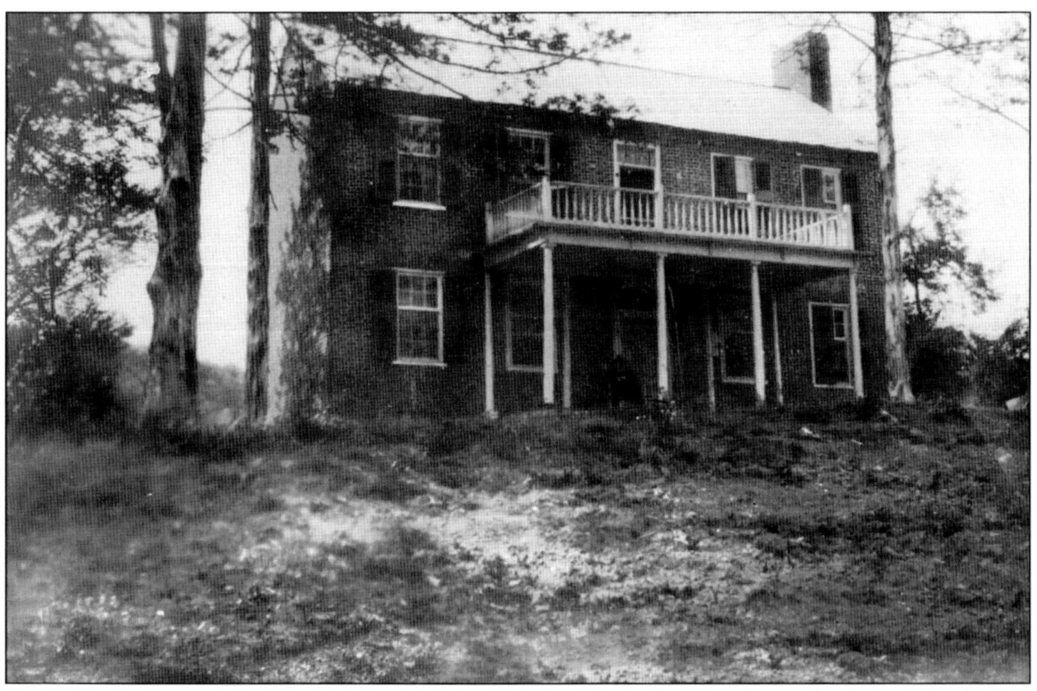

FAIN HOUSE. Located on East Main Street in Rogersville is the Fain house built in 1830. Today it is known as the Cope home and has been restored to its former grandeur.

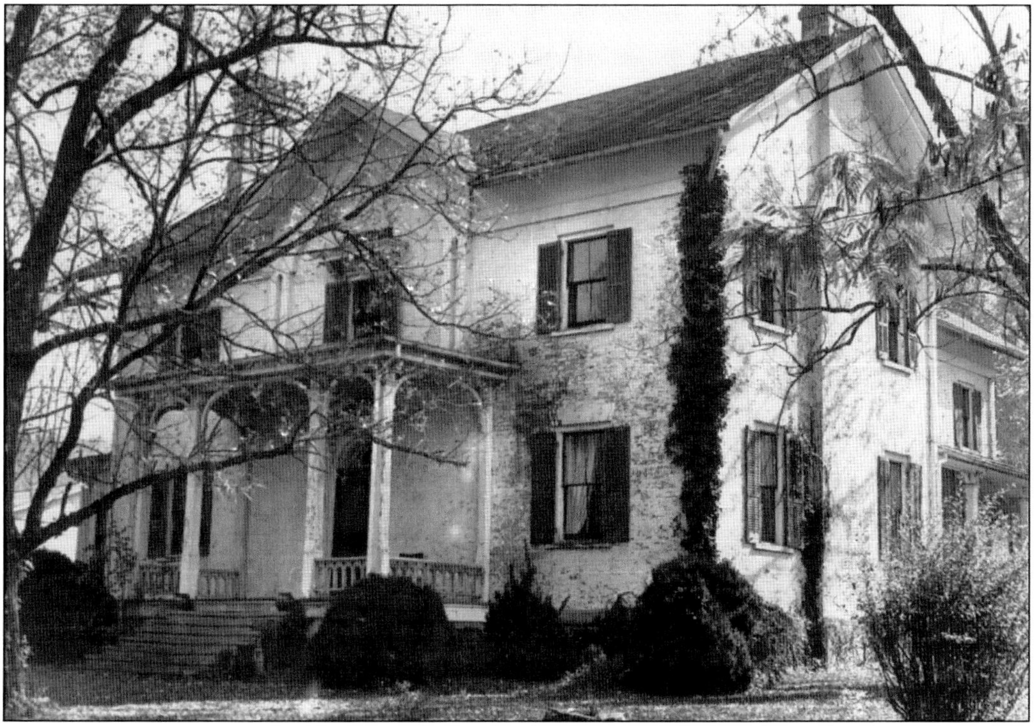

THREE OAKS. This 1845 mansion was built by prominent Irish lawyer and wealthy landowner John A. McKinney. The first log structure was built in 1830 and burned down shortly thereafter. The house derived its name from the 200-year-old oak trees on the property.

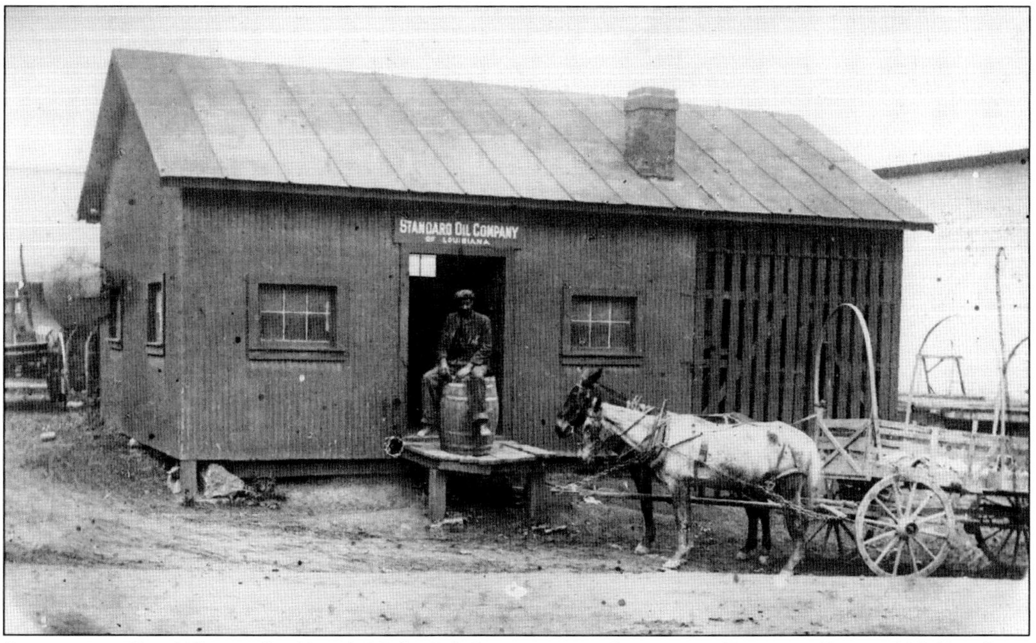

STANDARD OIL. This is the Frank Hale Oil Company in downtown Rogersville in 1895. Brothers Frank and Arthur Hale opened several businesses in the county over the years, including an electric plant, an ice plant, and a creamery.

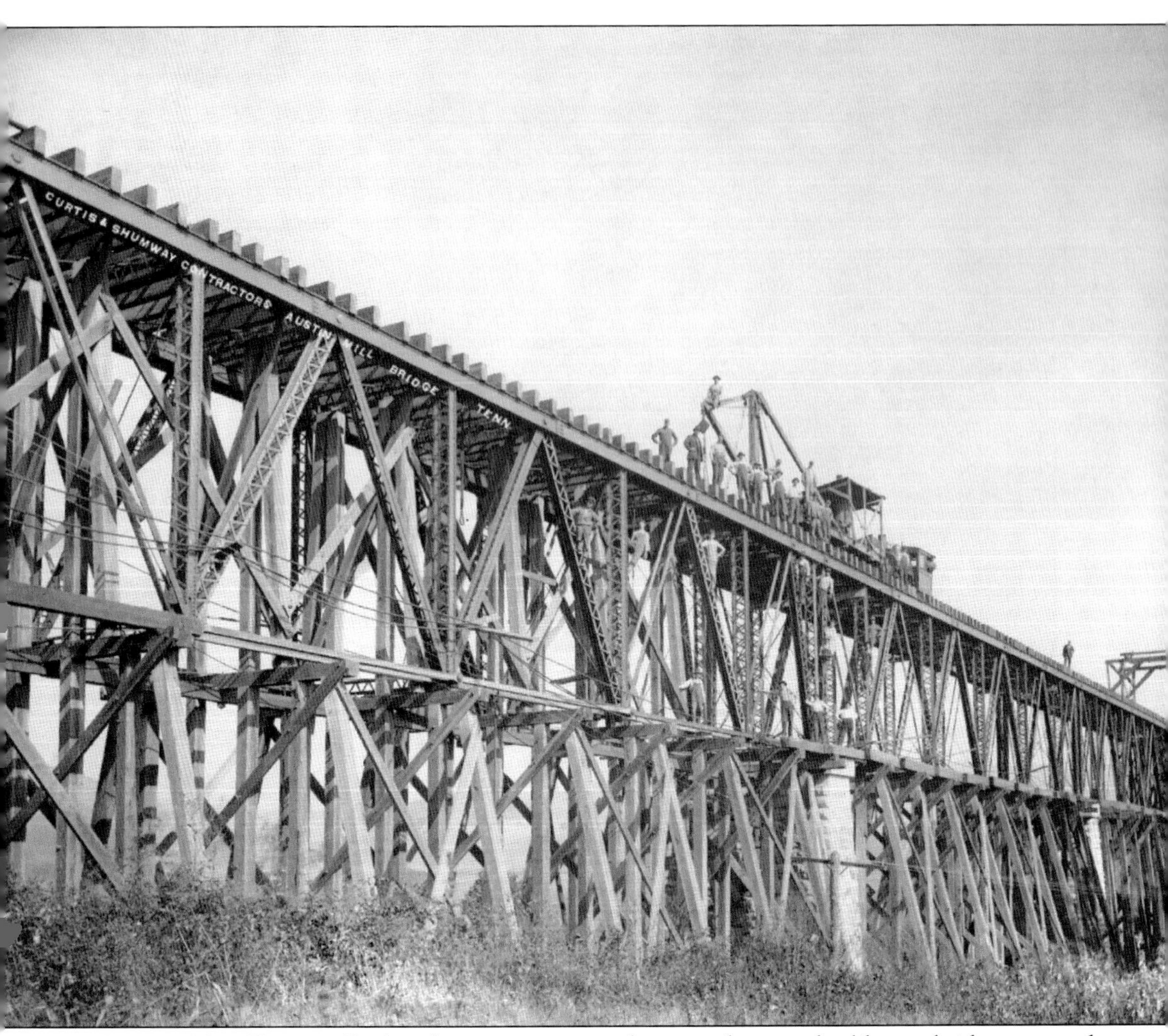

AUSTIN MILL BRIDGE. Railroad construction workers can be seen building a bridge across the Holston River in 1901. Constructed in the Austin Mill community, it served the railroad for 97 years until the train to Rogersville was discontinued. The bridge was torn down shortly thereafter.

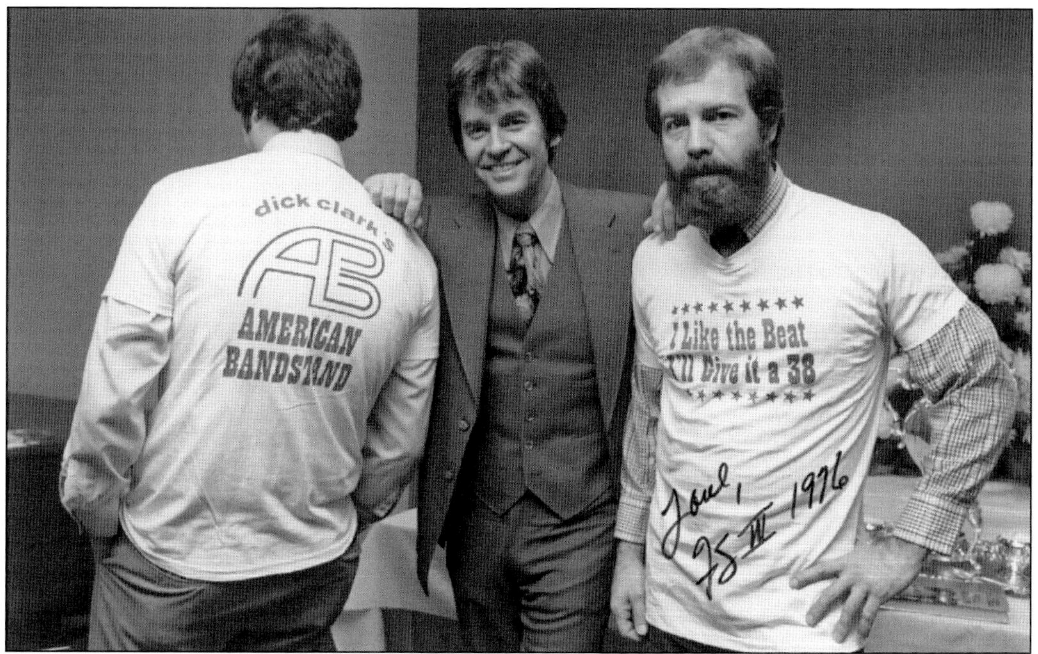

Band Stand. Rogersville native William "Skip" Frank Smith III was an advertising executive in Hollywood, California. The firm handled many television shows including the perennial favorite *American Bandstand*. Here he is shown in the 1970s with "America's oldest teenager," Dick Clark. (Courtesy of Jan Smith.)

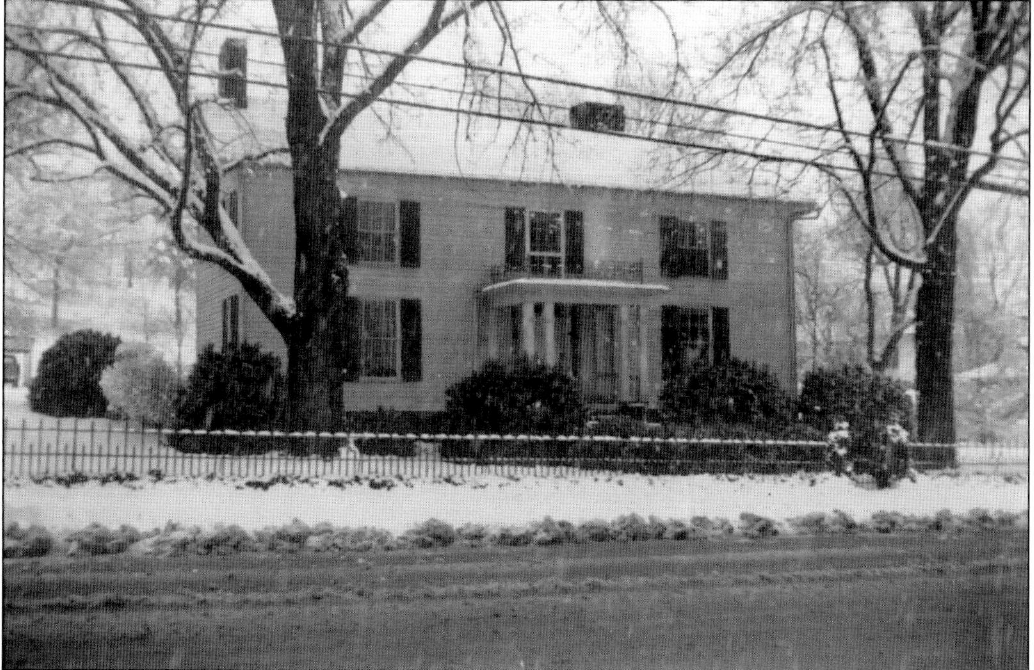

Kenner–Smith House. This house on West Main Street was built in 1824 by William Kenner and later converted into an inn. In 1935, it was purchased by Col. Frank Smith and wife, Miss Doodle, and completely renovated. (Courtesy of Jan Smith.)

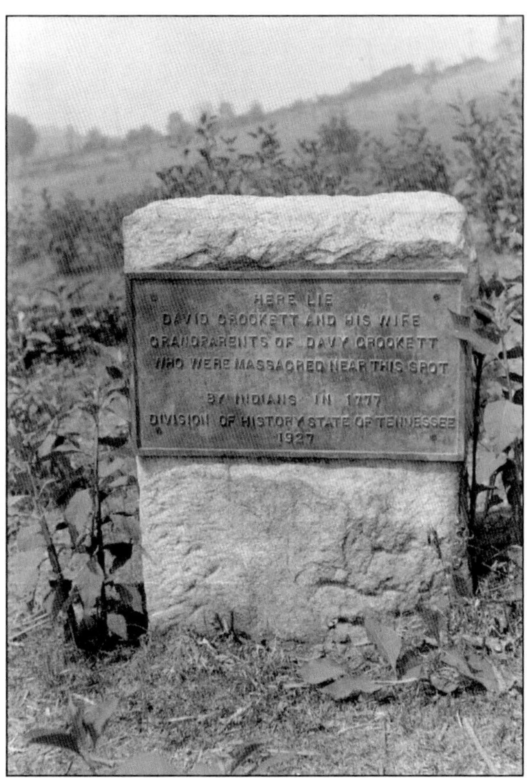

David Crockett. The David Crockett family was massacred by American Indians in 1777 and is buried near the site of this marker. David was the grandfather of Davy Crockett, the frontiersman and hero of the Alamo. Rogersville founders Joseph and Mary Rogers are also interred in this cemetery.

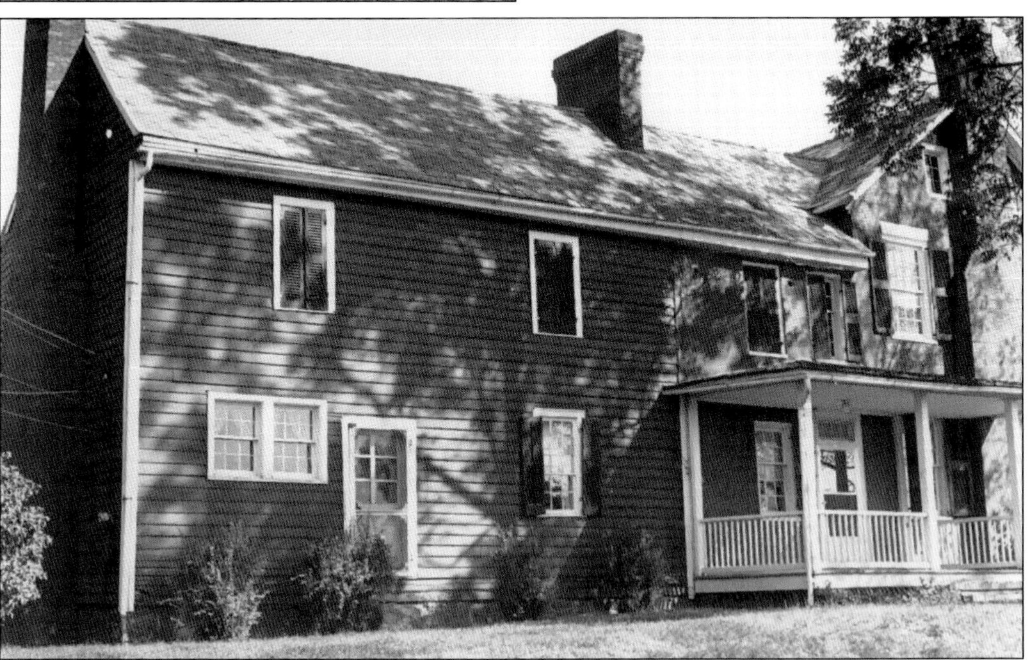

Blue Springs. The log section of this beautiful old home on the outskirts of Rogersville was built by George Hale in 1819, and the front brick section was added in 1832. Colonel Hale and his wife and two children are buried near the house. Ernest A. Trent and his wife, Sally Bea, were the last owners of the residence.

African Art. Born in Hawkins County in 1906, Ruth Cobb Brice graduated Swift Memorial College and went on to establish the Knoxville Art Center and the Dulin Art Gallery. Today many years after her death, her artwork is highly collectible. (Courtesy of Ada Rogers.)

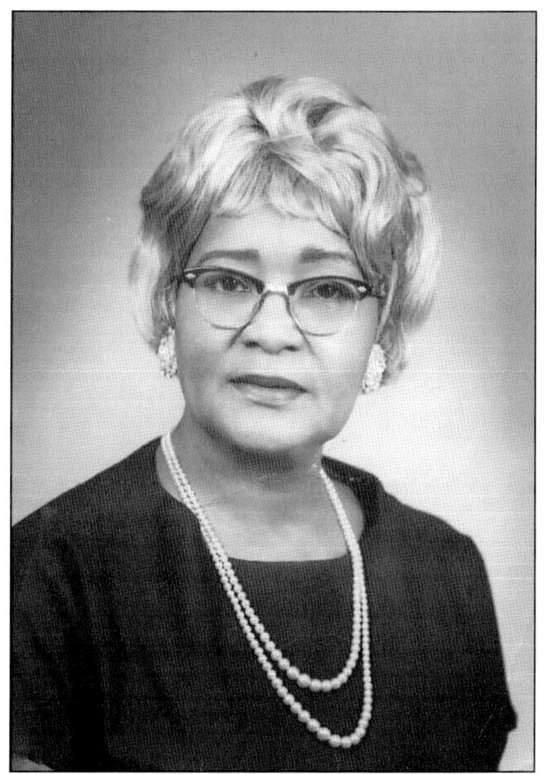

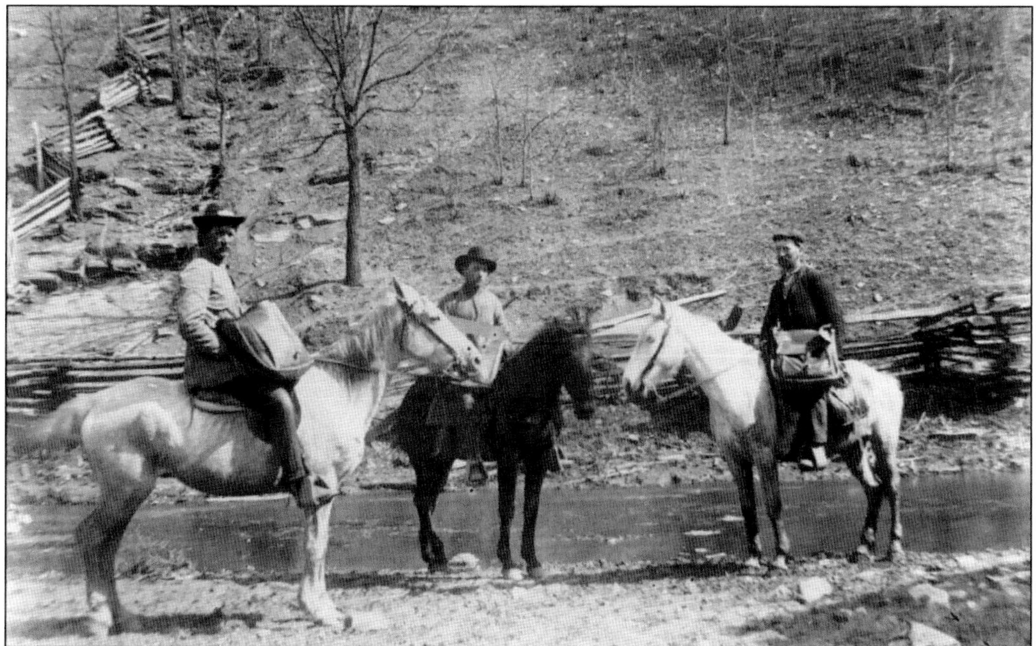

String Town Postmen. Here are three of the first rural letter carriers in the String Town community in Clinch Valley at the turn of the century. From left to right are John Moneyhun, Amos Anderson, and Thomas James Davis. Davis was a farmer in Edison and a representative in the Tennessee Legislature from 1950 to 1956.

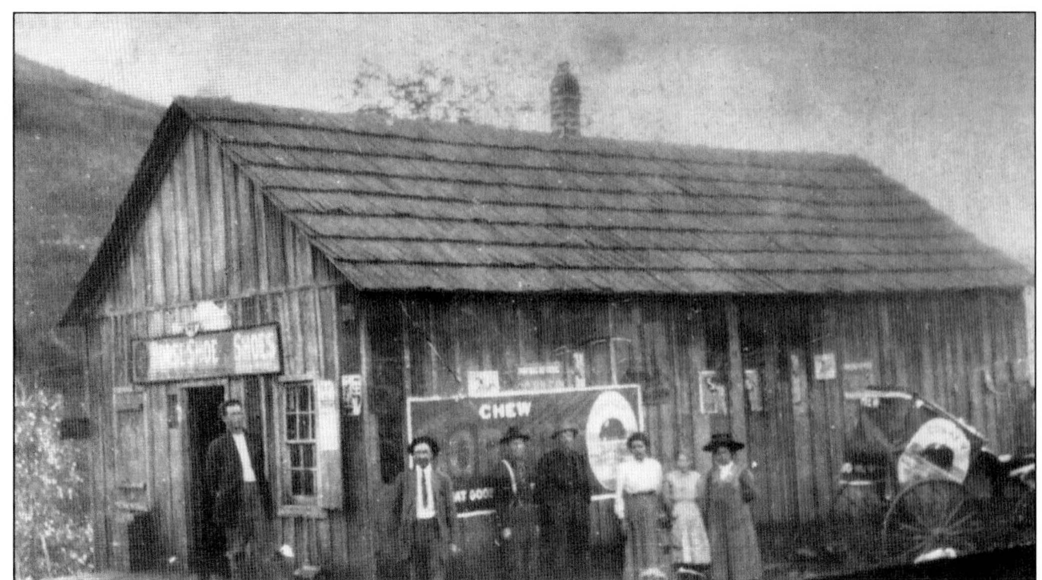

Pumpkin Valley. Here is the Cope store in Pumpkin Valley. E. A. Cope was not sure if it should be spelled "Pumpkin" or "Punkin," but at the U.S. Register of Deeds Department's old records, it was spelled "Puncheon."

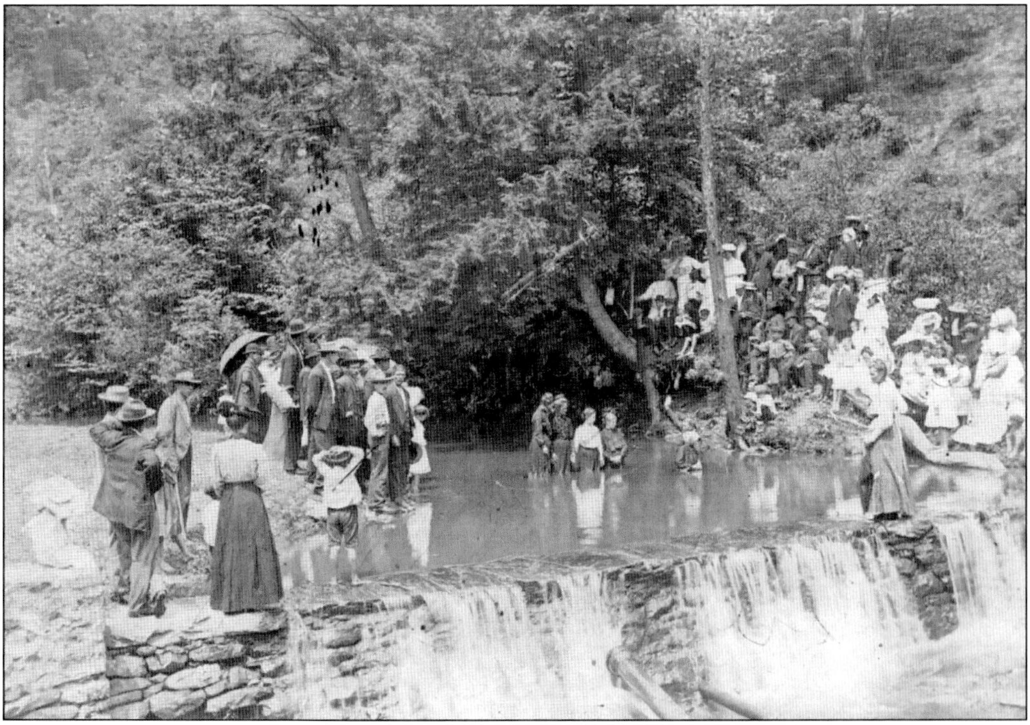

Baptizing. This shows an 1898 baptism on Beech Creek after a two-week tent revival. Beech Creek carried the unfortunate label of being a corrupt and unlawful community in the 1800s.

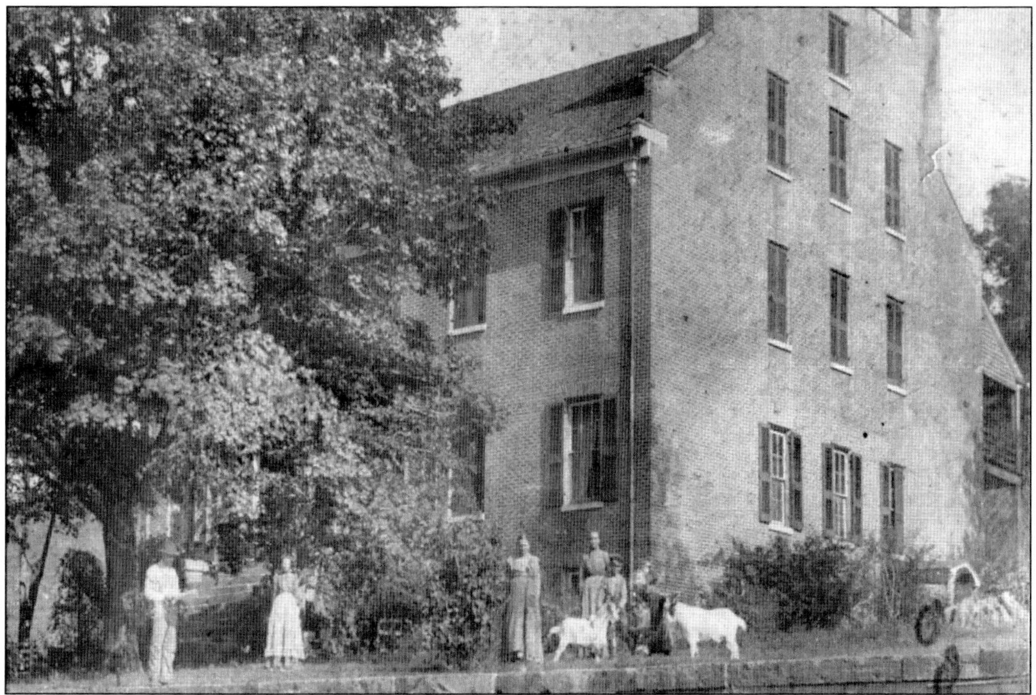

MARBLE HALL. Orrville Rice built this palatial 22-room mansion in 1848. All the floors in the house were laid with marble, and it was considered the most elegant home in East Tennessee. The house was the scene of a double murder in 1881 and was destroyed by fire in 1907.

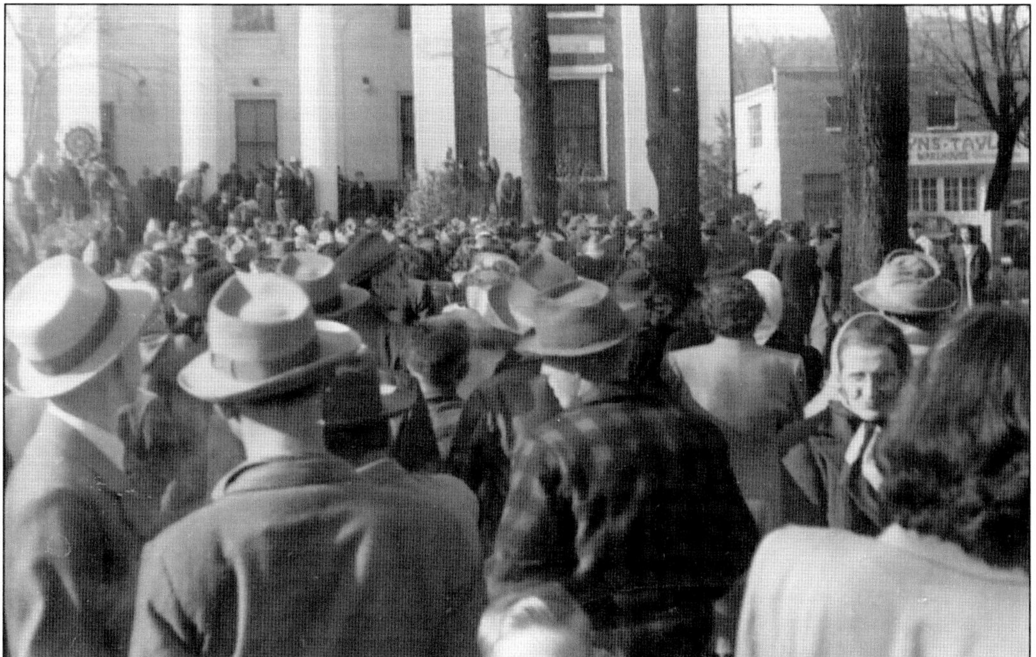

DECEMBER 7, 1941. A crowd gathers in downtown Rogersville on the day that will live in infamy. When Pearl Harbor was attacked in December 1941, many people came into town to hear the latest news.

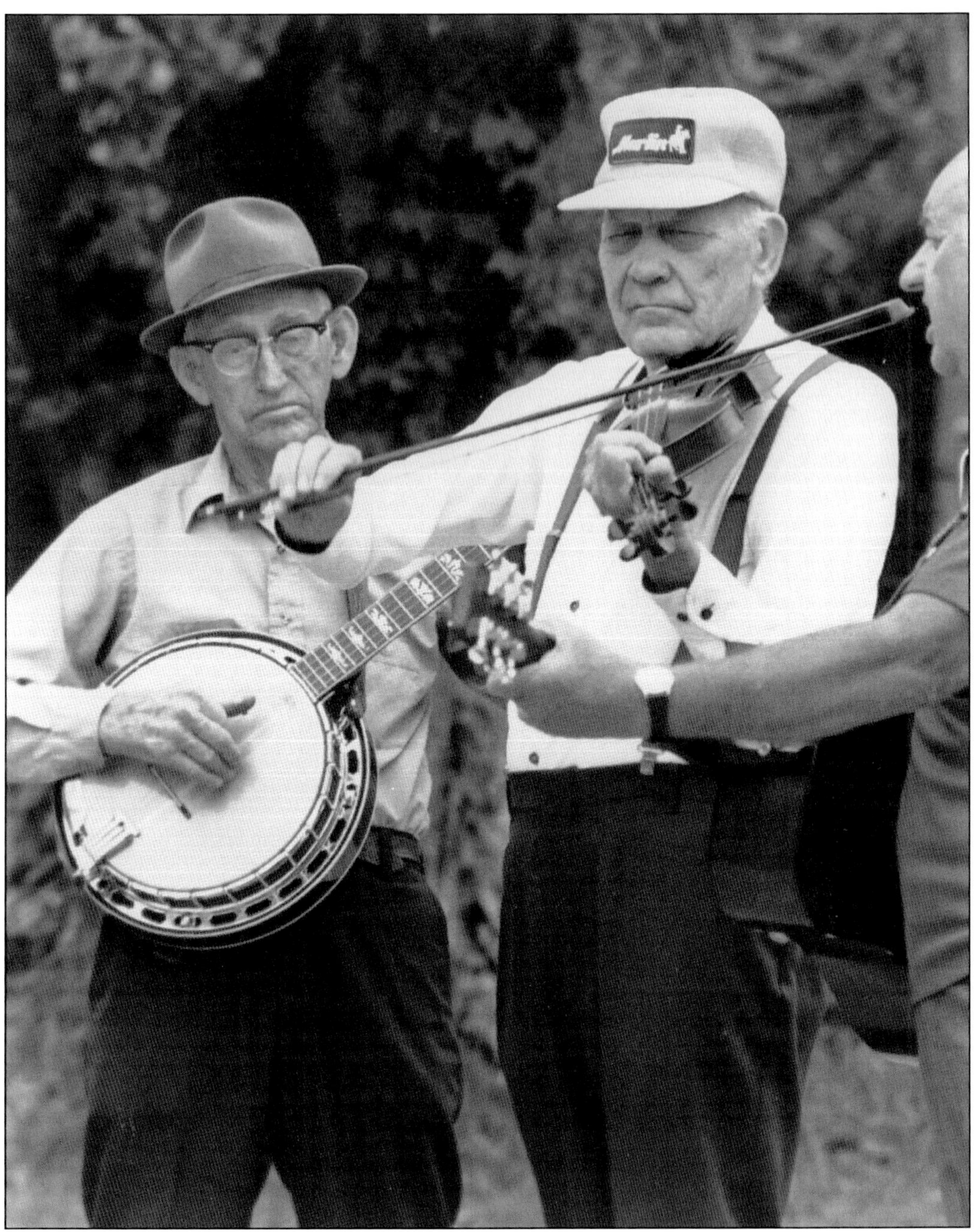

OLD-TIME MUSIC. Music came to the Appalachian Mountains with the early Scotch-Irish settlers. Hawkins County has never had a shortage of talented performers. (Photograph by Randy Ball.)

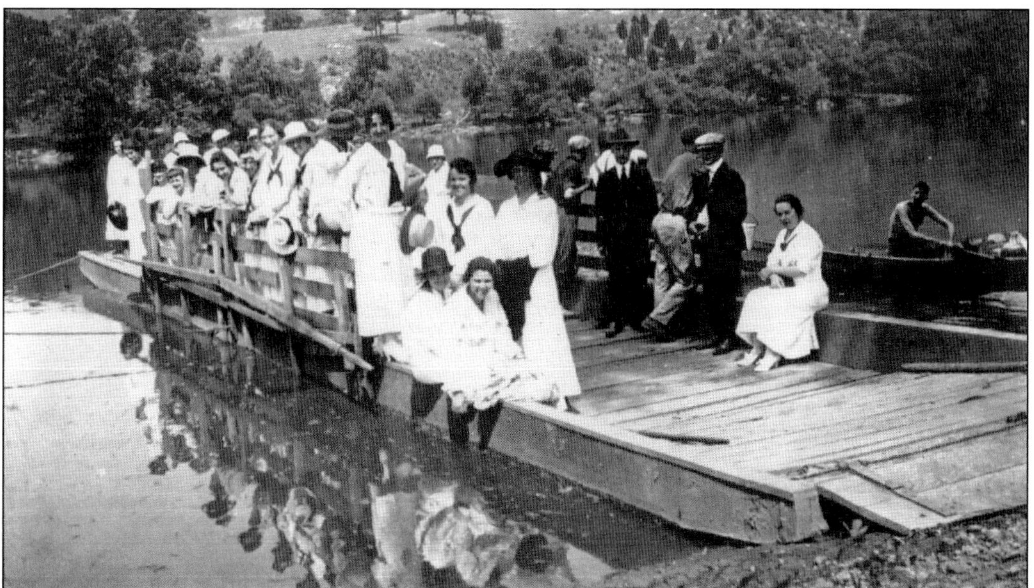

Melinda's Ferry. In this image is a large church group seen crossing the Holston River on the Melinda's Ferry. Located in the Marble Hall community, it was named for Amos Melinda, a horse trainer hired by Orrville Rice for his plantation.

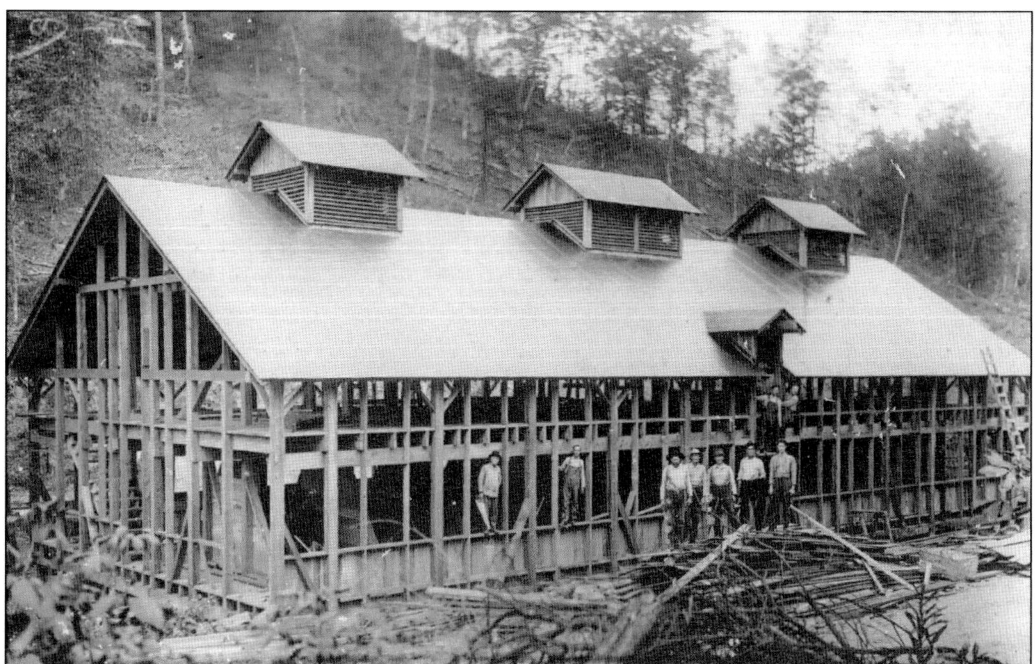

Barn Raising. Neighbors gather to build a dairy barn in the Long's Bend community near Surgoinsville. Barns once dotted the landscape in East Tennessee but today, not so much.

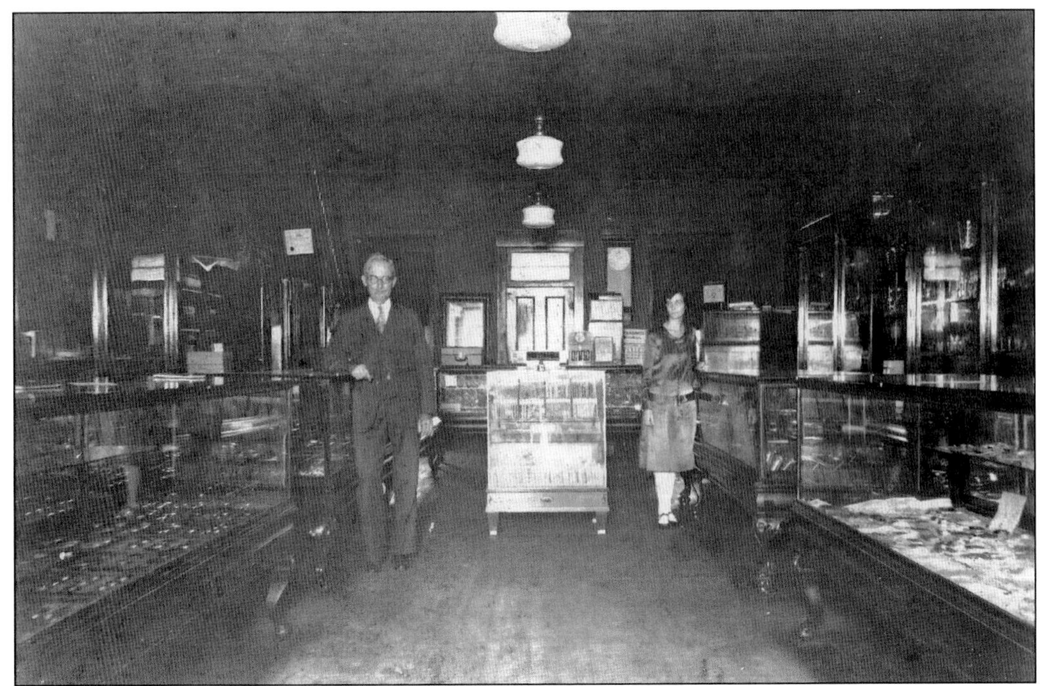

Clifton's Jewelers. E. S. Clifton (left) opened up Clifton Jewelers in 1909 and ran the jewelry store for over 50 years. The large Clifton Clock that hung above the front of the store was a Rogersville landmark. Many people set their watch by it each day.

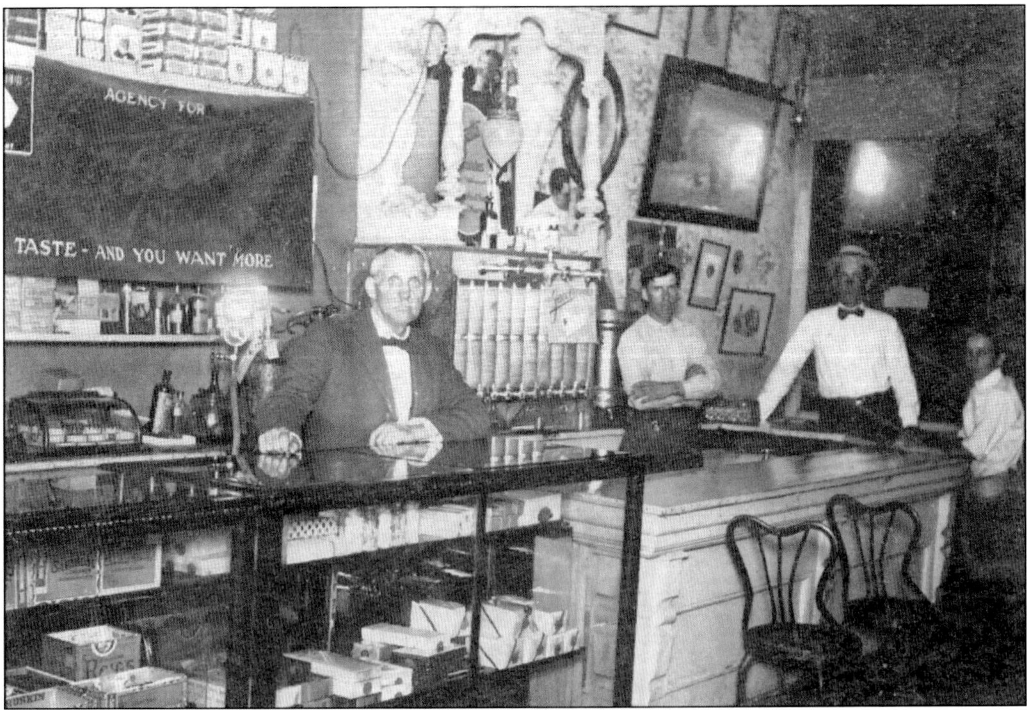

Nelson Drug Store. This is an interior view of Nelson's Drug Store, with Henry J. Nelson behind the counter. The young boy at the end of the counter is Lewis L. Poates.

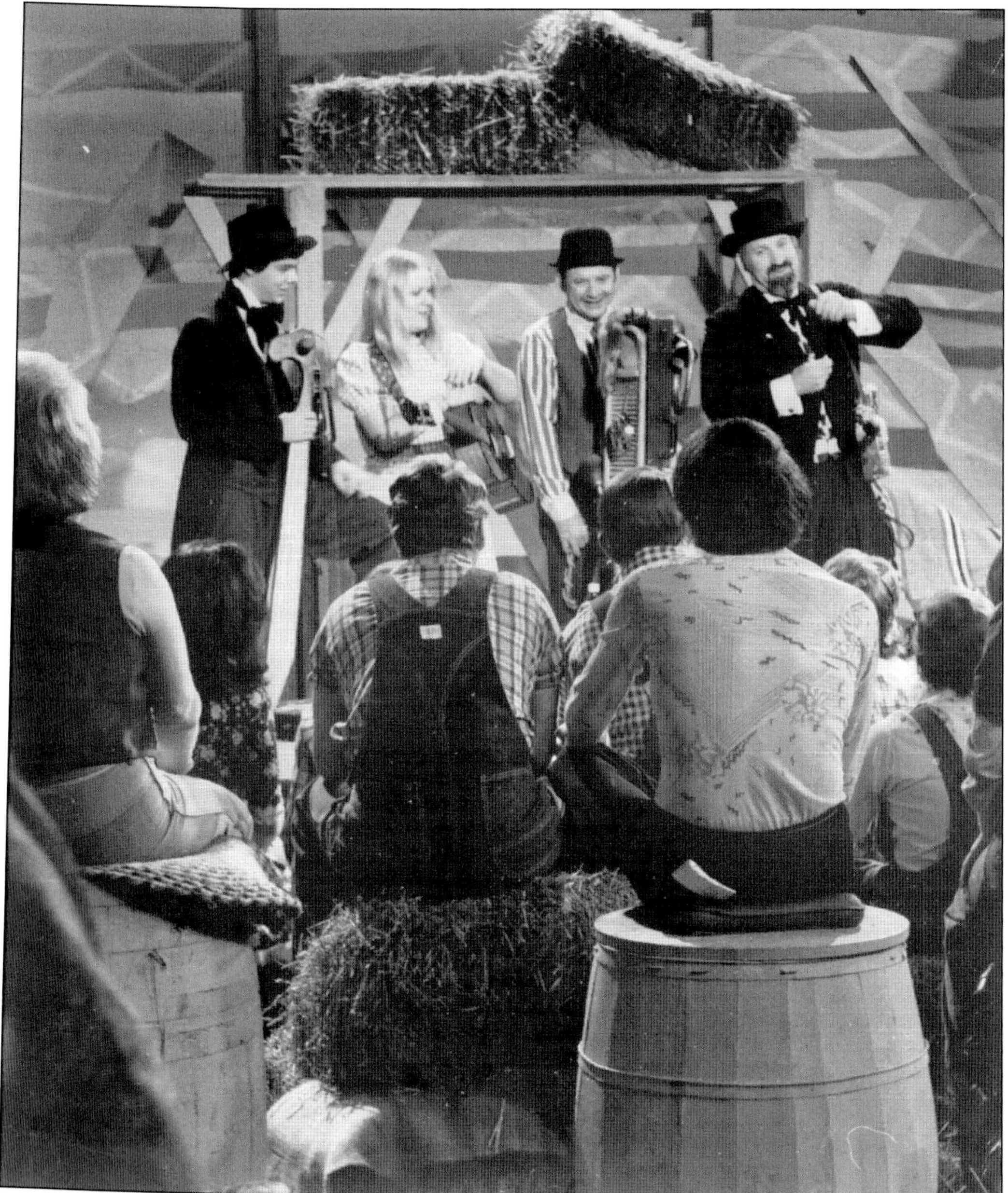

HEE HAW. In 1975, Doc McConnell's *Old Time Medicine Show* traveled to Nashville to debut on the nationally syndicated television show *Hee Haw*. From left to right are Joe Selby, Hannah McConnell, E. C. "Steamer" McConnell, and Doc McConnell. (Courtesy of Guerry McConnell.)

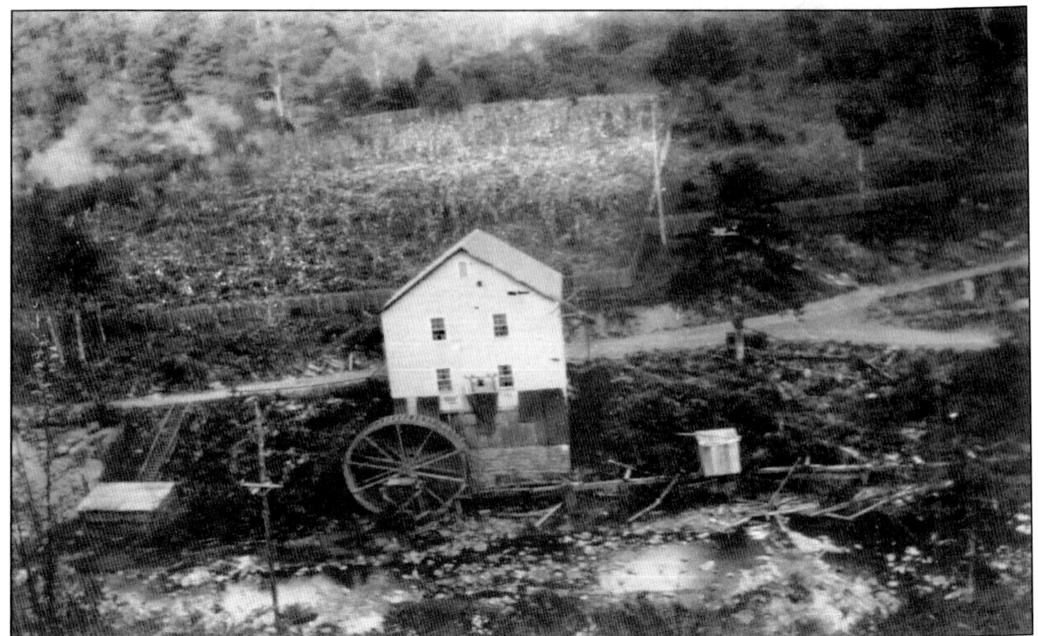

Poor Valley Mill. This lumber mill was located near the Pressmen's Home community in Poor Valley. The lumber from this mill was used to construct many of the buildings in Pressmen's Home. The structure stood on Poor Valley Creek.

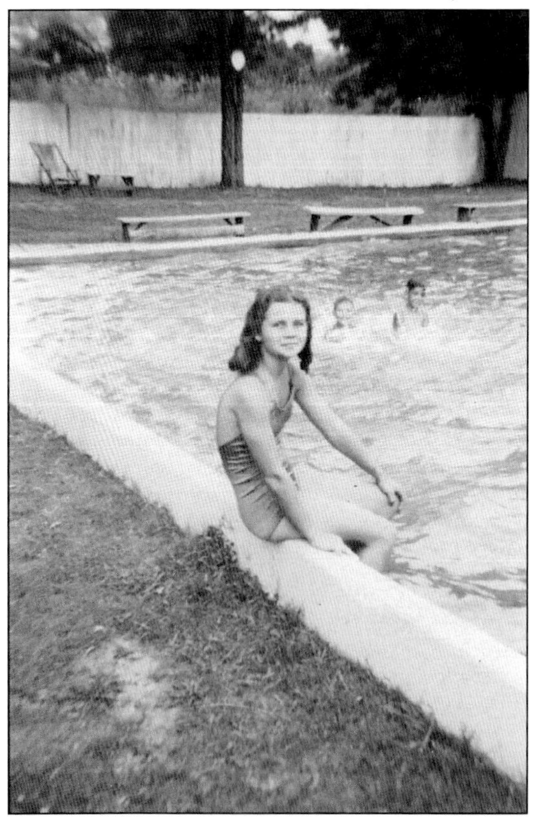

City Pool. Most people are sure to remember the old Rogersville Pool. Located in the present-day Joseph Rogers Park, the spring-fed water hole was an oasis for the young and old alike for many years.

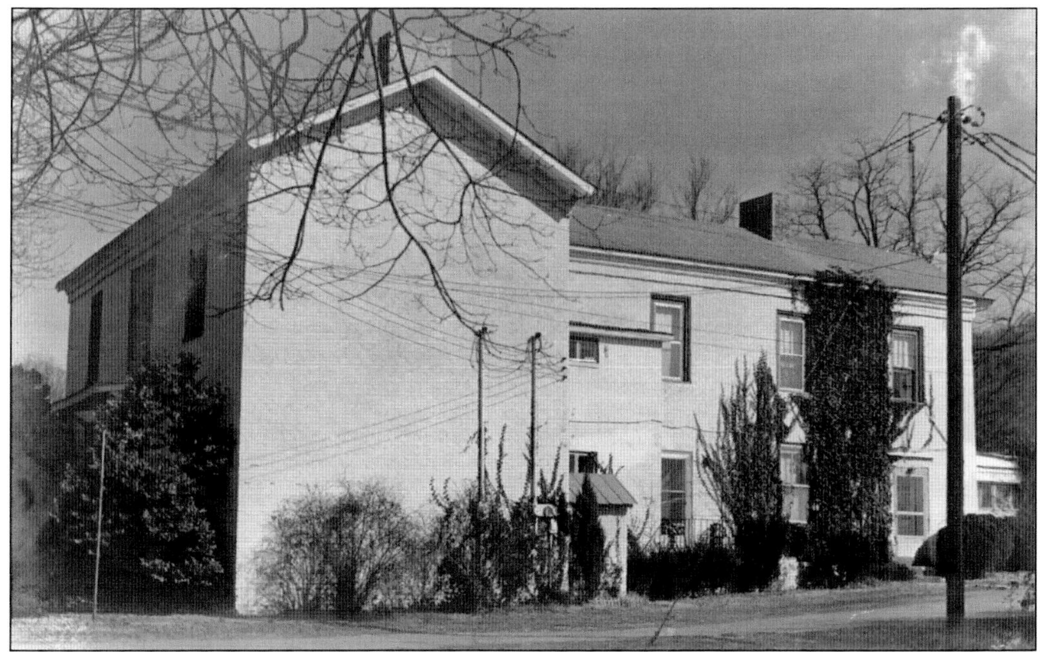

Hampton House. This house on West Broadway in Rogersville was begun by Charles McKinney in 1845 but not completed until after 1865. It was believed that, during the Civil War, the house was occupied by soldiers who slept in the front and stabled their horses in the rear. During a 1930 renovation, horse bones were unearthed, giving proof to the story.

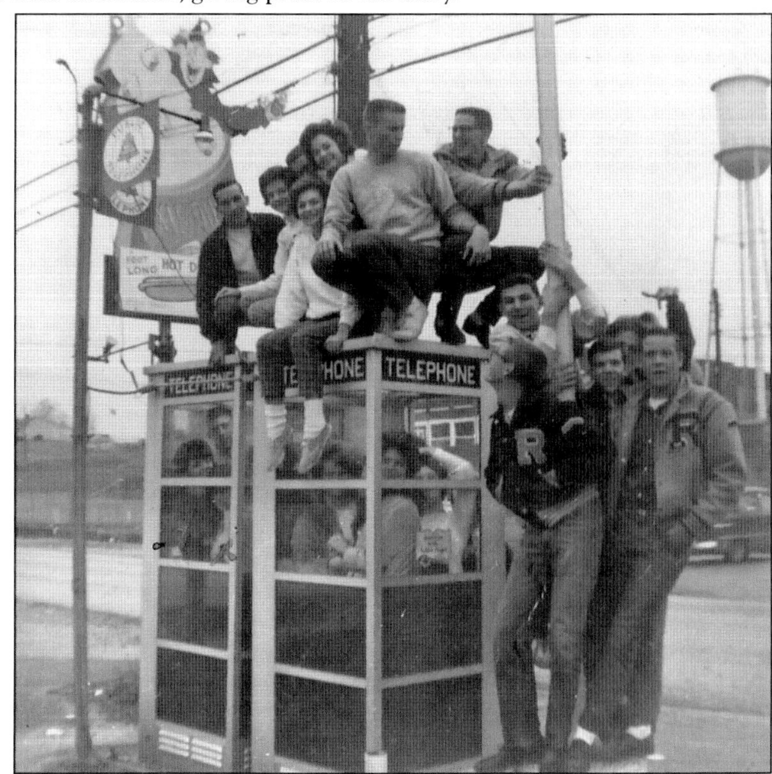

Dixie Queen. The Dixie Queen restaurant on West Main Street in Rogersville was a popular hangout for high school teens. In this photograph, the 1963 graduating class is clowning around under the clown. (Courtesy of Susan Farrow.)

Consistent with our mission to preserve history on a local level, this book was printed in South Carolina on American-made paper and manufactured entirely in the United States. Products carrying the accredited Forest Stewardship Council (FSC) label are printed on 100 percent FSC-certified paper.

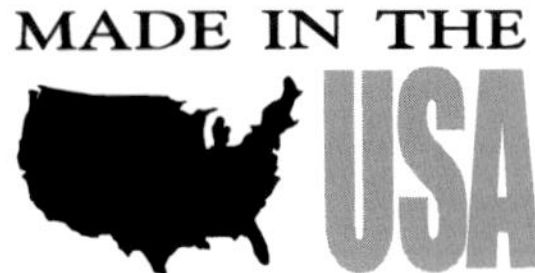